Assessing and Addre~~ssing~~
and Compliance in You~~r Law Firm~~

Related titles from Law Society Publishing:

COLPs Toolkit, 3rd edition
Michelle Garlick

COFAs Toolkit, 2nd edition
Jeremy Black and Tom Vose

Data Protection Toolkit, 2nd edition
Alison Matthews

Anti-Money Laundering Toolkit, 2nd edition
Alison Matthews

Titles from Law Society Publishing can be ordered from all good bookshops or direct (telephone 0370 850 1422 or visit our online shop at **www.lawsociety.org.uk/bookshop**).

Assessing and Addressing Risk and Compliance in Your Law Firm

Rebecca Atkinson

The Law Society

All rights reserved. The purchaser may reproduce and/or store the contents of the disk that accompanies this publication for the firm's internal practice management purposes only. The publication may not be reproduced in whole or in part for resale or commercial use, or for distribution otherwise to any third parties.

Note that the precedents, templates and checklists in this publication are intended as a guide and are to be adapted or modified for particular factual situations. Practitioners should ensure that individual precedents, templates and checklists are up to date and legally accurate. Whilst all reasonable care has been taken in the preparation of this publication, neither the publisher nor the author can accept any responsibility for any loss occasioned to any person acting or refraining from action as a result of relying upon its contents. Precedents, templates and checklists are used at your own risk.

The views expressed in this publication should be taken as those of the author only unless it is specifically indicated that the Law Society has given its endorsement.

© The Law Society 2020

ISBN 978-1-78446-150-8

Published in 2020 by the Law Society
113 Chancery Lane, London WC2A 1PL

Typeset by Columns Design XML Ltd, Reading
Printed by TJ International Ltd, Padstow, Cornwall

The paper used for the text pages of this book is FSC® certified. FSC (the Forest Stewardship Council®) is an international network to promote responsible management of the world's forests.

To Helen Archibald for taking a chance and giving me my first risk and compliance role, Paul Millett for giving me my second and teaching me so much, Craig Emden for his continued unwavering support and to my brilliant risk team who always reply enthusiastically when I suggest we take on yet one more area of risk and compliance.

Contents

About the author xii

Abbreviations xiii

Introduction xv

PART 1: WHAT ARE THE RISKS?

1 Complaints and insurance 3

    1.1 Complaints 3

    1.2 Notification to insurers and claims handling 5

    1.3 Insurance renewal 9

    1.4 How much insurance to buy and limiting your liability 11

2 Data protection 15

    2.1 Data protection compliance, officers and the Information Commissioner's Office registration compliance 15

    2.2 Emailing unintended recipients – how to prevent and mitigate, what to do when it happens and when to report a data breach 18

    2.3 Data subject access requests 20

3 Cybercrime 25

    3.1 Types of cybercrime 25

    3.2 Risk mitigation 26

4 Anti-money laundering compliance 32

    4.1 The MLRO, the MLCO and AML queries 32

    4.2 Centralising CDD gathering, PEPs, sanctions and adverse media checking and file opening ownership 33

    4.3 Sanctions and 'reverse sanctions checks' 34

    4.4 Firmwide AML risk assessment 35

    4.5 Risk assessments on clients and matters, high-risk registers and ongoing monitoring 36

    4.6 Controls you need to consider including screening employees and an independent AML audit 37

	4.7	Client and matter risk assessment completion audit and MLCO audits	38
	4.8	SAR filing and record maintenance	38
5	**Statutory compliance**		40
	5.1	New compliance requirements and how to stay on top	40
	5.2	Modern slavery compliance	41
	5.3	Criminal Finances Act 2017 compliance	45
	5.4	Anti-bribery and corruption compliance	49
	5.5	Whistleblowing legislation and your firm's policy	51
6	**Regulatory compliance**		53
	6.1	Practising certificate renewal and Solicitors Regulation Authority reauthorisation	53
	6.2	SRA Codes of Conduct queries, and in particular conflicts	55
	6.3	Ethics queries	56
	6.4	SRA Accounts Rules compliance and queries	56
	6.5	Price transparency	57
	6.6	SRA digital badge/clickable logo	59
	6.7	Reporting obligations and whistleblowing protection	60
	6.8	Gathering and publishing equality and diversity data	63
	6.9	Information on letterhead, email and website	64
	6.10	Other – compliance training, regulatory investigations and production orders	65
7	**Risk management**		69
	7.1	Audits and registers	69
	7.2	Policy writing and ownership	71
	7.3	Partners, consultants and employees becoming a director or an interest holder of a non-client or client company	72
	7.4	Procurement process	75
	7.5	Supplier contract and terms reviews and 'outside counsel' terms	76
	7.6	Sorting files that are sent externally	78
	7.7	File destruction, archiving and record amendments	79
	7.8	Guidance and analysis	81
	7.9	Inductions	84

	7.10	Engagement letter and terms of business ownership	85
	7.11	Email disclaimer	88
	7.12	How you send bank account details	89
	7.13	Business continuity	89
	7.14	Technical training to ensure competence	91
	7.15	Committees	91
8	Additional areas to consider		93
	8.1	Trainee secondment and work experience students	93
	8.2	Accreditation scheme maintenance – Lexcel and CQS	94
	8.3	Lender panel membership and maintenance	94
	8.4	Responding to audit letters	95
	8.5	KPIs, objectives and feedback on colleagues	96

PART 2: ADDRESSING RISK

9	Addressing risk in your firm		99
	9.1	Gap analysis	99
	9.2	Plan of action	100
	9.3	Risk registers	101
	9.4	Risk roles – outline of COLP and COFA roles in the firm and other types of roles	101
	9.5	Convincing the firm to invest money in risk and compliance	102
10	Risk management – how other firms do it		104
	10.1	Small to medium London firm	104
	10.2	Medium London firm	106
	10.3	Large international firm	107
	10.4	Medium regional firm	108
	10.5	Small regional firm	110
	10.6	Medium London firm	111
	10.7	Large international firm	112

PART 3: CONCLUSION

APPENDICES

1	Template client-facing complaints procedure	119
2	Template internal complaints procedure	121
3	Template professional indemnity insurance notification form	124
4	Template attendance note – own interest conflict and professional indemnity notification and rectification	126
5	Template professional indemnity insurance declaration	127
6	Template guidance to the professional indemnity insurance declaration form	129
7	Template client and matter risk assessment	131
8	Guidance to the client and matter risk assessment	136
9	Template data protection policy	142
10	Template password policy	148
11	Template email policy	149
12	Template privacy notice for employees and workers	151
13	Template acceptable use policy	156
14	Data subject access requests – a practical guide – internal only	159
15	Table of cybercrime events and whether insurance would cover any losses	163
16	Template anti-money laundering policy	167
17	Template anti-money laundering firmwide risk assessment	179
18	Template ongoing anti-money laundering/risk monitoring form	182
19	Template money laundering compliance officer audit questions	183
20	Flowchart from Legal Sector Affinity Group anti-money laundering guidance	184
21	Template suspicious activity report	185
22	Template modern slavery and human trafficking statement	186
23	Template modern slavery and human trafficking policy	188
24	Template Modern Slavery Act 2015 guidance note	191
25	Template Criminal Finances Act 2017 risk assessment	193
26	Template anti-tax evasion policy	196
27	Template anti-bribery and corruption policy	200

28	Template whistleblowing policy	203
29	Template conflicts of interest policy	206
30	Template guidance: Am I providing a banking facility to the client?	209
31	Guidance note: SRA reporting obligations – what are they and when do they kick in?	211
32	Firmwide risk register	213
33	Annual declaration of business/organisation interests	216
34	Template procurement/supplier questionnaire	218
35	Template risk and compliance action plan	221
36	Template letter to auditors	222

About the author

Rebecca Atkinson is director of risk and compliance for London law firm Howard Kennedy LLP. Rebecca heads up the risk function at her firm and is the money laundering compliance officer (MLCO), money laundering reporting officer (MLRO), data protection officer (DPO), whistleblowing officer (WBO) and anti-bribery and corruption officer (ABCO). Rebecca was called to the Bar in 2006 and recently qualified as a New York attorney. Rebecca is a regular writer of articles on the subject of risk and compliance and you may hear her deliver podcasts and webinars.

Abbreviations

ABCO	anti-bribery and corruption officer
AML	anti-money laundering
AML regulations	Money Laundering, Terrorist Financing and Transfer of Funds (Information on the Payer) Regulations 2017, SI 2017/692
BA 2010	Bribery Act 2010
CDD	client due diligence
CEO	chief executive officer
CFA 2017	Criminal Finances Act 2017
CGT	capital gains tax
CMA	Competition and Markets Authority
COFA	compliance officer for finance and administration
COLP	compliance officer for legal practice
CPD	continuing professional development
CQS	Conveyancing Quality Scheme
D&O	directors and officers
DBS	Disclosure and Barring Service
DDOS	distributed denial of service
DPA 2018	Data Protection Act 2018
DPO	data protection officer
DSAR	data subject access request
E&D	equality and diversity
EDD	enhanced due diligence
ESOS	energy savings opportunity scheme
EU	European Union
FATF	Financial Action Task Force
GDPR	EU General Data Protection Regulation (Regulation (EU) 2016/679)
HMRC	HM Revenue and Customs
HR	human resources
ICO	Information Commissioner's Office
ID	identification
IHT	inheritance tax
IT	information technology
KPI	key performance indicator
LeO	Legal Ombudsman
LLP	limited liability partnership
LSAG	Legal Sector Affinity Group
LSB	Legal Services Board
MLCO	money laundering compliance officer
MLRO	money laundering reporting officer
NCA	National Crime Agency
OFSI	Office of Financial Sanctions Implementation

OPBAS	Office for Professional Body Anti-Money Laundering Supervision
PA	personal assistant
PC	practising certificate
PEP	politically exposed person
PI	professional indemnity
PII	professional indemnity insurance
PIDA 1998	Public Interest Disclosure Act 1998
POCA	Proceeds of Crime Act 2002
PQE	post-qualified experience
PR	public relations
PSC	people with significant control
PSR	professional standards and risk
REL	registered European lawyer
RFL	registered foreign lawyer
RIDDOR	Reporting of Injuries, Diseases and Dangerous Occurrences Regulations 2013
SAR	suspicious activity report
SDT	Solicitors Disciplinary Tribunal
SRA	Solicitors Regulation Authority
UN	United Nations
VAT	value added tax
WBO	whistleblowing officer

Introduction

Who this book is aimed at

This book is aimed at anyone who has the pleasurable task of assessing and addressing risk and compliance in their law firm. You, the reader, might be a member of your firm's risk and compliance team or you may be the compliance officer for legal practice (COLP) or you may be a practitioner in a totally unrelated area and have been asked (or told!) to take on responsibility for management of risk and compliance in your firm, and it is now all yours to own. So, what do you need to do? Where do you start?

This book is written to be your 'go to' guide on how to assess and then address risk in your firm and ensure compliance with the various and numerous rules. We will first briefly discuss the history of risk management in law firms before delving into what kind of risks you need to be thinking about. We will then explore how to conduct a gap analysis in your own firm and how you might address the risks you find. Finally, we will explore how other law firms handle risk and compliance from a team perspective – what do their risk teams handle? What do their team formations look like? How large are their teams?

Along the way, the book provides you with draft risk registers, policies and procedures. If you need to use them, these should be adapted to fit your firm.

This book can be read from cover to cover or simply used as a reference guide. It is intended to be accessible for anyone who wants or needs to know what types of risk and compliance their firm should be thinking about. Please note that the term 'risk' is very wide and this book does not cover every aspect of law firm risk – such as health and safety, lateral hire risk or financial risk. This book is intended to help those who look after and/or are responsible for compliance with the regulatory regime faced by law firms and the risks that emanate from that space.

Risk management in law firms – then and now

It is hard to generalise how firms have managed risk in years gone by. However, it is possible to say how *some* firms have undertaken the task and whether this has changed.

Historically, risk management was undertaken by a senior partner in the firm, someone with experience and who could offer wise counsel to those who needed it. Some partners retire into the role and become a consultant. Some firms still have this arrangement and that works for them.

There is a new generation of risk professionals who have come into risk and compliance as their first-time career or have previously worked for regulators or the Law Society. These individuals often do not have the experience of practice (unless they started in practice, went to a regulator say and then have come back) but they do bring with them thorough technical knowledge of the regulations and an insight into how the institutions they have come from work. Some in risk and compliance have been practising solicitors and wish to leave behind the time-recording culture and become 'in-house' as it were.

The compliance officer roles have been a requirement of the Solicitors Regulation Authority (SRA) since 2012 and it is quite possible that since then there has been a significant increase in the number of people that work within the risk and compliance space and an increase in the size of risk teams. Why is this, then – is it because until that time risk wasn't taken seriously? I don't think so. However, with no one before the birth of the COLP and the compliance officer for finance and administration (COFA) roles required to be designated to look after risk management, there wasn't as much emphasis on it. Further, with COLP and COFA roles comes great personal responsibility and COLPs and COFAs want to ensure they have the right time and resource to dedicate to risk management lest they be before the Solicitors Disciplinary Tribunal (SDT).

There is also now more attention by regulators on anti-money laundering (AML), as they in turn are under the spotlight from the Office for Professional Body Anti-Money Laundering Supervision (OPBAS – known as the super regulator). As a result, more resource is being ploughed into this area of compliance.

Risk and compliance has become a specialist subject just as much as any other area of business services within a firm such as HR, IT and business development. As a result, some firms have changed their management of risk and compliance to build a team that was not there to begin with, expand the team or bring in new professionals from different types of businesses.

The stakes are higher now also. The SRA regularly takes regulatory action for non-compliance and the SDT has whacked out some whopping fines in the last few years. Even more reason to spend money on compliance. Better spending the money there than handing it over to a tribunal.

Research by market intelligence company JWG found that the banking sector spends 15–20 per cent of its revenue on risk and compliance (as reported in *Forbes*, 'Taming the high costs of compliance with tech', 22 March 2018). That is a staggering amount. If law firms were to do the same, that would mean a £10 million turnover firm would be spending £1.5 million minimum. For a firm that turns over £1 million, this would mean a cost of £150,000 minimum. A recent survey of senior staff at asset managers, brokers and banks suggests that financial firms spend around four per cent of their turnover currently on risk and compliance, and this could increase to 10 per cent (as reported in *Financial News*, 'Compliance costs to more than double by 2022', 27 April 2017). Will law firms go the same way? Are we already there?

The way to tackle compliance is to be as smart about it as possible, and this book should help you do that.

Gap analysis of risks – why do it?

Whether you are scoping out what needs to be done in your firm from a risk and compliance perspective for the first time, or have already done it and are reviewing your work, a gap analysis of areas to tackle is best undertaken before you begin or carry on. If you have an overall list of areas that you need to tackle, you will be able to prioritise them (you may even want to risk rate them in a firmwide risk register – see **7.1.2**) to decide which ones to tackle first.

Your gap analysis can be used to show regulators and insurers how important you consider risk and compliance to be and that you are working towards being better. Do not underestimate the power of a good plan. It not only gets things done, but it is a tangible document that insurers like to see – and rather than it highlighting your issues to your detriment, it shows how serious you are about this subject. Trust me, it will help with your insurance premium in the long run.

At **9.1** I set out in more detail how to conduct a gap analysis. Before you start that, you need to consider what risks there might be.

Assessing what risks there might be

In **Part 1**, we go through the areas of risk and compliance that should be thought about in each law firm and covered off either by a designated risk team or those tasked with ensuring compliance across the firm (normally the COLP). The contents here are by no means exhaustive – risks change and new rules to comply with are released on a frequent basis. It is each firm's responsibility to keep on top of regulatory requirements, and unfortunately ignorance is still no defence. That said, there are some 'mainstay' areas that are not going to go away. Be aware of them and ensure that your firm is compliant with these rules – **Part 2** will help you to take steps to tackle these areas.

PART 1
What are the risks?

1 Complaints and insurance

1.1 Complaints

1.1.1 What are the requirements?

The Solicitors Regulation Authority (SRA) Standards and Regulations require that solicitors have a procedure for handling complaints in relation to the services provided. (The SRA Standards and Regulations came into effect on 25 November 2019, replacing the SRA Handbook.) That complaints procedure needs to be communicated to the client in writing at the time of engagement, and further that procedure needs to set out the client's right to complain about the services and charges, how a complaint should be made and to whom. The procedure also needs to set out that the client has the right to complain to the Legal Ombudsman (LeO) and when that complaint needs to be made by (i.e. the time limits).

The SRA Standards and Regulations further set out that when clients have made a complaint and it is not resolved to the client's satisfaction within eight weeks following the making of the complaint, the client is reminded in writing of any right they have to complain to LeO, the timeframe for doing so and full details of how to contact LeO. Further, if a complaint has been brought and your complaints procedure has been exhausted but you are unable to settle the complaint, then you must set out the name and website address of an alternative dispute resolution approved body which would be competent to deal with the complaint and whether you agree to use the scheme operated by that body.

The SRA Standards and Regulations lastly set out that you must ensure complaints are dealt with promptly, fairly and free of charge.

1.1.2 Client-facing complaints procedure

The requirements are for you to set out your complaints procedure in writing at the outset of the matter to the client. Some firms choose to do this in the engagement letter sent at the outset (see more guidance on engagement letters in **7.10.1**). The rules do not say that the procedure needs to be in the engagement letter and some firms do not like the tone it might appear to set. An alternative is to place the complaints procedure in your firm's terms of business which are sent to the client with the engagement letter at the beginning of each matter. Wording for your engagement letter or terms can be taken from the sample client-facing procedure referenced below.

It is good practice to also have a client-facing complaints procedure that provides more detail on how the firm handles and treats complaints. This can be sent to the client either on the client's request, or upon the client expressing some form of dissatisfaction. You will find a sample client-facing complaints procedure in **Appendix 1**.

A complaint that requires the invocation of the complaints procedure will sometimes be clear and sometimes not so clear. A client who asks for the procedure should be sent the procedure as soon as possible. However, some complaints sound more like a minor grumble and it is not necessarily clear whether a complaint such that the procedure should be invoked is being made. For example, a client who is complaining about a time entry that can be explained by the conducting fee earner is probably not raising a complaint such that the procedure needs to be sent. The point is to be sensible about it. However, note that LeO's definition of a complaint is that it is an expression of dissatisfaction and so the threshold is rather low.

1.1.3 Internal process

As well as having a client-facing procedure there is merit in having an internal procedure that clearly defines for all staff what a complaint is, what to do when one is received and who in the firm needs to be notified. This will make clear to everyone what is expected of them when a complaint comes in and also serve as an education piece as to what a complaint might look like. A sample internal complaints procedure can be found at **Appendix 2**.

In terms of who investigates, the procedure should be clear about this. It is sometimes appropriate for the head of the team, supervising partner or similar person to respond in the first instance and then if the client is not satisfied for a separate person to investigate. Alternatively, a wholly independent person either within the firm or if you are a sole practitioner outside the firm might be an appropriate person to conduct the investigation. Whatever you decide is right for your firm document it and stick to it so everyone internally and clients know where they stand. Many firms have their COLP take overall responsibility for complaints handling in the firm and in some firms they conduct the investigation, while in others this is delegated to someone by the COLP. This will very much depend on the size of firm and the resources available.

It is tempting to ask the fee earner being complained about to draft a reply to the complaint with the person overseeing complaints in the firm signing the letter of response. This should be avoided at all costs as it makes a mockery of the complaints procedure which should be independent and further the conducting fee earner may not be responding to the complaint in the way it deserves and perhaps has a biased viewpoint.

Best practice is to thoroughly investigate complaints that are received and 'front load' the reply in case LeO is the client's next port of call. What I mean by this is to reply in a way that is a full response that tells the full picture with documentary evidence attached. Set out the background of the retainer, what the complaint is, what evidence has been reviewed, what the fee earner says, what the independent reviewer's views are and why and whether the complaint is upheld or not. If you do this, then when the client goes to LeO and LeO gives you a list of documents it requires as long as your arm (which comprises 90 per cent of the file but LeO insists on not being sent the file which would be far easier for everyone including LeO), you can start by giving your response to the complaint and the documentary evidence attached.

Remember to record complaints that are made. You will need this data for reauthorising the firm with the SRA (see **6.1**) and it is sometimes requested for pitches or in lender panel applications but more importantly it will help you spot trends so you can put procedures in place to nip behaviours that create complaints in the bud (see **7.8.3** for more on that). There are pieces of software out there that can help you with your recording but, depending on the size of firm, a spreadsheet is likely to do the job nicely. Ultimately it is up to you to decide what to record. You may decide to record each minor grumble; it isn't required though it can provide useful insights as to where things are not going as well as they could be.

1.1.4 *A note about who has the right to invoke your procedure*

Note that only those to whom you provide a service have the benefit of your complaints procedure. In practice, sometimes a non-client will complain. In that instance you are not obliged to follow your complaints procedure as required by the SRA Standards and Regulations but you may wish to respond in the spirit of the procedure. Certainly, where the complainant is not technically a client but likely to be seen as a quasi-client by LeO (for example, a beneficiary of an estate where the solicitor within the firm acts as executor) it is best practice to invoke the firm's complaints procedure and you may then gain a favourable view from LeO for doing so.

1.1.5 *Further guidance*

The Law Society has a number of useful practice notes to help you in this area. On its website you will find practice notes on client information requirements; handling complaints; and what to do when a complaint goes to LeO (**www.lawsociety.org.uk/support-services/advice/practice-notes/**).

1.2 Notification to insurers and claims handling

An unfortunate side effect of legal practice is legal malpractice. Sometimes things go wrong. This is why we have rubbers on the ends of pencils and professional indemnity insurance (PII). Handling notifications to insurers and rectifications correctly is vital to not only your PII but also your firm culture.

The culture in your firm must be a blame free one. Yes there will be times when a fee earner just keeps making the same mistake and that will need to be addressed but most of the time mistakes are just down to human error and if you are the person to whom people have to report their wrongdoing you need to be human about it and, above all, kind.

1.2.1 *When and what to notify?*

The timing of your notification can be crucial. Timing is key. From an insurer's perspective the time to notify is when an actual claim has been made or a circumstance has arisen. A circumstance is a matter which may give rise to a claim.

By definition 'circumstances' are an incident, occurrence, fact, matter, act or omission which may give rise to a claim in respect of civil liability. 'Circumstances' include not only an intimation of an intention to claim but also an awareness you may have of a failing or doubt as to the effectiveness of performance where such failing might give rise to a claim.

In other words, you must always notify circumstances where you are aware of a negligent act even if the client may be oblivious to the problem.

By way of practical illustration, here are some possible scenarios which could give rise to a circumstance and therefore be reportable to insurers:

- A client complains about or indicates unhappiness with your service. Even if you consider that the issue raised is no more than a complaint with or without substance, you need to consider whether you need to notify it to your insurers.
- You realise the firm has given negligent advice or in some other way breached the terms of the contract with the client even if the client is not yet aware of the error.
- The client has not complained and you do not consider the firm has done anything wrong, but nonetheless there is a possibility that a claim will arise.

Take the cue from your insurers and brokers on what they would want to see notified. Most insurers want their insured to take a cautious approach and notify if they are unsure. Ultimately insurers can always reject the notification as unnecessary but at least you will have made the attempt should there be a dispute later on.

It is important to note that the number of notifications does not mean a higher premium. It is not that simple or basic. Notifications which are purely precautionary (i.e. something might happen but might not and you are notifying insurers out of an abundance of caution) show insurers that you have a healthy culture in the firm where issues, possible errors and client unhappiness are openly discussed and it also shows that you take these issues seriously. Of course, if each and every notification was a claim yes that would affect your premium in the long run but if you are notifying insurers as you should the ratio of actual claims to precautionary notifications will be low. In my experience, I have notified more matters to insurers year on year and the premium has gone down and down. This seems to blow the minds of those who think notifying insurers is 'bad'. It isn't. It just isn't.

A few words about timing. Generally speaking, as soon as a circumstance has arisen then a notification to insurers should be made. However, there may be occasions where the matter arises on a Monday and is resolved on the Tuesday – should you notify? If the chances of a claim against the firm and policy are slim to none then you may well take the decision not to notify and most insurers would be relaxed about that. However, I wholeheartedly recommend that you still record it somewhere. You cannot nip in the bud patterns of behaviour which are leading to mistakes if you do not have the data before you to see it.

1.2.2 How to notify?

The method of notification will be down to your brokers and insurers. However, at **Appendix 3** you will see a template notification form which you may wish to adapt and adopt. By formalising your notification process, you will be able to record and spot trends more easily. Some insurers are relaxed and are happy to take an explanatory email from you and some insurers have a form similar to the one found here in this book. Even if you do not notify many matters, formalise your reporting technique and record the notification in a spreadsheet or data capture piece of software (such as Riliance). Having a notification form will also force you to ask how the circumstance happened, how you can prevent it going forward and whether it can be rectified.

1.2.3 Should you rectify?

Paragraph 3.5 of the SRA Code of Conduct for Firms (part of the SRA Standards and Regulations) sets out:

> You are honest and open with clients if things go wrong, and if a client suffers loss or harm as a result you put matters right (if possible) and explain fully and promptly what has happened and the likely impact. If requested to do so by the SRA you investigate whether anyone may have a claim against you, provide the SRA with a report on the outcome of your investigation, and notify relevant persons that they may have such a claim, accordingly.

This is clear that when a mistake has been made that the client is informed about it and where possible the matter is rectified. Two large warnings here.

First, always seek the agreement of your insurers before you admit any errors to the client. Insurers are sensible about this and they understand that you have regulatory obligations. However, they may have to pay out on any claim or the monies you may pay will erode your excess and for these reasons you must respect their position and ask for their approval before admissions are made.

Second, you must think very carefully about rectification in light of your other Code obligations and the *Howell-Jones* case (SDT case No. 11846-2018). In that case, Howell-Jones (HJ) acted for a matrimonial client. After realising that they might have under-settled their client's case, they took counsel's advice who confirmed they had been negligent. They informed the client openly and frankly about their negligence and gave the client the choice of either taking the matter elsewhere and suing the firm, or allowing the firm to rectify the matter by returning to court to seek a setting aside of the settlement agreement. HJ offered to write off fees, pay for the rectification work and pay any adverse costs order that might occur from the application they were offering to undertake. The client agreed to their rectification, as most clients would, and HJ made the application to court. However, things didn't go well. The judge refused to set aside the settlement agreement and the client complained. No doubt the firm and insurers subsequently dealt with a negligence claim. The client made a complaint and the SRA investigated. The matter went before the Solicitors Disciplinary Tribunal (SDT) who held that HJ should not have attempted to rectify the matter as there was an own interest conflict. It seems that while HJ advised the client that he should take independent legal advice, they did not insist upon it. Presumably if they had insisted, HJ would have had to pay for that.

This is not a popular decision and subsequent SDT cases may undermine it, but it does highlight that when faced with a negligence matter that is capable of rectification you must carefully consider whether you have a conflict of interest. I urge you to document your thought process on a case-by-case basis, and at **Appendix 4** you will find a template attendance note for your use. If in doubt, seek insurers' help as they will be grappling with this question on a daily basis.

1.2.4 Annual declaration prior to renewal

Each year before you renew your insurance you need to make sure that insurers are informed of every circumstance that they should be aware of, and further you will need to declare that you have completed this exercise to brokers and insurers before renewal. To complete this process, it is advisable to send out an annual declaration to all fee earners (to include trainees, paralegals and consultants). You will find a template declaration at **Appendix 5** (and explanatory note at **Appendix 6**). You may wish to place this on your firm's intranet or find more whizzy ways of asking fee earners to complete it. I would recommend you send this to your fee earners six weeks before renewal and ask that they complete it within three weeks (to allow for holidays). You need to allow yourself time to explore the potential notifications to insurers that come back.

You may wish to obtain other types of declaration at the same time. Perhaps a declaration that the client account is not being used as a bank account or in respect of any other area of risk and compliance that has proved problematic or concerning.

I would not recommend sending this declaration at any other time – e.g. every quarter or monthly – as you may create a culture where fee earners do not tell those in risk management roles about a matter straight away but instead will wait until the declaration comes around to be completed. This you do not want. Ultimately if you complete your annual declaration process and have very few new matters to tell insurers about, that suggests you have a culture where matters are notified throughout the year.

1.2.5 Claims handling

A very brief note on claims handling. Some insurers offer a claims handling service as part of the insurance policy or defence costs may be paid by insurers. You may also have someone in the firm who would be willing to handle claims on behalf of the firm. While this might look more cost effective, depending on your firm, it quite often isn't. Naturally you will want a partner or senior associate to handle the claim against the firm. Their hourly rates will often be higher than those of external professional indemnity (PI) panel solicitors. Also, external solicitors are independent and bring a fresh view to the matter. Any internal personnel have an interest in the firm and may not be able to see or take the more commercial line they might take with a client. Finally, your fee earners are busy trying to reach the target the firm sets. PI claims do not fall within this and so often the firm gives itself a second-rate service. It is best to consider instructing external solicitors always.

1.3 Insurance renewal

Insurance renewal and its handling is crucial to a lower premium. Yes, claims history cannot be erased – but it can be rolled in a little glitter, and how you present your past and where you are going in your future really makes an impact on who wants to insure you and at what cost. In this section, we will go through tips on how to have a successful renewal.

1.3.1 Seek help from your broker

Seek help from your broker when preparing for your renewal. Ask brokers what you should be providing; whether there is a specific way to approach renewal; and how to approach each insurer. Also speak to your broker about meeting insurers for a renewal chat. Your brokers are there to help you and to achieve the best renewal terms on your behalf. You pay them a fee, so use them.

1.3.2 Give a good impression

First impressions count. It is important to be ready and have all paperwork in order. A good but short presentation on the firm goes down well.

1.3.3 It's all about you

Really explain to prospective insurers what your firm is all about. Who are your clients? What is the work you do? Is it niche? Is it unique in any way? Are you an 'all services' firm? What is the vision? What is the strategy? Do you plan on merging? Do you plan on growing organically? Do you plan on staying the same size? What is the culture of the firm? What is changing? The key here is to not hold back.

1.3.4 Face your issues

Be honest about the issues that you have within the firm. Be ready to explain to insurers what has happened and what steps have been taken to rectify and prevent further occurrence.

If you have a particularly bad claim on record, speak about it with insurers and explain what happened. Insurers are going to spot the bad claim anyway and ask about it so why not get in there first? If necessary, write a short document explaining what has happened.

The worst thing to be is a 'politician' about what has happened and try to be clever with the truth. Be honest and be ready to talk.

Be ready to talk about any regulatory issues that you have. If you have reported material breaches to the SRA, tell your insurer at renewal time and be up front about what has happened. What is important here is that you explain what you have done to improve the situation to ensure it doesn't happen again. If the firm is currently being investigated by the SRA, explain why and what stage the investigation is at. Likewise if an investigation has been undertaken and concluded, explain the outcome.

1.3.5 Go beyond the renewal form

The renewal form, as large it may be, does not always enable the entire picture to be reflected. Don't be afraid to put together a pack of information which goes beyond the renewal form. This could include the firm's business plans, information about strategic projects, plans in relevant business service areas such as risk and compliance or professional support and knowledge enhancement, any internal risk publications or guidance pieces, any information about the development of risk management in the firm, any minutes from risk management committee meetings or the like.

Without question it is important to explain what has happened over the prior year but it is equally important to explain what is coming up and for the firm to explain what its plans are.

1.3.6 Look at claims summaries well in advance of your renewal meeting

It's important to start renewal discussions with an up-to-date notification and claims position. Review all the open matters no matter how old and ask insurers and brokers to close them off if the matter has been resolved, settled or nothing has happened. At the same time, look at the reserves placed there by insurers – do you agree with them? If you feel they are incorrect speak to your broker or insurer about amending the amount. This information will be used by the underwriter when deciding premium levels.

Once you have completed the clean-up, ask for a fresh claims summary and include this with your renewal documentation or ask your broker to do so.

1.3.7 Cybercrime

Be ready to discuss cybercrime. There are many cybercrime insurance policies out there and if you haven't considered obtaining cover, do so before you meet your insurers or prospective insurers. If you haven't read about cybercrime (where have you been?) read up on it. Nothing is more unimpressive about a firm than if it isn't on top of its topics. Even if you decide that a cybercrime policy is not for you, that is ok, just explain why. Also be ready to answer questions on your IT security, how you approach cybercrime messaging and training.

1.3.8 Ask insurers about themselves

I know I said it's all about you, but it isn't really. Ask insurers what is going on in their world and what renewal is looking like this year. Will they be expanding their client base or are they seeking to shrink it? What do they see are the major issues facing firms when it comes to PII? What are the claims trends that they have seen over the past year and what do they see as the trends of the future? What risk management support can they offer you? Insurers often have support they can give in the form of guidance, articles, training and the like.

A bit like a job interview, be ready to ask questions back. After all, you are interviewing your prospective insurers too.

1.3.9 Insurance Act 2015

The Insurance Act 2015 came into force on 12 August 2016. While it didn't alter the renewal process in any dramatic way, it did mean that insurers will be required to ask the right questions to get the information they need. You may therefore have seen a longer proposal form and have been asked more questions after submitting it. The flip side of this is that you also have an obligation to be able to evidence that you have made enquiries across the firm to obtain relevant information for the purposes of renewal. Therefore keep notes and emails of what you have asked people to provide. See **1.2** about notifications to insurers; and a template annual declaration form can be found at **Appendix 5**.

1.3.10 It's not War and Peace

In the light of all of the above, you may think I am advocating that you provide *War and Peace* to insurers. Definitely do not do this. There is nothing that makes someone not want to read a pack of information more than a folder of documents the weight of a small child. Be succinct and be precise. It's not the time to write a risk management thesis. Make it relevant, informative – and interesting to read.

1.4 How much insurance to buy and limiting your liability

When you renew your insurance, consider whether the level of insurance is right for you and your practice. This section sets out how you might go about deciding the level of cover you need.

1.4.1 Regulatory requirements

The SRA requires all firms to take out a minimum level of PI cover in accordance with the Minimum Terms and Conditions of Professional Indemnity Insurance in the SRA Insurance Indemnity Rules 2012 at £2 million, or £3 million in the case of a limited liability firm.

Outcome 7.13 in the previous SRA Code of Conduct 2011 stated that:

> you assess and purchase the level of professional indemnity insurance cover that is appropriate for your current and past practice, taking into account potential levels of claim by your clients and others and any alternative arrangements you or your client may make.

This Outcome has not fully translated to the new 2019 Codes in the SRA Standards and Regulations – though there is a general requirement at paragraph 2.5 of the new SRA Code of Conduct for Firms, which sets out that you must 'identify, monitor and manage all material risks to your business, including those which may arise from your connected practices'.

As happens when a new code arrives, we still use prior codes for guidance when they do not contradict or pull against a new code. After all, many of us are still using the old 1999 Code as guidance (including the SRA). It is therefore a good idea, in my view, to still take note of Outcome 7.13 of the SRA Code of Conduct 2011.

1.4.2 Assessing your firm

The first step is to assess your firm. Some factors can include:

- The size of your firm.
- What types of work you do. Crime may be considered to be low risk but real estate high. Brokers can help you here and often brokers and insurers will be able to provide you with statistics on the types of work that give rise to the most claims.
- Your firm's claim history.
- Whether the level of your cover is similar to that of other firms of your make-up and size. Again your brokers can help you here.
- Your ability to meet uncovered claims. For example, if you are a limited liability partnership (LLP) and you were to receive a £3.5 million claim and had cover for £3 million, could your firm sustain a top-up payment to cover what your insurance could not?

1.4.3 Assessing your risk

The level of cover that you need depends on your risk profile. Your risk profile is derived from many factors but there is no magical formula. Questions to ask can include:

- Does your firm conduct work in a high-risk area such as real estate or corporate? If so how much of that work creates your total revenue? A firm that derives five per cent of its revenue from real estate is going to be lower risk than a firm that derives 50 per cent.
- What are the values of the transactions that your firm handles? Are these values over and above your PI cover today?
- Are you coming up against opposition to the limitation of liability that you are placing on your retainers, i.e. maybe from banks who ask you to limit your liability to the value of the loan they are providing?
- How much money do you hold in your client account at any one time? Remember PI covers client monetary loss. Do you hold more in your client account than your level of PI insurance?

Taking the above into account, the ultimate fear-inducing question to ask is:

- If you/your firm were negligent on a matter, what is the maximum possible loss that the firm could cause and does that exceed your insurance cover?

As this question needs to be asked on a case-by-case basis (I would suggest factored into your client and matter risk assessment – a template can be found at **Appendix 7** and guidance at **Appendix 8**), considering the level of cover is an ongoing exercise and not one that is completed just at renewal time.

1.4.4 Limiting your liability

Under the previous SRA Code of Conduct 2011, Indicative Behaviour 1.8 set out the requirement that:

> if you seek to limit your liability to your client to a level above the minimum required by the SRA Indemnity Insurance Rules, ensuring that this limitation is in writing and is brought to the client's attention;

This has not found its way into the 2019 SRA Standards and Regulations but as indicated elsewhere in this book, old rules are good guidance so long as they do not contradict the current rules we are bound by. Further, if you have any hope in holding a client to a limitation of your liability then you need to have this set out in your engagement letter and terms of business.

Limitations of liability are only good if they are reasonable and proportionate. If you are handling a transaction worth £250 million and any negligence caused by you could amount to half that then a limitation of your liability to £3 million is probably not enough. You need to negotiate more. How much depends on how much damage could be caused by negligence. A client may claim the total value of the matter should be covered by your insurance (this is often the claim of banks who are lending) but this would not be the loss you could cause. For example, if your client is purchasing real estate for £50 million, is it reasonable that they want your insurance up to £50 million? Probably not because even if you were negligent that will not render the land purchased valueless – simply the loss will not be £50 million.

Sometimes clients (often banks who frequently aren't even the client but are receiving the benefit of your work) want unlimited liability. This is a judgment call for you to make. I would advise never to agree this. In my experience when you say no and ask the client to justify why they need it unlimited they cave in and agree a cap. If they really are insistent consider getting an outside opinion on the possible losses that could be caused by any negligence and whether it goes beyond your PI cover. Also consider getting another/second/third fee earner to check the work. Finally consider whether you need to increase your insurance.

Try and keep a record (a simple spreadsheet is all you need) of requests for increases of your limitation of liability so you can assess at each renewal whether your limitation is set right for the work you do and whether you need to buy more insurance.

1.4.5 Other aspects to note

Remember that claims are noted on a 'claims made' basis and so you need to maintain that level of cover until the possibility of a claim has passed, say six years.

The reality is that once you have increased cover you are unlikely to decrease unless your practice has changed. So it is important to consider whether you will continue to be able to afford your cover in future years.

Further, additional insurance can have different terms from those that apply to your primary layer of insurance. Be careful to check those.

The cost of top-up cover will vary depending on size of practice, type of work completed, claims history and so on. Consult your brokers for assistance.

2 Data protection

2.1 Data protection compliance, officers and the Information Commissioner's Office registration compliance

Your firm must be compliant with the Data Protection Act (DPA) 2018 and the EU General Data Protection Regulation (Regulation (EU) 2016/679) (GDPR).

2.1.1 How to comply?

Data protection compliance is a large area and too large in itself for full explanation here. However, below is a useful checklist that is a good starting point, and if you have not yet tackled any areas of this list, do so as soon as possible.

1. **Read guidance:** The Law Society and the Information Commissioner's Office (ICO) have very useful guidance. The Law Society also publishes an excellent *Data Protection Toolkit* (2nd edition, April 2019) which will help compliance. My recommendation would be to start with the Law Society guidance and go from there.
2. **Know what data you hold:** The first aspect of compliance is to know what data it is that you hold. This could be data about clients, employees, third parties such as suppliers. Put this information in a table/spreadsheet along with points 3 and 4 below.
3. **Know where your data is:** While thinking about what data you hold, do you know where it all is? It may be contained within your accounting system, HR system, payroll system, billing software and so on. It may be held physically. Are you aware of your staff sending client work to their home email? Question whether this happens, and if it does put a stop to it. Do you allow your staff to take files home to work on and if they do, do you have adequate protections and/or guidance/policies around this?
4. **Know how safe the data is:** Now you know what data you have and where it is, do you protect it? Sit down with your IT personnel and discuss virus protection, penetration testing of systems and IT security policies.
5. **Do you have a lawful basis for processing data (consent, necessary for a contract, legal obligation, vital to protect life, public interest, legitimate interests)?** You need to consider this and document it. If you cannot find a legal basis for having the data you need to think about disposing of it.
6. **Do you know how you would respond to a data subject access request?** Guidance on this can be found at **2.3**.
7. **How about a request for erasure?** Rehearse in advance how you will respond to a request for data to be deleted. Think about on what grounds you may refuse such a request such as data retention requirements either imposed by law or for insurance purposes.

8. **Do you have a data breach response plan?** Do people know who to contact? Draw up a plan with IT and test it!
9. **Review your IT security regularly:** Be sure that your firm has a thorough data security routine. How often do security upgrades occur? Data breaches can occur if update patches are not implemented. Do you have a policy on downloading software to a firm computer? Consider locking down that ability. Do you have a policy on USB sticks and discs?
10. **Apply data retention policies:** If you don't have a policy, put one in place. You are required to destroy data that you no longer need. Be brave and regularly destroy data, hard copy and electronic. This will ensure compliance but you will save money too.
11. **Train, train, train:** Keep messaging up! Make sure you train your people on data security and regularly message the firm about it. Perhaps aim to have a DPA message out across the firm every quarter. The more people see it, the more it will become part of everyday life.
12. **Finally, have your policies in place:** These need to be user-friendly, easily understood by the firm's population and clearly demonstrate compliance. There are a number of policies that you may have in the firm and these are but not limited to:
    - Data protection policy to include what types of data you hold, why you hold it, where it is, who has access and on what basis you hold it. The policy could also cover aspects of security such as whether data is able to be placed on a portable device and how long data will be kept for. You can separate information security into its own policy, but you don't have to.
    - Password policy.
    - Email policy.
    - Privacy notice.
    - Acceptable use policy.

A template of each of these policies can be found at **Appendices 9–13**. These are basic templates that will need to be adapted prior to implementation in your firm.

2.1.2 Do you need a data protection officer? What do they do?

Under the data legislation, you must appoint a data protection officer (DPO) if:

- you are a public authority or body (except for courts acting in their judicial capacity);
- your core activities require large-scale, regular and systematic monitoring of individuals (for example, online behaviour tracking); or
- your core activities consist of large-scale processing of special categories of data or data relating to criminal convictions and offences.

To decide whether you need a DPO, think about whether your core activities mean you process data on a large scale. It is likely that most firms will not consider themselves as large-scale processors of data. There is no defined size to the processing here, and so it will be a judgment call for most firms. If you decide not to appoint a DPO, you should document your thought process and review it regularly and at least once a year.

If you do not consider you need a DPO you are still able to appoint one voluntary.

The Law Society has very useful guidance on appointing a DPO and I encourage you to read it (**www.lawsociety.org.uk/support-services/practice-management/ gdpr/gdpr-for-solicitors/appoint-a-data-protection-officer/**).

As to who should be a DPO, this needs to be someone who is able to dedicate time to the role and who ideally has knowledge of the data protection laws. The GDPR states that the DPO should be 'expert' in data protection law but this just cannot be practical for small firms who do not have the resources to employ someone in the role. If that sounds like your firm, then consider carefully whether you need a DPO at all and if you feel you do, appoint one and give them time to undertake the role and allow them to attend events, courses and seek external advice if needed. Law Society guidance sets out that if you do not consider you need a DPO you can as an alternative create a role for someone to lead data protection in the firm and they may not be a DPO but instead be a data protection manager or officer.

The DPO's role is to be the first point of contact for any data protection activities. They should have a direct feed into the top management of the firm and so should be senior enough.

The DPO's tasks are defined in art.39 of the GDPR as:

- to inform and advise the firm about its obligations to comply with the GDPR and other data protection laws;
- to monitor compliance with the GDPR and other data protection laws, and with the firm's data protection policies, including managing internal data protection activities; raising awareness of data protection issues; training staff; and conducting internal audits;
- to advise on, and to monitor, data protection impact assessments;
- to cooperate with the supervisory authority; and
- to be the first point of contact for supervisory authorities and for individuals whose data is processed (employees, customers, etc.).

The Information Commissioner's guidance sets out that it is important to remember that the DPO's tasks cover all personal data processing activities, not just those that require their appointment under art.37(1):

- When carrying out their tasks, the DPO is required to take into account the risk associated with the processing the firm is undertaking. They must have regard to the nature, scope, context and purposes of the processing.
- The DPO should prioritise and focus on the riskier activities – for example, where special category data is being processed, or where the potential impact on individuals could be damaging. Therefore, DPOs should provide risk-based advice to the firm.

2.1.3 Information Commissioner's Office – registration compliance

If you are processing data you need to be registered with the ICO. The ICO's website provides detailed guidance and also a questionnaire so you can decide whether you need to be registered. Registration is very likely to be needed as law firms are considered to be data controllers, they receive data and determine the purpose of that data and how it will be processed. Don't forget to consider all your legal entities, for example if your firm is made up of two separate legal entities and not just one.

Registration is simple and can be undertaken via the ICO website. Fees are staggered depending on size of firm.

Do not forget to register with the ICO, as failure to do so can result in a fine.

2.1.4 Further data protection guidance

As indicated at the beginning of this section, data protection is a large area for compliance and one that is too big for this book. The Law Society, however, has great resources for you and further the Law Society's *Data Protection Toolkit* provides excellent guidance and template policies and procedures.

2.2 Emailing unintended recipients – how to prevent and mitigate, what to do when it happens and when to report a data breach

Emailing unintended recipients is so very easy to do, especially in the fast-paced environment that we work in and when working on the move. The consequences of such a mistake can be catastrophic, as confidential information is breached with possible subsequent complaints and investigations by the Solicitors Regulation Authority (SRA) and the ICO. Procedures and preventative measures are therefore an absolute must. You can't control human error or eliminate risk entirely, but you can and should mitigate as far as possible. Below is some guidance on how to go about preventing such an event and what to do if it were to happen.

2.2.1 Prevention and mitigation

Prevention and mitigation are better than cure, and so here are some ideas for you to consider:

- Place a time-delay on your emails being sent to allow people to go back and delete the email before it is sent. Some firms have this in place and once the initial annoyance people feel has passed, I have been told that this has helped avoid emails being sent in error.
- Consider using technology which is able to detect when an unintended email recipient is going to be emailed and requests the sender to check before proceeding.

- Always make attachments password-protected. Therefore, if an attachment is sent in error, the unintended recipient will not have the password (unless that was sent in error too!).
- If you are working on a big transaction, think about whether the transaction could be given a project name to be used in emails (e.g. Project Blue) so that an unintended recipient will not know what the work relates to.
- When you are sending sensitive documents via email, use a secure email sender such as Mimecast Large File Send to add extra security and tick the box which provides a notification when the material is accessed, so that you can ascertain whether the recipient has opened any documentation before any link is disabled.
- Of course, always double-check the recipient – mistakes are easy when we are working quickly, advise your people to take time to read the email and the recipient list, and be very careful when using 'reply all'.
- Email addresses are stored and this is often why mistakes are made as the first email address to become available in the 'to' box is selected. It is possible to delete any rogue/incorrect/obsolete email addresses from your autocomplete list by pressing the X to the right of their name. Doing so means the address won't appear again.

2.2.2 What steps to take if an email is sent to the incorrect recipient

- Act quickly and urgently.
- Try to recall the email but do not rely on this working.
- Email the unintended recipient and ask that they do not read the email, do not open any attachments and that they confirm they have not read the email and that they have deleted it.
- If the attachment is sent using security software such as Mimecast Large File Send, immediately take steps to disable any link which contains the documents. Your provider will be able to provide guidance on this.
- Your people should be clear who to tell. You may wish to set up an email address for all data queries and breaches such as: dataprotection@firmaddress.com. Make sure your staff know who to tell so that the DPO can quickly consider whether a report to the ICO is needed (note the timescale to report a breach is 72 hours from the breach and not discovery).
- Finally, either the sender or the DPO needs to speak to the client partner or equivalent about whether and what to tell the client (if they don't know already). I would always argue that it is better to tell the client rather than they find out from someone else.

2.2.3 When to report a data breach

In a nutshell, whether you need to report a data breach depends on the facts.

The compliance officer for legal practice (COLP) will need to consider whether the data breach involves facts or matters which the COLP reasonably believes could amount to a serious breach of the regulatory arrangements (see paragraph 9.1 of the SRA Code of Conduct for Firms), in this case confidentiality in the main but other aspects of the Code might come into play.

The DPO (and the COLP too arguably under paragraph 7.7 of the SRA Code of Conduct for Solicitors, RELs and RFLs, which states: 'You report promptly to the SRA or another approved regulator') needs to consider whether a report needs to be made to the ICO.

Firms are obligated to report unauthorised disclosures of personal data within 72 hours of the disclosure (not discovery) to the ICO.

The ICO sets out the test for this as being one in which you consider whether the data breach poses a risk to people. The ICO further sets out that you need to consider the likelihood and severity of the risk to people's rights and freedoms, following the breach. When you've made this assessment, if it's likely there will be a risk then you must notify the ICO; if the risk is unlikely then you don't have to report the breach to the ICO. You therefore do not need to report every breach to the ICO, but I highly recommend you record it somewhere (a spreadsheet will do) so you can spot any patterns to enable to you consider future prevention.

2.3 Data subject access requests

As a firm which holds data you are susceptible to the receipt of a data subject access request (DSAR). The time limit for responding to a DSAR is very tight, and so you need to have a plan of action ready. This section aims to guide you through a DSAR and suggest ways in which you might handle this. This is also produced as a takeaway document found at **Appendix 14**.

2.3.1 Introduction

All data subjects have the right to make a DSAR. Under DPA 2018 recipients of a DSAR have one calendar month to respond with the data (unless the DSAR is extensive and complex in which case you may be able to extend for a further two months – but be warned, the ICO doesn't like it, so extend with caution) and there is no fee unless the request is 'manifestly unfounded or excessive' (whereas once there was a £10 fee no matter what). Just hope you don't get a DSAR in February or over Christmas then! Note that if the deadline to reply to a DSAR falls at a weekend, then the ICO has confirmed you can respond by the next working day.

Given the short timescale, it is very important to spot a DSAR quickly and act swiftly upon it. When you have potentially thousands of emails to go through, time will seem to vanish.

2.3.2 Determining whether you have a valid data subject access request

First things first – if you think you have a DSAR on your hands, inform the DPO immediately.

It is important to remember that a person is entitled to information about themselves only. So first consider whether what is being asked for relates to the individual making the request. It is possible for third parties such as solicitors to make requests on behalf of others, but the recipient of such a request must be satisfied that the request is ultimately coming from the individual and you may wish to get this confirmed by the individual directly.

If a person is making a request for data not about themselves but about a non-person such as a company, consider whether this is a valid DSAR.

The request for data should be in writing, but need be in no particular format. The request itself does not have to say that it is a request under DPA 2018 or that it is a subject access request. The request should be treated as such a request if it is clear to the reader that an individual is asking for sight of their personal data. This can on occasions be quite tricky, as a request to see personal data can be made among dealing with other matters such as a complaint or a grievance from an employee.

The request is also valid even if it is not sent to a designated person in the firm. An individual employee may consider it perfectly reasonable to send such a request to their line manager or supervisor.

Every request made should be acknowledged. If the request was made electronically then you should respond electronically unless otherwise agreed with the requester. Security of data should be considered.

2.3.3 Time limits, extending them and negotiating a narrow request

As indicated above, the time limit for dealing with DSARs is one calendar month from the date of receipt. When acknowledging the request, it is good practice to confirm when you consider the deadline expires.

It is important to consider carefully the request and ask for more information if you need it.

You can ask for enough information to judge whether the person making the request is the individual to whom the request relates. This could be, for example, asking for a certified copy of the individual's passport or driving licence.

You can ask for information that you reasonably need in order to action the request. This could be, for example, clarity on the request itself or more information about it. Until such information is provided the organisation is not required to respond to the request and the time limit does not begin to run. This point should be made clear to the requester in writing. However, asking for more information where this is not needed should never be used as a tactic to buy more time.

Given that the timescale for responding to DSARs can be very tight, it is wise to narrow the request if possible, by writing to the requester within seven days of receipt and proposing a narrowing of the search criteria.

You must, however, be cautious doing this. The requester is not obliged to respond to any such request from the organisation, nor is the requester obliged to agree. The request can be as narrow or as wide as the requester likes. Do not therefore wait for agreement for too long, but prepare the material or you will run out of time very quickly.

If, however, the request can be considered to be extensive or complex, time can be extended by two months so long as it is explained to the requester within the one calendar month period – but note the word of caution above.

2.3.4 Unfounded and excessive requests

You can decide to charge a requester a reasonable fee for responding to their DSAR if the request is unfounded or excessive. In addition you do have the right to refuse to reply. However, this should not be a decision taken lightly and legal advice might be needed. We are in a world where the right for a person to have their data trumps many other interests (or so it seems) and so to ensure compliance with the legislation you need to respond to the DSAR as far as possible.

2.3.5 How to search for and sift information

The nature of the request often dictates where and how one should look for the personal data being requested. Below are some examples:

- **Files:** If you hold data about the requester in paper form, then you will need to consider whether the information is covered by the DSAR. Whether or not the data is relevant depends on the relevant filing system and whether you have been provided enough information to locate it. A relevant filing system is where the filing has been undertaken with reference to the individual and is structured in such a way that information about the individual can be found. An example of this would be a personnel file of an employee.
- **Emails:** As most communication is undertaken by email, most searches will involve searching incoming and outgoing emails. Your IT department (if you are lucky enough to have one) should be deployed to assist. Depending on the DSAR, search terms could include the requester's name. If you have been able to narrow the request by reference to an act then a date range could be inserted which would decrease the number of emails returned significantly.
- **Other electronic forms:** A document search should be made using the relevant search terms which could be the name of the requester. Thought should be given to any other electronic system where personal data is recorded about the individual such as an HR system.

When sifting the information that has been returned from a search, you should document the agreed process internally. This is just in case a complaint is made by the requester later with the ICO.

It is important that those who are to undertake the sifting process understand what they are looking for and that is personal data. Personal data is the data relating to the individual who can be identified from the data or from the data together with other information which is in the possession or likely to come into the possession of the organisation. This definition is not always easily applied, and if in doubt you should seek guidance.

Depending on the nature of the DSAR and where thousands of emails have been retrieved the following process could be adopted:

1. The emails are split between the persons reviewing the data.

2. Each person siphons those emails into four separate sub-folders as follows:
   (a) 'disclose' because the email contains personal data about the requester;
   (b) 'redact' because the email contains data about someone else (please see below);
   (c) 'review' because the sifter is unsure;
   (d) 'do not disclose' because the email does not contain any personal data or is privileged or falls under a different exemption (please see below).

   (**Top tip** – don't put your 'disclose' and 'do not disclose' folders next to each other in case of misfiling.)

3. A designated person or persons within the group of people undertaking the sifting then spot-checks the 'disclose', 'redact' and 'do not disclose' folders and corrects any errors.
4. A designated person or persons within the group of people undertaking the sifting then reviews the items in the 'review' folder and moves each item into one of the other three folders.
5. The emails contained within the 'redact' folder are then printed and the data of others is removed by way of redaction/taking non-personal data or data of others out (or you can use some technological way of redacting) or if the data about the requester is small compared to the data of others then the data can be extracted and placed into a separate document appropriately labelled to ensure it is understandable.

The same process could be repeated for documents.

If the personal data that is retrieved is coded by reference to language that is used by the organisation, then the requester must be supplied with the relevant information to be able to read the information, e.g. acronyms.

2.3.6 What to do if the information contains third-party data

Very often, your search results will contain the data of others. For example, an email from HR to a line manager confirms the sickness absence of four employees including the employee who has made the data subject access request. This email will contain personal data about three other employees. If this is the case, then that personal data of those individuals should be redacted.

Where the person's data is a small part of a much larger data set (for example, a spreadsheet with 100 lines and 1 about your data subject) consider extracting that data and collating it into a separate document instead of redacting the 99 lines.

Where the request involves providing information that relates to the requester and another person, there is no obligation on the firm to respond to the request unless the other person gives consent or it is reasonable in the circumstances to comply with the request without that consent. In these situations, the firm will need to balance the rights of the requester to see their personal data and the rights of the other party in having their data disclosed.

If consent is required from a number of people, it is wise to start seeking consent as soon as possible so as to meet the one calendar month deadline.

If the third-party information is already known to the requester, say because the requester was the recipient of such information, then it can be disclosed.

2.3.7 Exemptions to providing the data

There are a number of exemptions to providing data. Some of these are:

- privilege – where either litigation or legal privileged applies, the data does not need to be disclosed;
- confidential references – this is information given in confidence; however if you are in receipt of a confidential reference then it may be caught under the request;
- information publicly available;
- personal data processed for the purposes of crime and taxation – for example, the prevention of crime or the prosecution of offenders;
- personal data that is processed for management purposes such as forecasting and planning in so far as to disclose such information would prejudice the organisation;
- negotiations with the requester – if negotiations are ongoing, the firm does not have to comply with the subject access request if to do so would prejudice the negotiations.

You must remember to write down your reasons for deciding whether data is captured by one of the exemptions. This will be useful if you are asked to defend your position with the ICO.

2.3.8 Finally – do you really have to respond?

Sometimes it seems (or at least it feels) that a DSAR is a tactic to slow down the recovery of fees or complicate a complaint or grievance. Although this may be true, it doesn't matter – you still have to respond. You can, though, try and get to the nub of what the requester is really after by communicating with them and asking. However, time is still ticking during those communications so be careful. If you have any doubts, always seek legal advice.

3 Cybercrime

Cybercrime is one of the largest threats to your practice. The risk of your firm being the subject of a cyber-attack is very high. Law firms are rich in valuable data and you need to understand fully the risks you face and how to mitigate them. Cyber-attacks can cause financial loss to you and your client as well as extensive reputational damage.

Set out below is a very brief explanation of the types of cybercrime. Please do not underestimate how large a subject this is. Below is intended to be a starting guide and to get you thinking about how you might begin to mitigate those risks. This area of risk is a joint effort between the risk management personnel and IT teams and should not be tackled in isolation of each other.

3.1 Types of cybercrime

The first thing to remember here is that cybercrime is not static and methods are always changing. As much as possible each firm should dedicate time to keeping on top of cybercrime types and trends. Below are some of the main types that your firm may become a victim of.

- **Email modification fraud – firm to client:** Under this method, cybercriminals intercept genuine emails between the firm and the client. The criminal can then amend the content of the email from the firm to the client and may for example request that monies are sent elsewhere. This is perhaps the most frequent method used by cybercriminals.
- **Email modification fraud – impersonating internal people:** Another method is emails from fraudsters pretending to be members of the firm, for example the chief executive officer (CEO) or managing partner, and requesting that monies are sent in various directions. Often these are easy to spot, but it is possible for members of staff to think they are real.
- **Phishing, spear-fishing and vishing:** These methods of cyber-attack involve criminals sending emails in order to obtain confidential information, such as passwords, bank details or other sensitive information, or enticing the email recipient to unintentionally download malicious software (malware) on to your IT system. Spear-phishing is an email fraud attempt that targets a specific organisation and appears to be from a sender that the firm knows.
- **Ransomware:** Here data is 'taken hostage' as a result of malicious software infiltrating IT systems, and ransom monies are demanded by the cybercriminals to release the data. Note though that paying the ransom does not always guarantee access to data and/or devices. Ransomware normally gains access through the recipient clicking on a link they have been sent.

- **Website vulnerabilities:** Your website is also vulnerable to attack and through websites, users can be infected. Website vulnerability is often not thought of and this needs to be considered by you when testing your resilience to a cyber-attack.

3.2 Risk mitigation

There are a number of steps that you can take to mitigate the risks of a cyber-attack. Below is an outline of some of them.

3.2.1 Penetration testing

Here you pay someone to try to hack you. A penetration tester will test your network and website to find security vulnerabilities that an attacker could use to attack your firm. The tester will gather information about your firm before the test and consider entry routes into the firm and then attempt to hack and report back on findings to the firm. From this report you are able to consider what actions need to be taken to tackle any vulnerabilities. Penetration testing should ideally be conducted annually.

3.2.2 Phish your own people!

An effective (and can I say fun) way of testing your vulnerabilities is to phish your own people in the firm. There are technology companies out there (and you may be lucky to have internal expertise) that can create fake realistic-looking emails that invite the recipient to click on a link. When the link is clicked nothing happens or an error message occurs but in the background data on who clicked is recorded. This data should be used not to punish but to educate, to see whether your training is effective and whether you have any vulnerable spots in the firm.

3.2.3 Create a clear route internally for reporting concerns

It is important that it is clear to whom in the firm people should report anything suspicious. This is so that internally you can understand the types of threats that you are facing and so that people in your firm have a place where they can ask whether it is ok to open a document or click on a link. You may want to consider setting up an email group with an appropriate title such as 'Cyber Concern' or 'Threats' and have an internal process whereby the email that is sent on is checked by your IT team and the member of staff is informed if the email is malicious and whether they are able to safely open any attachment or click on any link. Of course, your IT team will need the tools to be able to check such emails. If you do not have a dedicated IT team then you need to consider alternative ways of checking emails such as calling the sender and asking them to send the information in a different way.

The bottom line here is that it should be made absolutely clear what a recipient of a dodgy-looking email should do and for this reason training on this subject should be included in the induction process for new joiners to your firm.

3.2.4 Be clear with clients about cybercrime and how you share bank details or request payment

Cybercrime prevention is doubly hard because not only do you need to educate your staff but also you need to educate your clients. We are all well aware that a bank will not call its client and ask for their password. The reason this has been drummed into us all is because the banks tell us that they will not do it and if someone is calling purportedly from a bank and asks for your password you are advised to hang up (politely presumably) and call the bank using a trusted number.

As a law firm your aim should be to educate your clients as banks have educated theirs. The way to do this is to put sufficient wording on your email disclaimers, in your terms and when you send bank account details to your client. That wording should give clients sufficient warning about what to look out for. I am pleased to report that in my experience this works and clients are now becoming savvier to fraudsters impersonating law firms and requesting monies be sent to a different location.

The wording you use should fit your firm. Below is some suggested wording that you might like to include in your email disclaimers, your terms of business and also when sending your bank details (see **7.11** for more information):

> Please note this message has been scanned for viruses. However email is not a secure medium. Any reply to this message could be intercepted and read by someone else. Please carefully check all emails purportedly sent by this firm and do not hesitate to telephone us to query the content of emails.
>
> [*Name of firm*] **will not change bank details during the course of this matter. If during the course of this matter you receive an email or a telephone call purporting to be from us informing you that our bank details have changed, it is likely to be an attempted fraud. Please contact us by telephone to inform us of any such communication.**

As and when you receive emails from other firms or businesses, have a look at their disclaimers and see what they write.

3.2.5 Buy up similar sounding domains

Fraudsters will impersonate your firm by buying similar sounding domains and try to pass themselves off as your firm. Speaking from experience, my firm Howard Kennedy LLP has been impersonated using the domain HovvardKennedy.com and HowardKennnedy.com. Note here the first impersonation has two Vs in instead of a W and two Vs look like a W at a quick glance; and the second has three Ns in Kennedy.

To try to prevent fraudsters using these domain names to fool your clients and staff, buy domain names that sound like your firm as far as possible. They are usually inexpensive to buy.

3.2.6 Show when emails come from an external source

To counteract impersonation fraud, you may wish to set up your emails so that when they are received from an external source the email clearly indicates this. Fraudsters are able to make an email address from which the fake email is being sent look legitimate with the correct email address showing – once the recipient right clicks on to the sender's email or hits reply the fraudster's email address normally appears. However, in case this does not happen or the recipient does not notice, having a message on the email saying it has been sent from an external source and yet the sender is an internal person with an internal email address, should hopefully arouse suspicion in the recipient and they can act (or not act) accordingly.

3.2.7 Block emails coming in!

Of course, you should ensure your firm has sufficient protection from malicious emails coming into your firm.

3.2.8 Training

As with all important subjects you need to provide training. This should feature in your yearly plan of training. There are various ways to get the message across and what works will depend on your firm. There are online training module providers and also external trainers who will come and visit your firm to provide training. Think of also hitting training in 'softer' ways such as a 10-minute chat in team meetings or mentioning cybercrime at any firmwide or role-based meetings (i.e. all partners, all trainees, all secretaries) or putting out publications on your website or by emails or blogging on your intranet when news items highlight the latest cyber-attack to hit a business. Make messages about such subjects short and snappy but make them frequent. Frequent short edible training messages are far more effective than a once yearly long missive that no one wants to read.

3.2.9 Business continuity cyber-attack simulation round-table testing

Business continuity is mentioned in more detail in **7.13**. However, there is special mention here as law firms tend to think of business continuity tests as testing the office being unavailable due to flood, fire or electrical failure, etc. It is right you must discuss running your business without the office and have a plan. However, do not miss the opportunity to run through some cyber-attack events that could happen and discuss these in a round-table setting with those in the firm who would be making decisions in the event of a real attack. Below is a basic scenario which you could run through as a round-table cyber-attack simulation.

Event	It is 9am and your firm has been the subject of a cyber-attack. Client X's data has been taken and is being held to ransom. Client X is an important client to the firm and the firm needs the data to complete a large transaction next week. The fraudsters are asking for £20,000 in bitcoins to release the data back to your firm. They demand payment by midday.
Questions	What is your first step? Should you investigate now how this happened? Do you inform insurers? Do you tell the client? What data has been taken and how damaging is it to the client for someone else to have it? Do you need the data to complete the transaction or can you get what you need in a different way such as a data backup or from an alternative source? If you do not complete the transaction what loss if any will be caused to your client or the firm? Should you tell insurers about this potential loss? Can completion be put back?
Event update	It is now 1pm and the fraudsters get in touch. They are angry as you haven't paid when they asked. They now demand £40,000 in bitcoins.
Questions	All of the questions above again and should you pay? Do you have any insurance that you can claim against?
Event update	It is now 2.30pm and the fraudsters are impatient. They haven't increased their price but they threaten to release the information to other third parties if they do not receive payment soon.
Questions	Do you now pay? Should you discuss with the client the impact on them if the information is released? What damage would it do? Are you sure the fraudsters have the data? Do you communicate with the fraudsters?
Event update	It is now 3pm and the fraudsters having not received payment say they have placed malware on your computer network and are ready and waiting to take more data. They demand £40,000 in bitcoins by 4pm.
Questions	What do you do? Do you pay?

As you can see, the scenario can be as short or as long as you want. However, practising these scary events means that if or when they do happen (and I genuinely hope they do not happen to you) you will be rehearsed and not in a state of shock.

3.2.10 Cyber Essentials and other accreditation schemes

Cyber Essentials is a UK government led scheme operated by the National Cyber Security Centre launched in June 2014 that encourages organisations to adopt good practice in information security. The scheme includes an assurance framework and a simple set of security controls to protect information from threats. The scheme sets out five major security controls which are:

1. **Boundary firewalls and internet gateways:** Protecting your internet connection with a firewall effectively creates a 'buffer zone' between your IT network and other, external networks.
2. **Secure configuration:** New software is often set with everything switched on to make it as accessible as possible. Unfortunately, this makes it easier for cyber-attackers to gain unauthorised access. Altering your configuration will limit the chances of an attacker getting through.
3. **Access controls:** The aim here is to minimise the potential damage that could

be done if an account is misused or stolen by giving staff only the access they need to perform their role at the firm.
4. **Malware protection:** Via operating systems or whitelisting (where an administrator creates a list of applications allowed on a device and any application not on this list will be blocked from running) or sandboxing (applications are run in an isolated environment with very restricted access to the rest of your device and network so it should be beyond reach of malware).
5. **Patch management:** It is important that software is kept up to date at all times to ensure it receives the safety patches provided by the supplier to fix security vulnerabilities.

As well as offering good advice and a self-assessment, the scheme also enables firms to become Cyber Essentials Plus accredited, the cost of which is a few hundred pounds (though it may cost more to implement what is required). This accreditation comes with a logo. More clients are now seeking confirmation of cyber security measures and so showing you have been through this process is bound to be a good thing.

The elements of Cyber Essentials can be mapped against other accreditation schemes such as ISO27001, the Standard of Good Practice for Information Security (published by the Information Security Forum; this is a business-focused, practical and comprehensive guide to identifying and managing information security risks in organisations and their supply chains); and IASME (Information Assurance Standard that is designed to help improve the cyber security of small and medium-sized businesses).

If having read this section on cybercrime you don't know where to start or don't have the resources to dedicate extensive time and money to this topic, then visit the Cyber Essentials website as a starting point and follow its five security controls as outlined above as a minimum.

3.2.11 Reports to the Solicitors Regulation Authority, Scam Alerts and Action Fraud

If an attack is attempted on your firm you need to consider reporting requirements. If there are facts or matters present which the firm, one of its solicitors or the compliance officer for legal practice (COLP) reasonably believe could amount to a serious breach of the regulatory requirements then a report to the Solicitors Regulation Authority (SRA) will need to be made.

Aside from the obligation above, while there is no duty to inform the SRA of an attempted or actual attack on your firm, it is best to inform it anyway and ask that a Scam Alert be placed on its website if appropriate. Scam Alerts are there to warn the public of impersonations of law firms or those within law firms. There is no shame in having your firm listed on the SRA Scam Alerts, it just means your firm and those people within it are worth impersonating.

Finally, while you are not obliged to, you may wish to consider reporting the cybercrime event to Action Fraud, the UK's national report centre for fraud and cybercrime. While it may not be able to investigate, data on attacks will only help the authorities to fight cybercrime in the long run.

3.2.12 Cybercrime insurance and planning for the worst

To buy cybercrime insurance or not to buy cybercrime insurance – that is the question.

Each policy needs to be carefully considered with the assistance of your broker. However, speaking in general terms your professional indemnity insurance may cover client monetary loss as a result of a cyber-attack event and your crime insurance may cover firm monetary loss. Excesses on your professional indemnity insurance can be large and so if at all possible, firms should avoid making claims against it which will only increase the premium.

Neither professional indemnity insurance nor crime insurance will cover the costs of forensic investigation, retrieval of data and reputational/PR advice. In contrast normally cybercrime insurance will cover those costs (subject to excess).

Cybercrime policies are still in their infancy and are changing too quickly to be written about in this book in any great detail. My advice is to mock-up a document setting out the type of cyber-attack event, the likelihood of it happening, how to mitigate the risk of the event happening, the impact if it did and whether you have insurance to cover. Where there is a gap, plug it as best you can (you may also find you are doubly insured and don't need/want to be). You can find a table at **Appendix 15** with an example to get you started.

4 Anti-money laundering compliance

Anti-money laundering (AML) compliance is arguably the most challenging and costly area of compliance for law firms. This section is not designed to teach you what the AML regulations (Money Laundering, Terrorist Financing and Transfer of Funds (Information on the Payer) Regulations 2017, SI 2017/692) require of your firm, but rather how you might effect compliance in practice.

I would recommend you get printed and laminated the AML guidance of the Legal Sector Affinity Group (LSAG) and read it cover to cover: **www.lawsociety.org.uk/policy-campaigns/articles/anti-money-laundering-guidance/**.

4.1 The MLRO, the MLCO and AML queries

It must be absolutely clear in your firm who the money laundering reporting officer (MLRO) is and therefore where concerns of money laundering should be directed. Further you should appoint a deputy MLRO to handle concerns in the absence of the MLRO. Details of these people must feature in your money laundering policy (see **Appendix 16** for a template policy).

The MLRO's role is to report suspicious activity to the National Crime Agency (NCA) and where appropriate seek a defence to a money laundering offence if committed (note it is not 'consent' you are seeking or what you will be getting, though it is often called this incorrectly).

As well as an MLRO, the firm also needs a money laundering compliance officer (MLCO). The MLCO must be an individual who is a member of the board of directors (or if there is no board, of its equivalent management body) or of its senior management and is the officer responsible for compliance with the regulations.

There should be someone in the firm that is available to answer any AML compliance queries. This could be the MLCO or MLRO and depending on the size of your firm may be more than one person.

The requirements for compliance with the AML regulations have become stricter and the Solicitors Regulation Authority (SRA) is closely monitoring compliance. It is no longer acceptable, in my view, not to have a person that fee earners and support staff can escalate compliance questions to. Muddling through is not an option when it comes to compliance with the AML regulations.

4.2 Centralising CDD gathering, PEPs, sanctions and adverse media checking and file opening ownership

With the cost and importance of client due diligence (CDD) gathering and checking so high, there is a real argument for centralising the gathering of CDD, checking clients for politically exposed persons (PEPs), sanctions and adverse media and therefore centralising the onboarding of clients. Whether centralisation is right for your firm will ultimately depend on client type (your clients may be regulated in which case simplified due diligence is likely to be adequate or your clients might be complex trust or corporate structures that perhaps go offshore), size of your firm and whether there is a consensus that centralisation is a cost-effective way of handling the onboarding of clients as ultimately a person or persons will need to be employed for the role.

Many firms do now centralise this function. Centralising has the following benefits:

- correct CDD will be gathered and checked in the process;
- it enables full sanction, PEP and adverse media checking more easily as information is to hand (this can be done via an online platform or by using open sources and should be redone when each new matter is opened);
- it enables a risk-based approach to be taken in conjunction with the fee earner more easily;
- it ultimately saves fee earning time.

If you do decide to centralise the CDD-gathering function into a risk team or you have already done so, don't fall into the trap of leading or allowing your fee earners into thinking that they have delegated their responsibility under the regulations to those who gather CDD. They should be involved at each CDD-gathering stage and copied in to all emails.

Some risk teams in firms also own the file-opening process and will either open files on behalf of fee earners in the firm or approve that opening. Again, this will depend on the nature of your firm as to whether this is appropriate for you. The benefit is that someone whose job it is to open files will inevitably be quicker at doing so and therefore it will cost the firm less.

Consideration needs to be given to how much work a fee earner is able to undertake before CDD is completed. Your firm may take the view that no work is to be completed or that only preliminary work is to be undertaken. Certainly, no substantial work should be completed and no transactions completed before the CDD process has concluded. You may also decide to treat regulated work differently from unregulated work (i.e. wills, litigation). However, clients port over from one work type to another and no one then is keen to ask the litigation client for ID so property work can be conducted. You may take the view, like a lot of firms do, that it is best to adopt the same high standard for all.

4.3 Sanctions and 'reverse sanctions checks'

Where possible, clients should be checked for sanctions. You may decide to only conduct sanctions checks for those clients who may be deemed higher risk (this analysis should feature in your firmwide AML risk assessment (see below and **Appendix 17** for a template)). If you have the resource, check all clients. If you have the budget, buy an online checking tool that will enable you to conduct PEP, sanctions and adverse media checks at the same time. If you do not have the budget, use open tools as far as possible such as open sanctions lists (see: **www.gov.uk/government/publications/financial-sanctions-consolidated-list-of-targets/consolidated-list-of-targets**) and Google.

4.3.1 What are sanctions?

In a nutshell, sanctions are financial constraints put in place by the United Nations (UN), the European Union (EU) and sometimes the UK in order to coerce, constrain, signal disapproval or protect the value of assets. Implementation of sanctions is undertaken by the Office of Financial Sanctions Implementation (OFSI). This organisation also enforces sanctions.

HM Treasury has enforcement powers to punish breaches which include a financial penalty which could range from 50 per cent of the total breach up to £1 million. The Policing and Crime Act 2017 increased the maximum term of imprisonment for offences to seven years' imprisonment.

The view of the OFSI is that it is the firm's responsibility to check sanctions lists and take appropriate steps.

If you find your client is on a sanction list, you need to determine what type of sanction it is and whether it applies to your firm. As sanctions are very serious, you may wish to take independent legal advice at that time and I would recommend you have an external adviser on hand ready to assist you.

If the client is on the OFSI's list and you already act, you must report to the OFSI. If you hold monies for the client, you must in effect 'freeze them' and not move the monies unless you can show an exemption in the legislation applies or you have applied for and obtained a licence from the OFSI. When reporting to the OFSI, you need to consider privilege, and further you need to consider whether you should make a suspicious activity report to the NCA.

Sanctions are serious business, and you are encouraged to visit the OFSI website for full guidance.

4.3.2 Reverse sanctions checks

Sanctions lists are updated regularly and I would recommend that you sign up to be notified when the lists are released, and then names contained on newly released lists are run through your database to ensure one of your clients is not now sanctioned. Better to know and seek the relevant licence than not to know and commit a criminal offence (for here ignorance is no defence).

4.4 Firmwide AML risk assessment

Under regulation 18(1) of the AML regulations, your firm is obliged to undertake a firmwide AML risk assessment to identify and assess the money laundering risk in your firm and to consider and put in place policies, controls and procedures to tackle those risks. The LSAG AML guidance has detailed and well-written guidance and I refer you to that rather than repeat the content here. I will, however, just highlight some aspects for you to consider.

- The SRA has produced a template risk assessment for you to consider. It does not mandate that you use this template and there are many ways of writing your assessment down. You may decide to do it by way of spreadsheet and/or table or in a written form consisting of paragraphs. You need to do what is best for the type of firm you are. At **Appendix 17** you will see a suggested template and you are encouraged to review the SRA's template found on its website.
- If you have not conducted a firmwide risk assessment, you must do one straight away. Do not wait for the SRA to ask you for it. Also, do not simply copy a template with no thought behind it. Make your assessment bespoke to your firm.
- Make a space on your assessment to note when it was reviewed last so you can show you are regularly reviewing it. There are no set review times, but I would advise at least once a year, and two or three times a year is definitely more preferable. While you are reviewing the assessment you can review your firm's AML policy and record that also.
- Before you start your assessment, you need to take into account the information about AML risks available to you. I would recommend you read the SRA's guidance and stance on AML and also the UK's National Risk Assessment, which is a comprehensive assessment of money laundering and terrorist financing risk in the UK undertaken by the government (**www.gov.uk/ government/publications/national-risk-assessment-of-money-laundering-and-terrorist-financing-2017**). Mark on the assessment itself that you have done this.
- Your assessment needs to take into account the following:
    - your clients, where they are based, where their assets come from, whether they operate in high-risk sectors, are PEPs, sanctioned or have adverse media against them, are high-cash businesses and so on;
    - countries and geographical areas in which your business operates;
    - the services you provide and the transactions your firm is involved with – for example, company formation, trust formation, sham litigation, tax havens;
    - how you deliver your services, i.e. face-to-face or not;
    - nature of your suspicious activity reports (SARs) and the disclosures that are made to the MLRO.
- Set out in your assessment how the risks you have identified are mitigated by way of policies, controls and procedures and what work there is to do. Diarise that work, set deadlines and carry those tasks out.

Please see the LSAG AML guidance and the SRA guidance for more information: www.lawsociety.org.uk/policy-campaigns/articles/anti-money-laundering-guidance/.

4.5 Risk assessments on clients and matters, high-risk registers and ongoing monitoring

4.5.1 Client and matter risk assessments

The AML regulations require a risk assessment to be undertaken on each client and matter (again for regulated work types though you may decide to adopt the same standard throughout). There is no set template client and matter risk assessment to complete and you should design your assessment around the money laundering warning signs either generically or specifically to the type of work. Again, the LSAG AML guidance provides good guidance on money laundering signs.

You may decide to implement a risk assessment for all types of client and work or you may decide to create a risk assessment that is specific depending on client and work. The latter can be time consuming to set up and can lead to multiple versions of the assessment that would need to be maintained.

At **Appendices 7** and 8 you will see an example client and matter risk assessment with guidance that you may want to adapt to suit your firm. This example assessment is split so that a central CDD-gathering function forms part of the risk assessment. This may not be how you wish to undertake the assessment at your firm and so you will need to adapt the template. There is no definitive way of devising your client and matter risk assessment.

You should already have client and matter risk assessments implemented in your firm. If you do not this needs to be rectified with urgency.

4.5.2 High-risk register

Each firm should also maintain a high-risk register where clients who are considered to be high risk are placed and monitored. A client can be considered to be high risk because they are a PEP (remember this includes domestic PEPs), sanctioned, have adverse media against them, operate from a high-risk jurisdiction or their activities are considered to be higher risk (for example, art dealing).

Your high-risk register need not be anything more than a spreadsheet. It should, however, be maintained and looked after properly. Maintenance could entail a recheck of the entries for PEPs, sanctions and adverse media every month or more frequently where faster paced work is being conducted such as property transactions.

Have a policy for when high-risk register entrants are suspended from the ongoing checking process and they can perhaps be placed in a suspended tab in your spreadsheet. Do not delete the entry as you may need to demonstrate that the client was on your register at one point and so it is a good idea to document why they were taken off.

Do not forget to inform the acting fee earner of any PEP, sanction or adverse media entry, what it means and that the client will be placed on the high-risk register. Each new fee earner who starts to work for the high-risk client should be informed of the results found and the client's entry on to the high-risk register.

4.5.3 Ongoing monitoring

The AML regulations require that risk is assessed at the outset and throughout the retainer. You may therefore want to create space on the client and matter risk assessment for the conducting fee earner to write down their ongoing monitoring assessment. Further guidance should be issued and the firm's process on ongoing monitoring set out in the firm's AML policy.

You may also want to centralise some form of ongoing monitoring to assist fee earners (though they need to understand it is ultimately their responsibility). This could be a member of the risk team calling the fee earner and asking a series of questions about the transaction and whether any suspicious activity has occurred. You will find at **Appendix 18** a simple ongoing maintenance form which you may want to adapt.

Also part of ongoing monitoring is the rechecking of CDD during the time the firm is acting for the client. There are some clients for whom the firm will act for many years and therefore CDD documentation may be out of date or the client structure will have changed. You need to decide what your process is around this. You may want to recheck clients on each new matter (which is likely to be too onerous unless long periods of time elapse between matters); at certain intervals, e.g. every two years; or at a frequency set depending on the type of client or work.

Ultimately, you can create something very complicated with these processes. Try not to. Make it as simple and proportionate as the AML regulations will allow.

4.6 Controls you need to consider including screening employees and an independent AML audit

Regulation 21(1) of the AML regulations sets out the controls that you must consider and apply depending on the size and nature of your practice. We briefly go through them here.

1. Appointing an individual as the officer responsible for the practice's compliance with the Regulations. This is referenced at **4.1**. The individual must be either a member of the board of directors (or equivalent management body) or senior management. A member of senior management means an officer or employee with sufficient knowledge of your practice's money laundering and terrorist financing risk exposure and sufficient authority to take decisions affecting that risk exposure.
2. Screening relevant employees prior to *and during* the course of their employment in relation to their skills and knowledge and their conduct and integrity. The LSAG AML guidance sets out that screening could mean having regard to

a person's qualifications, any regulatory, professional and/or ethical obligations to which the person is subject, checking a person's references.

A 'relevant employee' is someone whose work is relevant to your practice's compliance with the Regulations or who is otherwise capable of contributing to the identification or mitigation of money laundering and terrorist financing risks to which your practice is subject, or the prevention and detection of money laundering and terrorist financing in relation to your practice.

You may want to carry out criminal records checks on all incoming and current employees but this is not a requirement under the Regulations (consider whether current employees are able to provide freely given consent in an employee/employer position – I would argue they cannot give consent freely and therefore you are unable to undertake criminal records checks on existing staff).

For screening of existing staff you may want to conduct adverse media checks by simply Googling their name (consider whether this needs to be included in any documentation about what data you process and hold on your people) and having an annual declaration (however, be aware that any person who lacks integrity is likely to lie on such a declaration and so consider whether it is something you want to do).

3. Independent audit function to examine, evaluate and make recommendations regarding the adequacy and effectiveness of your firm's policies, controls and procedures. Have in mind the size of your firm, work type and type of client. The audit does not have to be carried out by someone outside the firm and it can be costly to do so. It should however be carried out by someone not involved in the day-to-day due diligence gathering and so not your central risk team if they gather and sign off CDD gathered. If there doesn't seem to be anyone within your firm that seems suitable, contact a similar size firm and see if it would be prepared to audit you and you audit it.

4.7 Client and matter risk assessment completion audit and MLCO audits

Of course, there is merit in auditing all types of AML compliance and I would suggest that the MLCO does this. At **Appendix 19** you will find a simple question set which could be used by the MLCO to audit files each month for compliance.

Completion of client and matter risk assessments is such a crucial part of AML compliance that it gets a special mention in this book. It is not possible of course to audit every assessment on every file but some form of audit to check completion rates should take place. You could weave this into your normal file review, place it within the MLCO file review or give it a standalone check.

4.8 SAR filing and record maintenance

It is vital that you record not only your SARs made, but also conversations that did not lead to a SAR. In other words, all suspicions should, if possible, be recorded and noted down. The SRA is keen to understand the conversion rate from reported suspicions to the MLRO to SARs filed, and can ask you for this data at any time. A simple spreadsheet will do, but also supplement this with a decent filing system for all email correspondence about the suspicion.

The decision of whether you have a suspicion and therefore you need to file a SAR can be very tricky. The LSAG AML guidance has a flowchart which can help you make the judgment – this can be found at **Appendix 20**.

Once you have decided you have a suspicion, you need to report, you then need to decide whether you need to submit an intelligence-only SAR (i.e. you are simply passing information to the NCA) or whether you need a defence SAR. Remember you are not asking for 'consent' from the NCA. That would be fantastic to have, but that is not what it is there to give you and so don't ask for it or your SAR may be rejected. The NCA is there to provide a defence to a money laundering offence should one occur.

Drafting a SAR can be tricky and there is plenty of criticism about the SARs that solicitors submit. At **Appendix 21** you will find a very simple template that you can follow. Below are some tips on how to draft your SAR.

- Remember the reader of your SAR is coming at this cold. They don't know you, who you are, who your client is, anything about the retainer and so on. Tell it like a story.
- Be clear about the act that you are concerned will potentially cause a money laundering offence to be committed. Be specific and in no way theoretical.
- Be clear which money laundering offences you are concerned will be committed and specifically state which Proceeds of Crime Act 2002 (POCA) offence with section references.
- Give a timeframe during which the payments will be made. The NCA does not like to give defences with no details about when the act might take place.
- Lastly consider fungibility – the idea that the 'bad' money taints the 'good'. If you take in what you consider might be proceeds of crime, does this taint a pool of money that your client might be using for ongoing purchases? Consider whether another SAR is needed.

5 Statutory compliance

5.1 New compliance requirements and how to stay on top

One of the aspects of the role of compliance officer for legal practice (COLP) is to ensure they are on top of the compliance requirements and then put in place adequate measures in the firm to implement those requirements. So how do you stay on top?

Time needs to be dedicated to reading publications, attending events and training. Easier said than done I know (all too well). One possibility is to share the load. If possible, give personnel their own area of compliance to be experts in. It can be part of their role to make sure they are up to date on the compliance requirements in that area and update the COLP for further discussion about requirements and implementation plans. Very often the COLP is a full-time fee earner and rarely a full-time COLP. When the latter is the case the law firm is usually a large one where the COLP will also have the benefit of a team to assist them in their role. Often there is too much for one COLP to do, and so share the load with risk team members or keen fee earners who are happy to help.

So where can you get information from to be able to keep up to date? If you are reading this and work in risk in your firm, sign up (if you have not done so already) to any publications the Solicitors Regulation Authority (SRA) and the Law Society can offer you. Further, hook into the SRA consultations which will give you a glimpse of what might be coming up.

Then I would recommend you be selective. There are many free publications/ newsletters out there and it is very easy to feel bombarded. Legal Risk LLP (established specifically to offer legal advice to lawyers on risk issues in the UK) and other law firms have newsletters you can sign up to and they are good for keeping on top of what is coming up, so sign up to them.

Further, consider subscribing at cost to the Law Society's Risk and Compliance Service, a service for people who manage compliance, which provides news and also free webinars and podcasts.

Events to attend are also numerous, and often free. Events hosted by technology suppliers are really events about their product which you may well be interested in, but if not then I would caution against attending those.

Your online module training supplier will often have a newsletter and events that you can attend as part of your package, so ask about those.

Ask your insurer or broker whether they have any publications you can receive or events you are able to attend. They often host events and they will be impressed by your enthusiasm.

If you are new to the risk and compliance space then try to attend events that give you a baseline knowledge and work from there. Law Society events are fantastic at providing great foundation training and you will meet like-minded people.

Above all else, network as much as you can. When networking, you will meet people in the same boat. Sometimes compliance can feel like a lonely space and so having on hand a few people you can run something by or bounce an idea off will always help. Risk and compliance is also a non-competitive environment between firms. All firms are in the same spot, trying to be compliant. Networking and meeting people in risk and compliance means when you need to put in place a policy or want to work out how to tackle an issue, someone in your network will have already been there and done that and will readily help you. Staying on top of everything required in law firm regulation is tough, so where possible do not try and reinvent the wheel each time. Reach out to your network and someone will help.

5.2 Modern slavery compliance

This may not apply to your practice due to your size. However, if you have a turnover of £36 million or more you need to ensure you are compliant with the Modern Slavery Act 2015.

5.2.1 The purpose of the Modern Slavery Act 2015

The Modern Slavery Act 2015 seeks to tackle modern slavery by creating criminal offences of:

- slavery, servitude and forced or compulsory labour;
- human trafficking: arranging or facilitating the travel of another person with a view to that person being exploited;
- exploitation: slavery; servitude and forced or compulsory labour; certain sexual offences; removal of organs or tissue; and obtaining services or benefits by threats, force or deception.

These apply whether or not the offences take place in England and Wales.

The Act seeks to address the role of businesses in preventing modern slavery from occurring in their supply chains and organisations.

The Act requires businesses in the UK with a total annual turnover of £36 million or more to report annually (by way of statement – see below) on steps taken by the business to ensure that slavery and human trafficking are not taking place in either its business or its supply chains.

5.2.2 Which organisations must publish a slavery and human trafficking statement?

The reporting obligation applies to companies, limited liability partnerships (LLPs) and partnerships which:

- carry on a business or part of a business in the UK;
- supply goods or services; and
- have an annual turnover of £36 million or more.

An organisation's turnover for these purposes includes the turnover of that organisation and all of its subsidiaries, whether those are located in or outside the UK.

Each organisation within a group that conducts business in whole or in part in the UK and exceeds the turnover threshold is required to publish a slavery and human trafficking statement. There is the option, however, to take a group approach to this requirement, say where a parent company and its subsidiary are both required to produce a statement, one statement can be published as long as it covers the supply chains of both.

What if turnover drops below £36 million? The government recommends through its 'Transparency in supply chains etc. A practical guide' (para.7.6) that the organisation should continue to report and publish a statement (**https://assets.publishing.service.gov.uk/government/uploads/system/uploads/attachment_data/file/649906/Transparency_in_Supply_Chains_A_Practical_Guide_2017.pdf**).

5.2.3 When and where must the statement be published?

The statement must be published following the end of each financial year of the business. Government guidance ('Transparency in supply chains etc. A practical guide') states that:

- Organisations should publish their statements as soon as possible after the end of the financial year and at most, within six months of the organisation's financial year end.
- Organisations may wish to publish the statement alongside their annual or non-financial reports.
- It is recommended that historic statements from previous financial years should remain available online even when new statements are published to permit the public to compare statements from different years (my advice is that if you do not want to do this you could set out in your current statement that prior statements are available on request and to whom such a request can be made).

If the firm has a website, it must publish the statement on that website and include a link to the statement in a prominent place on the homepage. The link should be clearly labelled so that the contents are apparent, so no hiding it behind another area of the site – it needs to be right up front.

If your firm does not have a website then you must provide a copy of the statement to anyone who requests it in writing, within 30 days of receiving the request.

The Home Office has done checks to make sure those who should publish a statement have done so.

5.2.4 What must the statement contain?

The minimum legal requirement is to set out the steps taken by the business in the relevant financial year to ensure that slavery and human trafficking are not taking place in either its business or its supply chains or, if no such steps have been taken in that financial year, to specify that no steps have been taken.

For corporate entities, the statement must be approved by the board and signed by a director. An LLP's statement must be approved by its members and signed by a designated member. A partnership's statement must be signed by a partner.

The statement may also include information about:

- the organisation's structure, business and supply chains;
- relevant policies, including supplier due diligence, auditing and procurement processes;
- training provided to those in supply chain management;
- key risks related to slavery and human trafficking including how those are evaluated and managed;
- relevant key performance indicators to enable readers to assess the effectiveness of the business' anti-slavery activities.

The organisation is not required to guarantee that there is no slavery or human trafficking in the business or its supply chains, and businesses are encouraged to take a risk-based approach to their management of the risk of slavery and human trafficking.

You will find a template statement attached at **Appendix 22**. This is just one way of writing your statement. When writing your statement, you may want to consider the statements of other law firms and also different types of businesses such as retail (John Lewis is a good example, see: **www.johnlewispartnership.co.uk/meta/modern-slavery-statement.html**). How far you go with your statement depends on your firm. If your firm conducts work in the charity or human rights sectors then you may want to make your statement very detailed.

5.2.5 Sanctions for non-compliance

The Secretary of State for the Home Department has the power to bring civil proceedings in the High Court for an injunction requiring an organisation to publish a statement. A subsequent failure to comply with any court order would risk the organisation being in contempt of court, punishable by an unlimited fine.

Of course, the biggest sanction is bad PR. Negative attention because a firm does not have a published statement would be severely damaging, especially if it matters to the firm's client base due to the type of clients a firm has and work the firm does.

5.2.6 Practical guidance

If you have not tackled this area of compliance yet, or not tackled it fully, then you need to do so as soon as humanly possible. There are in effect two aspects to compliance. First, getting up to the level of compliance that is required and second, having a process in place going forward to ensure ongoing compliance.

Achieving compliance

For the first step of bringing you up to the level of compliance, below is a suggested plan of action.

1. Analyse supply chains.
   (a) Ask your finance/accounts team to run off a report showing those you have been supplied to by reference to turnover and country.
   (b) Analyse those results and decide on the basis of turnover and/or country (as per the Global Slavery Index) whether to send the supplier a questionnaire. Suggested questions below.
2. Send questionnaire to current suppliers as identified in 1(b).
   (a) Compose a Modern Slavery Act questionnaire and send to selected suppliers. Ask for a response within 14 days and chase up to one month after sending.
3. Analyse the results of the questionnaires.
   (a) Consider responses to the questions and whether they give rise to a concern of slavery or human trafficking in the supply chain. If they do, consider next steps.
4. Review your policy or create one.
   (a) Review and devise a modern slavery policy. See **Appendix 23** for a template policy. Republish this policy each year to your staff.
5. Training.
   (a) Decide what training will be provided to those who are involved in procurement. If no training is being provided, then consider a guidance note. See **Appendix 24** for template guidance note.
6. Create a Modern Slavery Act statement (see **Appendix 22** for suggested template) to include:
   (a) organisation's structure, business and supply chains;
   (b) what you have done to audit your supply chains, what vetting procedure there is going forward and what policies you have;
   (c) what training those involved with procurement have had or will receive;
   (d) what your ongoing auditing will look like and what are the key performance indicators.
7. Publish the statement.
   (a) Reconsider guidance and publish statement in accordance with requirements, i.e. on website.

Suggested questionnaire questions for suppliers:

1. In which industry do you operate?
2. In which countries do you operate?
3. Can you trace every stage of the production process for your goods/services?
4. What is the composition of your workforce? i.e. women, migrants, etc.

5. What do you know about how the workers in your supply chain are paid?
6. What do you know about how the workers in your supply chain are recruited?
7. Do you have an anti-slavery and human trafficking policy and what does it say?
8. Who in your organisation is responsible for compliance with the Modern Slavery Act?
9. What key performance indicators (KPIs) has your organisation set to track your progress with ensuring there is no slavery or human trafficking in your supply chains?

Ensuring ongoing compliance

To handle the second aspect of compliance and make sure Modern Slavery Act compliance is present moving forward, you should consider incorporating a set of questions about Modern Slavery Act compliance into any procurement process adopted by the firm (you may decide to use the questions set out above). See **7.4** for further information about procurement.

5.3 Criminal Finances Act 2017 compliance

This section sets out the requirements of the Criminal Finances Act (CFA) 2017 on law firms and how you can ensure compliance with the Act in a practical and straightforward way.

5.3.1 What does the Criminal Finances Act 2017 say?

CFA 2017 came into force on 30 September 2017 and creates a criminal offence for any entity that fails to prevent the criminal facilitation of tax evasion by associated persons (defined below). The offence is not so much about tax law but about behaviours which are dishonest.

In essence your firm is in the frame if it fails to prevent tax evasion by its associated persons. If there is tax evasion by your associated persons, the firm's defence is that it did all it could to prevent it from happening. Therefore, you need to do your best to ensure compliance so you can use that defence.

The offence of tax evasion will be committed where an associated person:

1. is knowingly concerned in, or takes steps with a view to, the fraudulent evasion of tax by another person; or
2. aids, abets, counsels or procures the commission of a UK tax evasion offence by another person; or
3. is involved in the commission of an offence consisting of being knowingly concerned in, or taking steps with a view to, the fraudulent evasion of tax.

There are three stages to the offence:

1. the criminal evasion of UK tax, i.e. the underlying tax evasion offence;
2. the criminal facilitation of this offence by an associated person to the firm;

3. the firm failing to prevent the associated person from committing that facilitation.

As well as a UK offence, there is also a foreign offence. This offence is the same as the UK offence described above but the tax evaded is non-UK tax. As well as the tax evasion being a criminal offence in the non-UK jurisdiction, it must also be an offence in the UK for it to be considered an offence under CFA 2017.

5.3.2 Associated persons

Now here is a really important element of this legalisation – the associated person.

An 'associated person' is defined as:

- a person who is an employee of the firm who is acting in the capacity of an employee (this would include partners and consultants);
- an agent of the firm who is acting in their capacity as an agent; or
- any other person who performs services for and on behalf of the firm who is acting in the capacity of a person performing such services.

Those acting in the capacity of an employee of the firm is a pretty easy concept to understand – but what about agents?

Those who act as an agent may be experts that you instruct, including counsel. These parties may therefore be construed as being associated persons. Most if not all such persons will be regulated persons, and so will be subject to their own regulators' requirements and CFA 2017. You may therefore decide to consider these associated persons as being low risk.

However, if you are instructing a non-regulated person to provide a service which may cause them to be seen as an associated person and they are providing advice which may include tax advice, you need to consider the risks of doing so and whether you need to ask some questions about their adherence to CFA 2017. If you do feel the need to ask questions about their compliance why not ask how they handle compliance with other aspects of regulatory law such as money laundering, anti-bribery, modern slavery and so on. See **7.4** on procurement for more ideas here.

5.3.3 So what do you need to do?

The first thing to do is to read the Law Society's practice note on CFA 2017 (www.lawsociety.org.uk/support-services/advice/practice-notes/criminal-finances-act-2017/). This note is a very helpful guide to the Act itself and the steps that should be taken to ensure compliance.

If you have not taken any steps so far to ensure compliance with the Act, you must do so as soon as possible. Initially HM Revenue and Customs (HMRC) indicated that while it did not expect firms to have had everything in place by 30 September 2017, it did expect that firms would have taken some steps and would have a plan to ensure compliance as soon as possible – to include communication of the Act and a plan of action to implement compliance with it. We are now far from 30

September 2017 and so you should be compliant by now – but if not, then that needs to rectified as soon as possible.

Whatever you do, remember to write it down. If something happens and HMRC or the SRA come asking questions about what your firm did to ensure you were compliant with the Act, you need to prove what steps you took. Keeping your plans in your head only has the possibility of looking to a regulator like you are 'winging it' when they come to ask what you have done. Show compliance by drawing up a plan, even if it is just a one pager. Note of caution – make sure you follow through with that plan.

Below is a plan of action for you.

Step 1 – Conduct a risk assessment

There is no set risk assessment to complete and you should tailor it to your own firm dependent on size, type of work conducted and clients. See **Appendix 25** for a template.

To help you, below is a set of questions you may wish to consider and then score accordingly (either by way of low, medium or high risk or by reference to whether the situation would arise be that never, rarely, sometimes or often).

Clients

- Do you act for clients whom you have reason to suspect of tax evasion in the past or present?
- Do you act for clients who may pose a particular tax evasion risk? For example, because they are cash based, have assets in higher risk jurisdictions or hold assets through complex or obscure ownership structures?

Services

- Do you advise clients on tax?
- Do you assist in creating corporate or tax structures which may be used to facilitate tax evasion?
- Do you act on matters connected to tax havens?
- Do you set up structures to minimise tax?

Employees

- Do you have a lack of supervision anywhere?
- Do you ensure that appropriate checks are carried out before employment?
- Is there a culture of compliance in the firm and can it be better?
- Do any employees display an ignorant attitude to compliance?

The Law Society practice note goes into detail on the risk assessment and so it would be wise to consult it.

You may want to consider tying this risk assessment up with your firmwide AML risk assessment (see **Appendix 17** for a template AML risk assessment). Alternatively, you could conduct a firmwide risk assessment covering money laundering, CFA 2017, bribery, modern slavery and so on (see **Appendix 32** for a template firmwide risk register).

After analysing the risk assessment, draw up a plan of any changes that need to be made and obtain approval of these changes and the risk assessment from senior management. These changes might include how you vet third parties you instruct; how and who you train; whether a new anti-tax evasion question forms part of your firm's file review/audit process; and so on.

Step 2 – Create a documented anti-tax evasion policy

You need to have a documented anti-tax evasion policy. See **Appendix 26** for a template policy.

As with the risk assessment, there is no set template to use and it should be tailored to your own firm. A good policy could set out:

- what a CFA 2017 says;
- what the commitment of the firm is – e.g. to do business ethically and in accordance with its obligations under regulations and relevant laws;
- what the firm expects of its staff/employees (this could include how you will treat the vetting of those the firm instructs such as counsel – remember that a risk-based approach can be adopted and so if the firm is instructing regulated persons you may wish to consider the risk to be low. However, if you are instructing non-regulated persons, the risk may be higher and so questions may need to be asked about their own policies, procedures and controls);
- what the facilitation of tax evasion is, how your staff/employees can unwittingly become involved, and how they can spot it ;
- the duty on all staff/employees to report and to whom (this could be tied in with your whistleblowing policy);
- practical examples of tax evasion in each practice area – e.g. delivering misleading or inaccurate bills which enables a client to evade tax; misstating the value of a property so that less land tax is payable; or assisting in the creation of corporate or trust structures designed to conceal taxable income. The more practical the examples the better, so your people really understand how it can happen in their everyday practice. It has to feel 'real' or it might just get ignored.

Again, this policy needs approval from senior management.

Step 3 – Communicate the policy

You now need to communicate the policy in the most appropriate way to your firm.

This could be by email, in a meeting, on your intranet, by internal memo – whatever suits your size, is proportionate and appropriate. You might want to adopt a different approach for different practice areas. For example, those who work in tax and private client could be called to a meeting as those practice areas may be considered to be higher risk for the purposes of the legislation and you may decide to simply email everyone else.

Whatever you decide to do document your thought process (remember that the firm's defence if an offence is committed by an associated person is that it took reasonable steps to prevent the offence occurring – so you may need to prove what you have done and why).

Step 4 – Provide appropriate training

It might be that not everyone in the firm needs to be trained and it might be that not everyone needs formal training. Training could be by way of online module, by way of meeting and a talk, seminar, webinar with a group of people watching and so on. How you train your firm is up to you. However, whatever you do, you must document it. So, if you consider that your firm did not require formal training, you need to document this.

5.3.4 Finally

Diarise to review the risk assessment, policy, relevant procedures and training in a year's time. It is all too easy to write clever policies and let them collect dust. Don't let that happen.

5.4 Anti-bribery and corruption compliance

Your firm must be compliant with the Bribery Act (BA) 2010 which came into force on 1 July 2011.

5.4.1 The Bribery Act 2010

BA 2010 creates three main offences:

1. bribing a person to induce or reward them to perform a relevant function;
2. improperly requesting, accepting or receiving a bribe as a reward for performing a relevant function; and
3. improperly using a bribe to influence a foreign official to gain a business advantage.

Under the Act, bribery by individuals is punishable by up to 10 years' imprisonment and/or an unlimited fine. If your firm is found to have taken part in bribery or to lack adequate procedures to prevent bribery, it too could face an unlimited fine.

A conviction for a bribery or corruption related offence would of course have severe reputational and financial consequences for your firm.

It is important to remember that bribery is not always a matter of handing over cash. Gifts, hospitality and entertainment can be bribes if they are intended to influence a decision.

The Law Society has a practice note on BA 2010 which provides more detail and good solid guidance (**www.lawsociety.org.uk/support-services/advice/practice-notes/bribery-act-2010/**). I urge you to read it.

5.4.2 Managerial responsibilities

Your firm should have a designated anti-bribery and corruption officer (ABCO) who is responsible for overseeing the firm's policy on anti-bribery and corruption and ensuring it is upheld in both word and spirit.

The ABCO's responsibilities should include:

- an annual review of the policy;
- an annual review of the risk assessment of issues relating to the policy;
- overseeing training and communications relating to the topic.

Although the ABCO has responsibility to oversee bribery compliance in your firm, you may want to make it clear that ultimately all partners of the practice remain accountable for your policy implementation and ensuring compliance.

5.4.3 Third-party due diligence

The scope of BA 2010 requires you to identify third-party business relationships which may give opportunities for a third party to use bribery while acting on the firm's behalf. To that end appropriate due diligence should be undertaken before a third party is engaged (please see procurement process at **7.4** which will help cover off this risk). It is important that third parties should only be engaged where there is a clear business rationale for doing so and with an appropriate contract. Any payments to third parties should be properly authorised and recorded as per your firm's process.

5.4.4 Gifts and hospitality

Your firm needs to have a policy on gifts and hospitality that is proportionate to the work you do and the clients you have.

Gifts and hospitality are commonly used in business to build relationships and market services or products. Hospitality often takes the form of entertainment, meals or tickets to events. If the provider of the hospitality does not attend, then it should be regarded as a gift.

While this is all normal practice, it should be recognised by your firm and reflected in your policy that gifts and hospitality can be used to influence and corrupt third parties, and on occasion to manoeuvre employees into a position of obligation. When considering whether to accept a gift, what matters is the intention behind it. If it is offered as a bribe it should be refused; but if it is offered as a genuine gift as, say, a thank you for a job well done, it may be accepted provided that all aspects of your firm's policy are complied with.

Ultimately, you want to prevent the giving or receiving of gifts, hospitality or paying of expenses if it might influence or be perceived to influence a business decision.

Accordingly, you need to decide what value of gifts, entertainment and hospitality either given or received must be reported to the ABCO and recorded by either the ABCO or other appropriate business services team such as business development/ marketing. This will allow you to monitor both the level and the number of instances to assess whether the nature of the relationship is appropriate.

5.4.5 Risk assessment

You need to conduct a bribery risk assessment to assess the extent and nature of the risk of bribery or corruption to which you might be liable in your activities. This assessment should record the type of risk and the means by which you can prevent or mitigate your exposure to such risk. The assessment should be reviewed each year and you may wish to combine it into your firmwide risk register (see **Appendix 32**) or tag it on to your AML risk assessment (see **Appendix 17**).

5.4.6 Communication and training

It is important that your people are all aware of your policy and stance on bribery. To that end, you need to clearly communicate your policy and provide training where appropriate. It is also a good idea to diarise to send out a bribery story or small piece of guidance once or twice a year in addition. You may decide to train via online module, face-to-face or by way of guidance note which you could designate as a mandatory read.

5.4.7 Finally

If you do not have an anti-bribery and corruption policy you need to implement one ASAP. Please see **Appendix 27** for a template to get you started.

5.5 Whistleblowing legislation and your firm's policy

The first thing to remember about the whistleblowing protection in law is that the whistleblowing must relate to disclosure of information *in the public interest*. The framework for this is set out in the Public Interest Disclosure Act (PIDA) 1998.

PIDA 1998 protects workers who make certain disclosures of information in the public interest (a 'protected disclosure') and gives them the right not to suffer a detriment or be dismissed as a result.

PIDA 1998 is part of employment legislation and specifically the Employment Rights Act 1996.

Under PIDA 1998, whistleblowing is the disclosure of information in order for past or current misconduct, or perceived misconduct, to be addressed in relation to any:

- criminal offence;
- failure to comply with any legal obligation;
- miscarriage of justice;
- damage to the environment;

- attempting to conceal any of the above.

The Enterprise and Regulatory Reform Act 2013 includes a requirement for whistleblowers to act 'in the public interest' but removes the need for the disclosure to be in 'good faith', leaving public interest as the primary test for any disclosure made in relation to protections under PIDA 1998.

Although not a regulatory requirement, the easiest way to ensure compliance as far as possible is to implement a firmwide whistleblowing policy. You can find a template policy at **Appendix 28**. This policy should align with the reporting requirements on the firm, individuals, the COLP and the compliance officer for finance and administration (COFA) and will demonstrate your firm's commitment to an open culture, that you take misconduct seriously, that you encourage reporting and will support it. Further, a good whistleblowing policy can help demonstrate compliance with anti-money laundering (AML) regulations and BA 2010 as it is one way to show you have policies in place to report such activities.

It is important that you communicate your policy effectively and train staff where relevant. You may not decide to train all staff on whistleblowing but certainly the COLP, COFA, HR team and perhaps line managers will benefit from face-to-face training about the whistleblowing framework that the firm operates in. (See **6.7** for the SRA's approach to whistleblowing and reporting obligations.)

6 Regulatory compliance

It is vital for anyone in risk and compliance in law firms to be aware of and stay on top of the regulatory requirements. While new requirements are added on occasion, there are some mainstay items and these are set out here.

6.1 Practising certificate renewal and Solicitors Regulation Authority reauthorisation

Each year a firm needs to reauthorise with the Solicitors Regulation Authority (SRA) and renew all its solicitors' practising certificates (PCs) on a bulk renewal basis. The application is completed online via mySRA and opens for completion on 1 October each year and has to be completed by 31 October.

If you are new to the responsibility of reauthorising the firm and renewing PCs, I encourage you to go to the SRA website and download the guidance that is ordinarily available there. I also set out below the categories of information that the firm needs to have available when completing the application (please note this list may change, and so is not a replacement for reading the SRA website which should be your first port of call):

1. largest, smallest and average client account balance for last accounting period;
2. the firm's turnover and whether more than 20 per cent comes from any single client, group of clients or referral source;
3. areas of work that make up your turnover i.e. conveyancing, family, personal injury;
4. professional indemnity insurance (PII) details;
5. information about associations (such as introduction arrangements);
6. details about any arrangements, relationships or connections that might influence the running of the firm;
7. details about separate businesses clients are signposted to and the like;
8. how many legally qualified and non-legally qualified fee earners the firm has;
9. how many claims have been made in the last indemnity period and how many claims have been paid out in the last indemnity period regardless of when the claim was made;
10. details about complaints that have gone through the firm's internal complaints process, what those complaints were about (e.g. delay, failure to advise, costs information) and which complaints went to the Legal Ombudsman (LeO);
11. details of solicitors for which a PC will be granted (see below).

In terms of PC renewal, the form within mySRA has ticked as standard for each solicitor that the individual is not subject to regulation 3 of the SRA Practising Regulations 2009 (www.sra.org.uk/sra/regulatory-framework/sra-practising-regulations-2009/); that they have complied with the continuing competence regime; and 'No' to a reduced fee. Let's take each of these in turn.

1. Regulation 3 of the SRA Practising Regulations 2009 refers to the requirement to make an 'application following certain events'. If a solicitor is applying for their PC (via the firm normally under bulk renewal) and has been:
   - subject to SRA reprimand;
   - subject to disciplinary sanction such as a fine or rebuke;
   - made the subject of an order under section 43 of the Solicitors Act 1974;
   - ordered to pay costs;
   - made the subject of a recommendation to the Law Society of England and Wales or the SRA to consider imposing a condition by the Solicitors Disciplinary Tribunal (SDT) or struck off or suspended;
   - bankrupt;
   - committed to prison;
   - charged with or convicted of an offence;
   - disqualified as a director;
   - made the subject of an intervention;

   or any of the other criteria apply, which are too lengthy to repeat here, then regulation 3 requires the applicant to make a separate application for a PC outside the firm's bulk renewal process which the SRA will consider. This will involve that individual making their own application.

   If you are responsible for handling the firm's bulk PC renewal process, you may decide that you would like all solicitors to confirm to you that regulation 3 doesn't apply. You may take the view that you would know if a solicitor fell within regulation 3, which might explain why the SRA pre-ticks the box on the bulk renewal form, and therefore you do not need to ask for confirmation from all solicitors.

   If one of your solicitors is subject to regulation 3 and is granted a PC, they are then able to come back into the bulk renewal process the next year and regulation 3 is not deemed to apply again.

2. Continuing competence – The previous continuing professional development (CPD) 16-hours-a-year requirement was replaced in November 2016 with the continuing competence regime. This regime requires solicitors to reflect on the quality of their practice and identify any learning and development needs (think very carefully about whether it is a good idea to tie this in with appraisal time in the firm as you may not (or you may) get honesty about what training is required). With no minimum hour requirement this was a sea change for practitioners, and you may have decided to keep your minimum hours in the firm. The continuing competence regime is a wide subject beyond the scope of this book and I encourage you to read more on it.

   By ticking the continuing competence box (or allowing the box to remain ticked), the authorised signatory for the firm (the person who ultimately signs the application off, normally the compliance officer for legal practice (COLP) or managing partner) is declaring on behalf of the solicitor 'yes' to the following question 'Have you reflected on your practice and addressed any identified learning and development needs?'. In my view, therefore, you need to be sure that the solicitor has completed their continuing competency plan or you cannot declare on their behalf and they cannot then get a PC. This has been a useful (but painful and tedious) stick to 'beat' solicitors with who do

not naturally reflect on their competence. There is no doubt that HR and senior management assistance is required here.
3. Reduced fee – Here you need to enter the dates of any maternity/adoption leave or any equivalent leave (shared parental leave would qualify) currently being taken or having been taken during the last PC year. This will result in a reduced fee needing to be paid.

My advice here is to *start early*. Obtain the guidance to the renewal form at the end of September and ask other areas of the business to assist you and have information back to you by the second week of October, and then start your application and submit in good time. *Never leave this to the last minute*. MySRA will be bombarded on the last few days of October and will inevitably be slow.

Remember your authorised signatory (normally your COLP or managing partner) has to sign this form off and submit it, and so prime them in good time to make sure they know their login details for mySRA. No one else can get this for them.

6.2 SRA Codes of Conduct queries, and in particular conflicts

6.2.1 SRA Codes of Conduct queries

Depending on the size of your firm you may wish to invest in personnel who are on hand to answer any queries under the SRA Codes of Conduct (Code of Conduct for Solicitors, RELs and RFLs and Code of Conduct for Firms). This is a task that is normally undertaken by a risk team, or maybe the COLP themselves. As the new SRA Codes of 2019 are now so short, it has left a lot of room for interpretation and uncertainty, and so if you are a COLP with no risk team, I recommend you try to either write some guidance to each section of the Codes or have on your intranet links to the SRA guidance and relevant Law Society guidance under each area of the Codes so that your fee earners are able to find guidance quickly.

6.2.2 Conflicts

Conflicts are an area that need frequent discussion and careful thinking through. Conflict scenarios can be relatively straightforward or horrendously complex. Consider having a conflicts policy which doubles as guidance together with a decision tree. Further, consider whether you want to have a conflicts committee in your firm where really challenging conflicts can be discussed. However, be aware that the more minds on the subject the more overall cost to the firm in lost fee earning time and also the longer it will take for decisions to be made and generally conflicts need to be considered rapidly.

See **Appendix 29** for a template conflicts policy with guidance which you may want to adapt and implement in your firm.

6.3 Ethics queries

Distinct from the 'can we' question is the 'should we' question. Ethics queries are becoming more frequent and fee earners are questioning more whether they should be taking an action or not as opposed to whether the Codes allow it.

At the heart of ethical considerations are the SRA Principles (see: **www.sra.org.uk/solicitors/standards-regulations/principles/**) and, as with Codes of Conduct queries, fee earners in the firm need to know who they can discuss these issues with. This can be the risk team or the COLP or it could be the fee earner's line manager initially.

Consider building a bank of questions and answers on ethical scenarios for your intranet (this is not only useful for fee earners, but also creates a bank of scenarios that the risk team or COLP can refer to as it is easy to vaguely remember something you were asked about some months ago that sounds similar to the query you have now).

Also consider running some ethical scenario training. In my experience this is really popular and fee earners particularly like it if it relates to scenarios that have actually happened in your firm. Remember: training should be informative, interactive and fun – and if possible, always feed people (if it is not lunchtime, provide cake!).

More and more cases are appearing before the SDT that turn on questions of ethics. Those in charge of the risk function in the firm need to ensure that fee earners understand ethical considerations and that when such considerations arise, fee earners have resources to help them consider the situation and have a place where they can discuss the ethical issue.

6.4 SRA Accounts Rules compliance and queries

Just as support is provided for compliance with the SRA Codes of Conduct, so support should be given to fee earners in understanding the SRA Accounts Rules (**www.sra.org.uk/solicitors/standards-regulations/accounts-rules/**). The 2019 SRA Accounts Rules have significantly reduced the requirements that are imposed here, but the reality is that most firms will stay relatively the same. Ensure that all fee earners and the accounts team have regular Accounts Rules training in one shape or another. This could be training every two years, say, plus a guidance piece or practical example of a particular rule in action. One particular rule that is here to stay is the non-banking rule (rule 3.3) and if you do not have guidance in your firm about this you need to put some in. This rule states: 'You must not use a client account to provide banking facilities to clients or third parties. Payments into, and transfers or withdrawals from a client account must be in respect of the delivery by you of regulated services'. See **Appendix 30** for an example of guidance that you may wish to give to your firm.

As the SRA Accounts Rules are now very reduced compared to what they once were, consider whether you want/need to create an accounts manual which sets out the processes and procedures that the firm adheres to. This will be useful if there is an internal challenge to how things are done – but be warned: your auditor is likely to judge you against it and so do not commit in your manual to work in a way which is too challenging and aspirational and that you are therefore unlikely to achieve.

6.5 Price transparency

The SRA Transparency Rules on prices came into force on 6 December 2018 (see: www.sra.org.uk/solicitors/resources/transparency/transparency-price-service/).

6.5.1 The requirements

In a nutshell, firms need to place in a prominent position on their website price information about the following types of service undertaken:

- For members of the public:

  - residential conveyancing (freehold sale or purchase, leasehold sale or purchase, mortgages and remortgages);
  - probate (uncontested cases with all assets in the UK);
  - motoring offences (summary offences);
  - immigration (excluding asylum applications);
  - employment tribunals (claims for unfair or wrongful dismissal).

- For small businesses:

  - debt recovery (up to £100,000);
  - employment tribunals (defending claims for unfair or wrongful dismissal);
  - licensing applications (business premises).

The information you produce and place on your website must include:

- what services are included within the displayed price;
- any services not included in the price that might reasonably be expected to be included;
- typical timescales and key stages for the given legal service (you are not required to provide cost information for each individual stage, just a total cost);
- the experience and qualifications of all individuals who carry out work within the areas specified under the Transparency Rules (think about whether the information already on your website is enough; also consider whether it is appropriate to set out a fee earner's post-qualified experience (PQE) as this could lead to discrimination);
- the experience and qualifications of those who supervise the individuals who will be carrying out the work, although you do not need to necessarily specify who supervises whom.

6.5.2 Why did these rules come in?

The SRA introduced the price Transparency Rules further to its own research conducted after the December 2016 report from the Competition and Markets

Authority (CMA) which concluded that there was an absence of sufficient information on price, quality and service and that this was hampering consumers' and small businesses' ability to choose the best option for legal support.

The SRA reported that its research found that price transparency is likely to help to overcome some of the key barriers that discourage small businesses from accessing legal services. The SRA's view is that the research also suggested that publishing prices may help firms to win more business, both from competitors (presumably they mean non-solicitors here) and from new clients who do not currently access professional support due to incorrect assumptions about how much the solicitor will cost.

Key findings from the research include:

- Small businesses said that a lack of readily available price information, and the complexity of the information that was currently available, were the main barriers to finding a new solicitor.
- Solicitors were perceived as being expensive.
- A portion of small businesses already spent time searching the internet when looking for legal service providers, and 75 per cent would spend more time doing so if more accessible information was available online.
- The SRA said it found evidence that by increasing price transparency solicitors would win more business from alternative providers and professions that do not publish their prices.
- Further, the SRA said that even where all potential providers publish pricing information, solicitors' potential market share was still likely to increase when they publish prices.

In its application to the Legal Services Board (LSB) to implement the Transparency Rules, the SRA stated (www.legalservicesboard.org.uk/what_we_do/regulation/pdf/2018/july/20180706_LSB_Formal_Application_Better_Info.pdf):

> Our objective is that consumers should have the information they need to make informed choices about the purchase of legal services. Specifically, we aim to ensure that consumers have the information they need about firms, the services they offer, the prices they charge and the protections they have in place. This will enable consumers to compare different providers and make informed choices about which provider will best meet their needs.

6.5.3 Hindrance or marketing opportunity?

Solicitors operate in a very competitive space and to have to publish prices may, one might say, reduce the number of clients rather than bring more in. Further, it might be thought that the published information could be used by a client as complaint fodder (wrongly of course, but it could still be used for that).

Some larger firms have adopted an attitude of 'Yes, we are expensive. If you want services cheaper, go elsewhere please'. However, that is not suitable for the majority of firms.

There is an opportunity, though, to sell and distinguish your services on your website.

Either way, it would be good if the SRA could repeat its research to see whether in fact what it set out to achieve (more clients for solicitors) has worked, and if it has not, maybe it might decide to change the decision to publish such information. Or maybe it will require firms to publish price information for *more* areas of work than they currently have to.

Watch this space.

6.6 SRA digital badge/clickable logo

The SRA conducted a study with LeO called 'Better information in the legal services market' which, it says, tested how people understand and use information about regulatory protections and complaints (**www.sra.org.uk/globalassets/documents/sra/research/better-information.pdf?version=4a1ac1**). In June 2018 the SRA reported that the study showed the following:

- Presenting information about regulatory protections not only increased people's awareness of protections, it also meant that people engaged with and used these to make decisions.
- An 'SRA regulated' logo had a significant impact on people's choice and has potential benefits for both consumers and firms. When people were asked to choose between providers in the trial, the providers with a logo were selected by an average of 14 per cent more people. Additionally, 79 per cent said they felt more confident in buying services from a website with the logo.
- People were also willing to trade off protections and price to choose the service that they believed was right for them. They did not simply select the cheapest option. For example, 54 per cent said that they would be willing to pay more for certain regulatory protections.

From 25 November 2019, all firms are required to display the SRA clickable logo (also referred to as the SRA digital badge) on their website. Firms should visit the SRA website for instructions on how to obtain the logo.

Once the logo is clicked on, the visitor is taken to an SRA page which confirms that the SRA regulates the firm and that the SRA sets the rules that the firm and the solicitors follow and 'will take action if these rules are broken'. It further sets out that this means the following:

- everyone who works for the firm must meet the high standards the SRA sets;
- the firm must have the right level of insurance to protect 'you' in case something goes wrong – note here the SRA says 'you' and not clients, which suggests that non-clients are able to make a claim against insurance;
- the person clicking may be able to claim through the Compensation Fund (a discretionary fund operated by the SRA which solicitors contribute to through a levy added to practising certificate fees) to have their money reimbursed if the firm or a solicitor working for it loses their money;
- the person clicking can complain to the SRA if they are concerned about the behaviour of the firm.

Further the message sets out that if the clicker of the logo has concerns about the service they receive they can also make a complaint to LeO and that the clicker can find out more about this firm by using the SRA's law firm search function.

6.7 Reporting obligations and whistleblowing protection

Whistleblowing from a regulatory perspective has become more important than ever (see 5.5). I say this because we are in an era of recognising and 'outing' bad behaviours and the reporting obligations on firms and solicitors have become more widely worded.

6.7.1 Reporting obligations

Section 3 of the SRA Code of Conduct for Firms sets out the reporting and notification requirements. These are similar provisions in the SRA Code of Conduct for Solicitors, RELs and RFLs (paragraphs 7.7–7.9) which are not reproduced here. The reporting obligations are:

3.9 You report promptly to the SRA, or another approved regulator, as appropriate, any facts or matters that you reasonably believe are capable of amounting to a serious breach of their regulatory arrangements by any person regulated by them (including you) of which you are aware. If requested to do so by the SRA, you investigate whether there have been any serious breaches that should be reported to the SRA.

3.10 Notwithstanding paragraph 3.9, you inform the SRA promptly of any facts or matters that you reasonably believe should be brought to its attention in order that it may investigate whether a serious breach of its regulatory arrangements has occurred or otherwise exercise its regulatory powers.

3.11 You do not attempt to prevent anyone from providing information to the SRA or any other body exercising regulatory, supervisory, investigatory or prosecutory functions in the public interest.

3.12 You do not subject any person to detrimental treatment for making or proposing to make a report or providing, or proposing to provide, information based on a reasonably held belief under paragraph 3.9 or 3.10 above or 9.1(d) or (e) or 9.2(b) or (c) below, or under paragraph 7.7 or 7.8 of the SRA Code of Conduct for Solicitors, RELs and RFLs, irrespective of whether the SRA or another approved regulator subsequently investigates or takes any action in relation to the facts or matters in question.

For individuals, their reporting obligation is discharged when they inform the COLP or COFA as per the SRA Code of Conduct for Solicitors, RELs and RFLs paragraph below:

7.12 Any obligation under this section or otherwise to notify, or provide information to, the SRA will be satisfied if you provide information to your firm's COLP or COFA, as and where appropriate, on the understanding that they will do so.

If the COLP/COFA and the person reporting the facts or matters which may amount to serious misconduct are in disagreement about whether a report should be made, then this will of course cause friction and external legal advice may need to be sought.

6.7.2 The old rule

The prior rule under the SRA Code of Conduct 2011 was as follows:

> **Outcome 10.4:** you report to the SRA promptly, serious misconduct by any person or firm authorised by the SRA, or any employee, manager or owner of any such firm (taking into account, where necessary, your duty of confidentiality to your client)

There has been a shift, therefore, from promptly reporting 'serious misconduct' to reporting 'facts or matters that you reasonably believe are capable of amounting to a serious breach'.

6.7.3 Why the change?

This particular rule has had extensive thought put into it by the SRA, including a consultation to take in the views of the profession – Reporting Concerns Consultation in 2018 (**www.sra.org.uk/sra/consultations/consultation-listing/reporting-concerns/**).

In its post-consultation document, the SRA set out that firms' and individuals' understanding of when the duty to report was triggered differed, and in particular the SRA identified that some considered that they did not need to report concerns until an internal investigation had occurred and a determination as to whether serious misconduct had taken place was reached. This is at odds with how the SRA considers matters should proceed.

The SRA says the reason for the shift from reporting 'serious misconduct by any person or firm authorised by the SRA, or any employee, manager or owner of any such firm' to reporting 'any facts or matters that you reasonably believe are capable of amounting to a serious breach of the regulatory arrangements by any person regulated by them (including you)' is to reflect that as a regulator it expects to receive information at an early stage where it may result in it taking regulatory action. The SRA say it does not want to receive reports or allegations that are unmeritorious or frivolous, but it does want to know whether it is possible that a serious breach of its standards or regulations has occurred.

Further, the SRA says in the consultation documentation that it agrees with one respondent's comment that: 'It is not the role of the Compliance Officer to make a final determination as to whether or not an act or omission amounts to a breach of the Code of Conduct.' The SRA wants to conduct its own investigation and wants the legal profession to report. This doesn't mean, however, that the COLP cannot or should not investigate but confirms that the decision about what is serious misconduct is for the SRA to make and not compliance officers or anyone in the firm.

That is clear then, isn't it? Maybe. It doesn't make the decision to report easier, though. There are situations that are clear cut such as 'hands in the till' or other forms of dishonesty. However, sometimes allegations are just that – allegations. It may not be known until an investigation has taken place whether the allegations are meritorious. Reporting is serious and should not be taken lightly.

The 'notwithstanding' wording in paragraph 3.10 implies that even if you do not consider a report should be made under the first part of the section because you don't think the facts are capable of amounting to serious misconduct, you still should report it to the SRA anyway as it may take a different stance.

6.7.4 Ensuring your firm knows what to report

The SRA said in its consultation:

> We do want to receive reports where it is possible that a serious breach of our standards or regulations has occurred and where we may wish to take regulatory action.

So, the first thing to guide your firm on is whether you have facts or matters which could amount to a *serious* breach. 'What is serious?' you may wonder. The SRA does not define serious, but the SRA enforcement strategy provides a guide on what indicates seriousness in its view. For example, nature of the allegation, intent, motivation, harm, impact, vulnerability, regulatory history, patterns of behaviour and remediation.

The rules do not provide clarity on when the reporting should happen. However, the consultation provides big clues as to what the SRA expects. In its 'Reporting concerns: Our post-consultation position' (January 2019) the SRA said (www.sra.org.uk/globalassets/documents/sra/consultations/reporting-concerns-post-consultation-position.pdf?version=4a1abb):

> ... it is important for us, as the regulator, to receive information at an early stage where this may result in us taking regulatory action [para.25].
> ... we require reporting of facts or matters which could comprise a serious breach, rather than allegations identifying specific and conclusively determined breaches [para.26].
> ... it is our job to investigate those concerns that are capable, if proven, of amounting to a serious breach of our requirements. Early reporting is important because it allows us to do so; and although a firm itself, having identified a breach may be best placed to gather evidence, this will not always be the case – for example where this sits in another firm or with a client [para.27].
> Early engagement with the SRA also allows us to make sure that we can understand any patterns or trends using information we already hold. Sometimes we will want to gather information regarding particular types of risk to consumers, to understand patterns and trends (eg cybercrime), even where this may raise no concerns about the conduct or behaviour of regulated individuals or firms [para.29].

So should you investigate first before you report? The SRA says:

> This is not to suggest that firms shouldn't investigate matters nor that compliance officers shouldn't exercise their judgment in deciding whether a potential breach has occurred – indeed we want to encourage firms to resolve and remedy issues locally where they can.

However, we are keen for firms to engage with us at an early stage in their internal investigative process and to keep us updated on progress and outcomes. In these circumstances, we are likely to be happy for the firm to conclude their investigation and to provide us with a copy of their report and findings. However, we may, on occasion wish to investigate a matter (or an aspect of a matter) ourselves – for example because our focus is different, or because we need to gather evidence from elsewhere [para.30].

This is clear. You can investigate of course, and in fact should do so – but you should *also* inform the SRA so that the SRA, rather than you, can decide what it does.

The reporting obligations are serious and are taken seriously by the SRA, and as such you need to ensure your firm and those within it understand their obligations. You may wish therefore to issue an internal guidance note (see **Appendix 31** for an example). This should, however, dovetail with the firm's whistleblowing policy.

6.8 Gathering and publishing equality and diversity data

The SRA requires your firm to report equality and diversity (E&D) data to it roughly every two years. The SRA provides the specific questions that you need to answer, and it is worthwhile setting those questions up in your HR system so that your people can provide the data in your own systems from which you need to ensure you can report, if you have a system that will cater for this (see: **www.sra.org.uk/diversitydata/** under 'collecting data' tab and then there is a document that can be downloaded). Alternatively, you can request that your people complete a questionnaire as and when the time comes. There are many providers out there that will help you to set this questionnaire up.

As well as gathering and submitting your E&D data to the SRA, you will need to publish it. To the SRA, publishing means making the data available to staff and externally. This can mean, therefore, that you choose to publish the data on your firm's website. However, the SRA guidance suggests that you may wish to put up a poster in your office or meeting rooms or publish an article in an external newsletter or bulletin.

If you are going to put the data on your firm's website, it needs to be easy to find and so no burying it in the depths of your website pages. The publication itself needs to have your data in an easy-to-read format with tables, diagrams or graphics including a summary of what those snazzy graphics show.

A word of caution: you should not publish data if to do so would identify individuals. This could happen for very small firms, and to that end you may find that you are unable to publish the data at all. If that is the case, document why you considered this to be the case.

Remember that it is not compulsory for those in the firm to take part in any data-gathering exercise, but the firm is obliged to try to collect the data. You do not therefore need to force completion, in fact that would be quite wrong indeed.

6.9 Information on letterhead, email and website

It is important that your letterhead, email and website contain the information that is required by the SRA. My suggestion is that this aspect of compliance is owned by the COLP or risk and compliance team, rather than those who look after the firm's brand.

Displayed on each of your letterhead, email and website should be 'authorised and regulated by the Solicitors Regulation Authority' followed by the firm's SRA authorisation number. Don't forget also that your firm is now obliged to house the SRA digital badge on its website (see **6.6** for more information).

If your firm is a partnership, you are not obligated to list the partners. However, if you choose to do so, then it must be clear that this is what you are doing; or if you wish, you may state that a list of partners is available for inspection at your offices. If your firm is an LLP, again you are not obligated to list members.

If your firm is incorporated, then the letterhead and website must include the registered office address, the company number, the part of the UK where the company is registered and what type of company you are.

The firm needs to describe accurately the fee earners within the practice. For example, the firm should not hold out a person as being a solicitor when they are not. If your firm employs foreign qualified lawyers, then consider making this distinction in the person's job title – e.g. 'solicitor (New Zealand qualified)'.

The firm will also need to ensure that it is compliant with the SRA's price Transparency Rules (see **6.5** for further guidance). Further, the firm will also need to consider publishing E&D data on the website (see **6.8**).

You will also need to ensure that you meet the requirements of the Provision of Services Regulations 2009, SI 2009/2999. These requirements are to make the following information available (this might be covered in your engagement letter and terms also (for information on engagement letters see **7.10.1**)). The provider of a service must make the following information available to a recipient of the service:

1. the firm's address and contact details;
2. the firm's VAT number;
3. details of your compulsory professional indemnity insurance;
4. details of how to access professional rules that apply;
5. details of how to complain or any other dispute resolution methods;
6. the legal status and form of the firm;
7. details of regulator and registration number;
8. the general terms and conditions;
9. which legal jurisdiction applies to the engagement;
10. costs of the service;
11. what the service includes if not obvious.

For further information about how to comply with the Provision of Services Regulations 2009, consider reading the Law Society practice note by the same name (www.lawsociety.org.uk/support-services/advice/practice-notes/provision-of-services-regulations-2009/).

Whatever you decide to put on your letterhead, email and website it must be accurate and not misleading in any way. The Law Society has a very useful and detailed practice note called 'Information on letterheads, emails and websites' which you should call upon (**www.lawsociety.org.uk/support-services/advice/practice-notes/information-on-letterheads-emails-and-websites/**).

6.10 Other – compliance training, regulatory investigations and production orders

6.10.1 Compliance training – online modules and face-to-face

A vital part of risk management in any firm is the compliance training. Depending on your size, you may wish to require your people to undertake online compliance training modules or you may wish to run sessions face-to-face. Face-to-face is always better for learning, in my view – but if you have a number of people to train this may not be possible or cost-effective. Consider, however, having some of the firm undertake certain compliance training online and some face-to-face on a risk-based approach. For example, for anti-money laundering (AML) training you may want to require those who do not undertake regulated work (litigation, for example) to complete an online module and those who do undertake regulated work (real estate for example) to attend a face-to-face training session with someone internal or external delivering the training.

Generally speaking, there is no set frequency as to when training should be undertaken. However, good practice means training your people every one to two years depending on the area of regulation or compliance to be taught. Below is a list of the training your firm should be undertaking, who might undertake it and when. The list below focuses on training on areas of regulation but don't forget also to run sessions on how to avoid a negligence claim and negligence trends (if you instruct external solicitors to handle your negligence matters they are normally very happy to run such sessions and also your insurers are usually happy to help here too).

Whatever you choose to do, make a plan each year and stick to it – but remember not to fatigue people with training. Your audience will switch off and just go through the motions if they are tired by all the training you are putting in place. If you select eight areas to train every two years, then one a quarter can be completed and this is achievable (but still may feel like a slog). Remember that not all training has to be formal, however, and a note to read or risk team/COLP attendance at a team meeting for 20 minutes to run through the subject might be enough.

Table 6.1 Training suggestions

Subject	Who	How frequent
Anti-money laundering	• Fee earners • Secretaries/PAs/administrators • Accounts • Risk and compliance • MLRO • MLCO • COLP • COFA • Consider other business services	1–2 years. Aim for every 18 months. Consider requiring new joiners to complete an online module within 1 month of joining the firm
Anti-bribery and corruption	All those in the firm	2 years. Consider requiring new joiners to complete an online module within 1 month of joining the firm
SRA Codes of Conduct – consider combining with ethics training	• Fee earners • COLP • Risk and compliance	2 years
Data protection	All those in the firm	2 years. Consider requiring new joiners to complete an online module within 1 month of joining the firm
Modern slavery	Those who undertake procurement and recruitment for the firm (HR for certain, but also maybe business services who are involved in procurement)	2–3 years
Anti-tax evasion	All those in the firm	2–3 years
Equality and diversity training	All those in the firm (you may not want to train about this formally and instead combine it with other firm initiatives such as work on culture and values – whatever you decide to do, make sure you cover this off)	2–3 years

6.10.2 Regulatory investigations and production orders

Regulatory investigations

It goes without saying that it is within the remit of the COLP to handle or delegate as appropriate any internal regulatory investigations and respond to any external regulatory investigations.

How an investigation should proceed rather depends on what the issue is. Further, other departments may lead the investigation with the COLP/risk team assisting such as a HR investigation of misconduct.

What is important, however, is the thoroughness of the investigation, and no sweeping under the carpet either actual or by perception. Here are some aspects to consider when faced with the need for an internal regulatory investigation:

1. Create a locked-down electronic workspace for all filing.
2. Consider whether there is a need to report the issue now to the SRA (remember the firm, the COLP and solicitors have a duty to report any facts or matters

which the reporter reasonably believes are capable of amounting to a serious breach of the regulatory arrangements and further the Codes also set out that notwithstanding your analysis here, the firm, COLP and solicitors need to consider informing the SRA of anything which the reporter considers should be brought to the SRA's attention in order that it may investigate (the catch-all)).
3. Consider getting external specialist advice early on. You may have internal expertise which you can use, but consider whether such internal advisers would feel conflicted and whether in reality client work will come before advising the firm.
4. Speak to your brokers and insurers and consider whether you need to make an insurance notification if the costs and any subsequent SRA/SDT penalty will be payable by insurers.
5. Conduct an independent investigation of the allegations or oversee/be involved with other areas of the firm investigating. If appropriate, consider external providers investigating.
6. Document your findings. Even if you decide not to report to the SRA, someone else might do so (i.e. a complainant) and when the SRA asks for the firm's response you will want to show what you have done by way of contemporaneous documentary evidence.
7. Consider learnings and implement them straight away. For example, if your systems have allowed unwanted behaviour such as misconduct or dishonesty then close/plug any gaps, implement training either to certain individuals or firmwide and consider as soon as possible whether the appropriate response to any findings should be sanctions such as warnings or dismissal. The firm's position will be much stronger if the SRA investigates and the firm has already implemented remedial measures.

Production orders

Production orders are what they say on the tin – they are orders to produce documentation granted by a court after application by authorities, normally the police. As a law firm, you are rich in information and so it is possible that you may receive a production order in relation to a client. Before a production order is made, you may receive a call from the police asking whether you feel that an order is necessary and that they are going before a judge shortly to obtain one. Whether a production order is necessary depends on whether you are able to obtain your client's consent to hand over the documentation wanted by the authorities. Sometimes the police do not wish you to approach your client to seek consent and so you must comply with the production order.

There is a very useful Law Society practice note called 'Responding to a financial crime investigation' (**www.lawsociety.org.uk/support-services/advice/practice-notes/financial-crime-investigations/**). If you receive a production order, I urge you to navigate to that practice note in the first instance and also consider the short list of aspects to consider below:

1. If the authorities/police call to ask whether you would be prepared to produce documentation without an order, your answer should be yes with client

consent, and no without consent. Generally, always opt for an order as this requires a judge to assess the merits of such a request and your client cannot reasonably be upset if you have been ordered to hand information over.

2. Consider whether the order has been drawn up correctly. Has the correct client, retainer or firm been named? Consider whether the order should be challenged in any way. You may need to take external advice.
3. Consider the wording of the order carefully and only produce what you are requested to produce, i.e. do not over-produce documentation.
4. Does the client wish to co-operate and give you consent to disclose the documentation sought? The police may have tried to obtain information from the client and this has not borne fruit and so it is possible the client will decline. However, a production order may change their mind. Carefully consider here your duty to inform the client of any relevant material and any wording on the order which prevents you from discussing the same with your client. Consider here tipping off and therefore involve the firm's money laundering reporting officer (MLRO).
5. Consider very carefully legal professional privilege, those documents caught by it and whether the crime/fraud exception applies. The order should state that the disclosure is subject to legal professional privilege and such documents are not to be disclosed. The practice note referred to above sets out a very useful analysis of what you need to consider.
6. Now that you have the order, consider whether you need to make a suspicious activity report, particularly in relation to other ongoing work. The MLRO will need to be involved here.
7. Whoever in the firm is responding to the order will need to provide a witness statement when producing the documentation. The police will draft this for that person to amend and sign off.

There are other types of orders and notices that are able to be made to compel disclosure by the firm, and guidance on these can be found in the aforementioned practice note.

7 Risk management

7.1 Audits and registers

7.1.1 File reviews/audits

File reviews are a good barometer of what is really happening on the ground and whether what people say they are doing they are in fact doing.

There are essentially two types of file reviews: one that looks at technical advice and whether it is correct; and one that looks at whether the firm's policies and regulations have been adhered to. You can of course combine the two, but I caution peers reviewing each other for important aspects like anti-money laundering (AML) compliance. You may have some keen fee earners who want to review colleagues' compliance with rules and regulations and are good at doing such a review (in which case can you send me their names because I'd like to meet these golden people) but in my experience these types of people are few and far between or really just don't exist. If possible, review compliance from a central location, possibly from your risk team, even if each fee earner gets one or two files reviewed each year. The compliance file review doesn't replace a technical review of the work conducted and if fee earners are already conducting peer-to-peer reviews of that type, keep that up but ensure that it is not just a tick-box exercise.

So what types of compliance questions should be asked?

There are, of course, no set questions and you should tailor what you ask for to your firm. However, there are some core areas that should be covered. Below are a set of questions that you may wish to consider and adapt.

- Are the client and matter details recorded correctly? (This will ensure conflict checking works.)
- Has client due diligence (CDD) been gathered in accordance with the AML regulations (see **Chapter 4**) and the firm's policy?
- Was a conflict check carried out?
- Were the conflict check results analysed correctly?
- Has the client and matter risk assessment been completed?
- If the client or work is considered to be high risk, is there evidence of ongoing monitoring?
- Where appropriate, has source of funds information been sought and obtained? Does the information look satisfactory?
- Was a client care/engagement letter sent covering all aspects of the retainer?
- Was the client care/engagement letter signed by the client? (If that is your firm policy)
- Was the best possible costs information given to the client at the outset and updated throughout?
- Have key dates been recorded properly and in accordance with policy?

- Have undertakings been given and recorded in accordance with policy?
- Has the matter been progressed properly? Any delays on the part of the firm?
- Where appropriate has a case strategy been agreed with the client?
- Is the file in good order and filing done according to policy?
- Were monies on account obtained? (If this is your firm policy)
- Was the client given an estimate for counsel/experts' fees before their engagement?
- Was the client billed in accordance with what was agreed?
- Are there are complaints, notifications or AML issues that have arisen and were they properly reported as per policy?
- Is supervision evident from the file?
- If the matter is at an end, has any residual balance been sent on, file closure letter sent, file closed and archived?

These are just some examples. If you do not currently conduct such file reviews, then I would recommend you start small and grow the process over time (I recommend that for most new processes, as it is easy to be daunted by the big task and therefore not start at all, so start small and add over time). You could, for example, only review the higher risk areas such as real estate and corporate, and ask five core questions. You could do that for, say, six months and then take stock and see whether you want to expand the questions, the areas of practice that are being reviewed or both. Alternatively, if your firm is conducting peer-to-peer file reviews you could make sure core compliance questions are included and then you could conduct a spot check of those reviews – say 5–10 a month to make sure they are being done correctly. If your firm is too big for compliance reviews from a central risk team or you do not have resource, consider instead thematic reviews based on trends.

There are many ways to slice and dice file reviews. They are not mandatory (unless you have an accreditation scheme that mandates it or it is a requirement of bank lender panel membership) but they are an effective way of testing that what should be happening is in fact happening.

7.1.2 Firmwide risk register

A good risk management tool is a firmwide risk register. By analysing risk across the firm, you will be able to consider what steps are available with a view to mitigating risks posed against the firm.

If you do not have a risk register, then start small. Risk registers can be daunting when you see one that has been completed. You will find a template risk register at **Appendix 32**.

Risks that you might wish to consider are as follows:

1. **Regulatory risks:** Failure to obtain professional indemnity insurance (PII) cover; supervision inadequacy; data security; money laundering compliance; cybercrime awareness; dishonest use of client monies; misuse of office monies; providing a banking facility for clients; breaching confidentiality; acting where

there is a conflict; inadequate complaints handling; misleading or inappropriate publicity; poor service; negligence; discriminatory behaviour; dishonesty; and so on.
2. **Operational risks:** Not getting on to or maintaining membership of accreditation schemes (see **8.2**) or lender panels (see **8.3**); recording key dates; loss of key personnel (especially if you are small or heavily reliant on key persons for revenue); fraud; being involved in the commission of a crime; lack of management competence; lack of financial competence; change in demands by clients; business continuity; keeping up with IT changes; lack of succession plans.
3. **Financial risks:** Lockup days being too long; cash flow issues; reliance on key clients and what happens if they are lost; competition in the market; pricing models and move away from estimates to fixed fees; increase in professional indemnity (PI) premium; economic downturn where clients have less to spend.

You will see from the template at **Appendix 32** that the purpose of the risk assessment is to consider the likelihood of the act happening; the impact if it did; and by multiplying these two you get a risk rating which indicates whether you need to take action and how quickly.

Your risk assessment should be reconsidered regularly. What that means for you is down to the issues you consider you may have to address. If you have assessed that you have some urgent issues to tackle then perhaps a review of your risk assessment more frequently to update it would be a good idea.

7.2 Policy writing and ownership

It is vital that the firm has a set of risk policies. This would normally be owned by the risk team or compliance officer for legal practice (COLP). Some policies are a regulatory requirement to have, and some are a matter of good practice. What is important is not to go overboard with your policies. Keep them short, understandable and to the point though where necessary set out the firm's ethical or philosophical stance. If the policy has to be long, create a summary to assist your firm. The summary is not a replacement for the policy itself but will assist in readers getting to the bones of the policy quickly.

Below you will find a list of policies that you either need to have (where indicated) or might consider having:

1. AML policy (required);
2. anti-bribery and corruption policy (required);
3. anti-tax evasion policy (required);
4. anti-slavery and human trafficking policy (required where applicable);
5. mortgage fraud policy (if appropriate to your practice);
6. data protection policy (required);
7. risk management and compliance plan (which sets out how the firm handles risk management);
8. client care policy which sets out how clients are served;
9. risk management of client files which sets out how clients are onboarded, who

to report issues of negligence to, how supervision works in the firm, file reviews, conflict checking, confidentiality, risk assessments of clients and matters, conflicts, file closure and so on;
10. complaints policy and process plus the client-facing complaints procedure;
11. equality and diversity (though this may sit within HR).

The business owner for these policies needs to review them each year and record on the policy that they have done so. This should therefore be diarised.

Collectively you may want to call these policies your Risk Management Manual. Whatever you decide to call it, the firm needs to ensure that the policies are read and understood especially those that are mandatory. To do this, (a) members of staff could be asked to read and sign a declaration setting out they understand their obligations, etc.; or (b) you could create a quiz or training module to test knowledge of the policies. Either way, if possible, make sure the policies/risk management manual get mentioned at least once a year.

7.3 Partners, consultants and employees becoming a director or an interest holder of a non-client or client company

There are a number of risk issues to consider when a partner, consultant or employee wants to undertake an interest-holding position with either a client or a non-client entity.

7.3.1 Becoming a director or an interest holder of a non-client company

Generally speaking, becoming a director or an interest holder of a non-client company normally requires no approval from your firm unless specified in your partnership deed, consultancy contracts or contracts of employment. However, such appointment can create conflicts of interest (for example, a client wants to sue a company of which one of your partners is a director) and so it is highly recommended to request that those in the firm complete an annual declaration (see below) which could be tied in with your reauthorisation and practising certificate (PC) renewal (see **6.1**) or PI renewal annual declaration (see **1.3**). The entities in which your people hold positions should then be entered into your database not as clients of course but as contacts and your conflict checking system should be designed to check against contacts as well as clients.

7.3.2 Becoming a director or an interest holder of a client company

There may be sound reasons for a person within the firm to hold the position of director or some other interest in a client company. However, there are a number of considerations to such an appointment as set out below.

Approval

Partners may need to seek approval of such appointment under the firm's partnership deed. Such approval should likely set out the name and nature of the company, the position to be taken upon approval, the duration of the position, analysis on whether a conflict of interests may arise and insurance cover. Decide who should consider this request if the partnership deed is silent.

If the proposed interest holder is a non-partner, then approval should be sought in line with the consultancy contract or contract of employment. If this is silent, consider amending such contracts and/or putting in place a policy which sets out that approval should be sought by either the client relationship partner or equivalent for the client, the person's line manager, senior management such as a board member, chief executive or the COLP/risk team. Again, enough detail needs to be given to allow those who are considering the appointment to deliberate the risks. Such information can include the name and nature of the company; the position to be taken upon approval; the duration of the position; analysis on whether a conflict of interests may arise; and insurance cover.

Once approval has been given, the company to which the appointment relates will need to be recorded in a way that it would show up on a conflict search, ideally by creating the entity as a contact (and not client) in your system.

Proper exercise of duties as director

Becoming a director should not be taken lightly. Directors have numerous duties to a company. These include:

1. to act within powers;
2. to promote the success of the company;
3. to exercise independent judgment;
4. to exercise reasonable care, skill and diligence;
5. to avoid conflicts of interest;
6. not to accept benefits from third parties;
7. to declare an interest in proposed transactions or arrangements.

Duties cannot be contracted out, but companies can buy insurance to cover instances of breach.

Duties are far reaching, and in effect directors are the agents of the company, appointed by the shareholders to manage its day-to-day affairs. Breach by a director of their duties can give rise to an injunction, damages or compensation. It is important, therefore, that when a person in the firm is becoming a director of a client company, they fully understand the duties they owe and you may therefore want to provide an advice note or direct persons to a friendly corporate lawyer in your firm who can advise.

Insurance

You need to consider whether your PII will cover the position held in the client company. Also consider the firm's directors and officers (D&O) liability cover;

however, generally this will only cover positions held in relation to the firm. Even if your PII does cover the position, consider whether you want your firm's insurance cover to be exposed in this way.

You may wish to make it policy that the director or interest holder of the client's company must ensure the company holds its own D&O liability insurance and that your firm will not provide insurance under its PII for the activities of such interest holder unless specifically agreed.

Conflicts of interest

Careful consideration needs to be given on a case-by-case basis to the possibility of a conflict of interest between the interest holder of the client company, the interest holder's role as fee earner and/or employee and the firm's interests.

By way of example, if a partner is a director of a client company and a fellow director does not agree the firm's fees, the partner will be in a position where they have duties to the company and the firm and these may well conflict.

Compliance with the non-banking rule

No interest holder should pay through the firm's client account monies that do not relate to normal regulated services provided by the firm, as to do so would breach the non-banking rule – i.e. rule 3.3 of the Solicitors Regulation Authority (SRA) Accounts Rules, which states: 'You must not use a client account to provide banking facilities to clients or third parties. Payments into, and transfers or withdrawals from a client account must be in respect of the delivery by you of regulated services'.

Although this might be open to debate because of the definition of regulated services (which states that this includes 'where appropriate, acting as a trustee or as a holder of a specified office or appointment'), my advice is that being a director or an interest holder is not part of regulated services and as such the day-to-day running of the company must not be conducted through the firm's client account. An example of this would be to pay accountants' fees for preparing the company accounts.

Monies which relate to your normal regulated services are able to be paid into and out of the firm's client account. An example would be if the firm were acting on the purchase of property for the company client then purchase monies can be paid into and out of the firm's client account.

Charging for being an interest holder

A client may be happy to pay for your partner's, consultant's or fee earner's time in being a director or an interest holder. As firms of solicitors, we are here to provide legal expertise. If in acting as a director or an interest holder the person is providing legal expertise then the interest holder should be able to charge the client company for this service payable to the firm. If no legal expertise is being provided then consideration needs to be given as to whether there is a reason for the appointment in the first place.

7.3.3 Interest holder's declaration

Never popular but very important is the interest holder's declaration. As set out above, this could be tied in with your reauthorisation and PC renewal (see **6.1**) or PI renewal annual declaration (see **1.3**). It is important to capture this information and record it for conflict-checking purposes going forward. Further, the SRA asks for information on other roles of partners during the reauthorisation process for which the answers given in such an annual declaration may be relevant.

You will find a template interest holder's declaration form and guidance at **Appendix 33**.

7.4 Procurement process

It is important for the firm to ensure that those it contracts with are not thwarting the firm's ability to meet its regulatory requirements. Also, those you contract with can be reflective of the firm and cause reputational damage if they were to be found to be engaging in unsavoury activities.

It is crucial, therefore, that when you are selecting those you contract with, the supplier is put through a procurement process. This needs to be owned by someone or a team in the business. That might be risk, or it could be facilities or operations. A procurement process could look like this:

1. The internal business owner for the product or service ensures they have budget approval and through a series of meetings or conversations with the supplier decides that this is the right supplier for the firm.
2. The business owner sends to the supplier the firm's procurement questionnaire and requests that this is completed and returned with the supplier's draft contract and/or terms.
3. Once these documents have been returned, the business owner looks through the terms to the extent of checking that the supply is correctly stated.
4. The business owner sends the documentation on to the reviewer in the firm (this might be risk or facilities or operations).
5. The reviewer reviews the questionnaire and any accompanying documents, the contract and terms, and suggests any amendments to the business owner or the supplier directly.
6. Any concerns with the questionnaire answers and amendments to the contract or terms are ironed out and agreed upon. The reviewer keeps a central record of the supplier contracts and negotiations for future reference.
7. Supply can now begin.

You will find a suggested procurement questionnaire at **Appendix 34**.

Your questionnaire could cover the following areas:

1. Details of directors and beneficial owners (you could check these for any adverse media).
2. Does the supplier have a business continuity plan? Important if they are going to be supplying core functions within the firm.
3. Does the supplier have a data protection policy?
4. Outline the information security measures that are taken to protect the data of the supplier and those who are being supplied.
5. Does the supplier have an AML policy and a money laundering reporting officer (MLRO)?
6. Does the supplier have a modern slavery statement and policy? Does the supplier assess that those in its supply chain are not involved in modern slavery and human trafficking?
7. Does the supplier have an anti-bribery and corruption policy and an anti-bribery and corruption officer (ABCO)?
8. Does the supplier have an anti-tax evasion policy?
9. Does the supplier have a whistleblowing policy?
10. Does the supplier have an equality and diversity policy?
11. Does the supplier have a health and safety policy for all locations? Are there written health and safety assessments in place? If appropriate, ask for stats on accidents.
12. Does the supplier have any accreditations such as ISO (quality management system accreditation)?

You may decide to use fewer or more questions depending on the type of supply. I would recommend, however, that you do not forgo the procurement process based on the cost of supply. Inexpensive supply can still cause damage especially if the supplier is handling firm or client data and things go wrong.

7.5 Supplier contract and terms reviews and 'outside counsel' terms

7.5.1 Supplier contracts and terms

Law firms enter into supplier contracts very frequently especially in the field of IT. Such contracts and/or terms need to be read and scrutinised. This could be done by one of the firm's lawyers of course but I advocate that the risk team look through those terms and also the data protection officer (DPO) if not within the risk team. Often, supplier contracts are hugely unfavourable to the firm and this becomes a problem when things go wrong. Aspects to consider when reviewing supplier contracts and terms are:

1. **Duration:** Ensure the duration of the contract suits the firm. Often suppliers will lock the other party into a two- or three-year term. If this is not suitable, ask the supplier to reduce the term or allow a break clause.
2. **Termination:** Often the reasons for termination are the insolvency of the firm, not paying for the supply or some other substantial material breach. Often the non-performance of the systems that are being supplied is carved out as not being a breach and there is no guarantee that the product your firm is buying

will work. Think about this carefully. This may be reasonable in light of the product your firm is buying, or it may be wholly inappropriate.
3. **Limitation of liability:** This is often limited to the value of the supply. If it is a small IT contract, that could be as little as a few hundred or thousand pounds. Think about what damage the supplier could cause and how much monetary loss that would be and ask for an indemnity near that. This is particularly important if the supplier is handling client data for which data loss could bring huge monetary losses. Most suppliers are happy to renegotiate this aspect.
4. **Data protection:** Ensure that the positions of data processor and data controller are the right way around. Check out the reporting responsibilities in the event of a data breach and whether the requirement to inform each other is in a reasonable timeframe. Also check whether the supplier will be sending the firm or client data outside the EU and check that if it does, your own terms reflect this.
5. **Controlling law and disputes:** Ensure that the law that applies to the agreement is in a jurisdiction you are comfortable with. Most agreements will be governed by the laws of England and Wales, but if the supplier is in New York, for example, it is likely to want New York law to rule and you need to ensure you are comfortable with this. Weigh up how likely a dispute will be but also check with any insurers that might cover a dispute as to whether they require you to change this aspect. Further, the method of resolving disputes is quite often set out. Arbitration is often a requirement. Again, consider whether you are happy with this. Also check whether your firm is being barred from bringing a claim in time. Some terms require a claim to be brought within, say, six months of the act when the statutory limit can be years after the act.

7.5.2 'Outside counsel' terms

More corporate clients are now requiring law firms to sign up to the client's terms as 'outside counsel' rather than the client agreeing to the firm's terms. This can cause a problem as the firm is required by various regulations to share information at the outset of the retainer.

When presented with the client's terms, and assuming the client is not prepared to forgo their terms in place of the firm's entirely, the client's terms will need to be carefully reviewed and challenged where appropriate. Aspects to look out for are:

1. **Conflicts:** Some clients will attempt to stop you working for competitors or any other party whose interests may be adverse to theirs, even though technically this may not be a conflict. You need to decide whether your firm is comfortable with this and work out how you will check you are not taking on such clients when conflict checking. Also, the client may extend this position to any of its subsidiary companies in which case you need to decide how the firm will ensure it does not act against the client's subsidiaries, which may mean creating the subsidiary as a contact in your conflict checking system.
2. **Data destruction:** Often clients want their data destroyed as and when they request it. The firm will need to retain data for regulatory and insurance purposes and so such clauses will need to be amended.
3. **Confidentiality:** Some client terms require that no disclosure of confidential

information is given either ever or without permission. This causes a problem with the firm complying with its regulatory obligations such as answering the SRA's questions, informing insurers of errors or reporting suspicions to the National Crime Agency (NCA). Such clauses therefore need to be carefully considered to allow disclosure where required by law, regulation or insurers.
4. **Billing and service requirements:** Often larger clients require billing to be undertaken in a specific way and sometimes with the client's own system. Also, clients sometimes require certain service standards to be met. Be aware of these requirements.
5. **Controlling law and disputes:** As set out above, ensure that the law that applies is in a jurisdiction you are comfortable with. Also check the position with your PI insurers if you are being asked to be bound by foreign law or resolve disputes abroad. If your insurers wouldn't agree, then better for you to find this out early and not when the dispute arises.
6. **Limitation of liability:** Clients might want unlimited liability. Consider whether your firm is prepared to give it or whether you need a cap.

If, after going through the client's terms, you discover that they do not contain the information you are required to impart, attempt to send your terms to the client with the request that where the firm's terms are at odds with the client's then the client's terms will prevail but where the terms are not, the firm's terms will prevail. That way you are still providing the information you are required to provide (i.e. data protection, money laundering information, how to complain to the Legal Ombudsman). Failing that, if you are frequently coming across clients who require the firm to sign up to their terms, consider creating a short information sheet containing key regulatory required information to provide at the outset.

7.6 Sorting files that are sent externally

Clients often ask for their files to be sent to them or new solicitors. As the reasons for this can be because a complaint or negligence claim is looming, often it is a good idea for the risk and compliance team to become involved. The risk team can either fillet the file in accordance with the below or instead give guidance to those who are doing the filleting in the firm. Often a trainee may be asked to go through the file before it is sent externally. This is fine (and a good learning experience) as long as proper guidance is given and there isn't a large claim approaching. If the latter, then perhaps it is better for the risk team to go through the file.

In terms of what should go with the file to the client or their new solicitors there is a Law Society practice note called 'Who owns the file?' (**www.lawsociety.org.uk/support-services/advice/practice-notes/who-owns-the-file/**) which refreshed the guidance given in Annex 12A of the previous *Guide to the Professional Conduct of Solicitors 1999*. That note sets out the following in terms of who owns certain contents of the file for you to decide whether to pass over the document in question:

- Documents in original form sent to the firm by the client belong to the client unless it was intended that ownership pass to the firm.

- Where the firm was acting as agent of the client and received documents in that capacity then those documents belong to the client. An example of this is correspondence with third parties such as counterparties.
- The final versions of documents produced during the retainer, and for which the retainer was the purpose, belong to the client. The same goes for final documents produced by third parties such as counsel.
- Documents produced by the firm for its own benefit or protection belong to the firm. These could be file copies of letters, drafts and notes as to time taken.
- Further internal emails and correspondence and accounting records belong to the firm.

While the above is all technically correct, I would advocate that you do not extract from a file those items that belong to the firm before you send the file on, unless you feel you really need to. Extracting documents in this way will make the file look disjointed and if your client is preparing to raise a complaint or a claim, taking out internal emails say between the fee earner and the accounts team giving an instruction for a payment could lead to some incorrect assumptions. Instead, therefore, most definitely check through the file but consider keeping those items that belong to the firm in. If you discover internal correspondence that is, say, unsavoury to the client, then reconsider your stance of keeping internal correspondence in the file before sending and separately address the issue of comments being made about clients and making their way into email (remember that if there was a data subject access request, such emails may well be disclosable).

Some final thoughts when receiving a file request. Consider whether you wish to exercise a lien over the file due to outstanding fees. If you receive a data subject access request (DSAR) from a client that owes monies, quite often the client thinks that this will get them the file without having to pay their outstanding fees (which they may be disputing). The client is wrong in this assumption, and remember that you do not need to provide documentation with the client's data in but instead can reproduce the data (though this may be very time consuming and so if the unpaid costs are not significant you may wish to just lift your lien and provide the file as part of your response to the data subject access request).

Consider also, if you have joint clients, whether the other client needs also to be sent the file. Permission from one client to release the file to the other should not be necessary, but careful consideration needs to be given where the clients are in dispute and you have perhaps ceased to act due to a conflict.

7.7 File destruction, archiving and record amendments

Normally the remit of either a records or archiving team, file destruction, archiving and record amendments are important from a risk and compliance perspective and so I recommend that the COLP and/or risk team get involved and set the firm's policy in this area.

In my experience, solicitors do not like to destroy files. However, also in my experience, it is far better to be in a position where you are unable to assist a former client who is asking for their file 20 years after the retainer rather than have to pull out a slip of a file which has information missing or could be incriminating.

Destruction dates should be kept to, not only to protect the firm from being in a position to assist many years after the limitation period but also because data protection laws require that data is destroyed when there is no longer a legal purpose for which it can be kept. Files should therefore be destroyed when the limitation period for any claim against the firm for the work that was conducted has passed. Generally speaking, for most types of work file destruction can happen at six years after closure or for some wiggle room say seven years. For other types of work, you may decide to keep files for longer. Also carefully consider how long to keep will files for. A client who instructs the firm to draft their will in perhaps contentious circumstances will not want their file destroyed after X number of years resulting in their executors being unable to defend a beneficiary claim upon death for lack of documentary evidence of the client's intentions and instructions. Of course, wills should be kept indefinitely and until death, but consider keeping the will files until a person has reached, say, age 100. This may mean keeping the will files for 50 years or maybe more.

Matrimonial files where the matter has ongoing financial maintenance issues also have a similar problem. A client whose settlement included maintenance for life will not want their file destroyed in case they need to apply to vary that maintenance. The same goes where there are young children who are to be maintained for the next 18 years.

The cost of archiving therefore can be very high. Consider whether you are able and want to offer the file to clients to take at your normal destruction time. You may not want to do this, and there may be good reasons not to. For example, the client could lose the file, the client may take it to another firm when they need advice and not back to your firm.

Alternatively, consider scanning files into your electronic system either at destruction time (some archiving companies can do this for you) or at file closure time instead of archiving the physical file. Alternatively, do not have physical files if you can help it or go 'paper lite'.

Of course, if you do archive files, they must be archived in a way that allows retrieval easily. Accurate recording of client name, matter description and file content is therefore essential. Also discourage in your firm as far as possible the running of multiple retainers on one file. If a claim comes in it can be very difficult to separate the multiple retainers making disclosure exercises very difficult and costly and the defending of the firm's position very challenging.

Record changes are very important from a risk and compliance perspective and if the changes are to be made by people outside the risk and compliance team then I would recommend they are trained to know what to ask and what changes to decline to make and those which need to be referred to risk and compliance. Here are some thoughts as to why:

1. **Change in client name:** The issue here is whether the firm has the relevant client due diligence (CDD) for the client, whether the firm's checks and balances have been circumnavigated, i.e. sanction, politically exposed person

(PEP) and adverse media and whether a new conflict check has been run. If an incorrect client record has been opened, maybe there has been a misunderstanding as to who the client actually is then it may be permissible to change the client record. However, if a fee earner was acting for X and is now acting for Y it would be wholly improper to change the client name as this erases the fact that the firm ever acted for X and a conflict in the future will not be spotted.

2. **Adding clients or separating clients:** If the firm has acted for Mr X and is now being asked to act for Mr X and Mrs X, the original client record must not be amended and a new joint client record must be opened. If the original record is changed, then it will appear that work done for Mr X was in fact done for Mr X and Mrs X when this was not the case.

3. **Joint venture partnership and special purpose vehicle clients:** This is a tricky one to get right. Often clients will not incorporate the company being used to purchase an asset until exchange. This means that until that point the firm is acting for a company that is not yet incorporated and it cannot open a file in the name of it. There are two ways to tackle this. The first way is to run the matter in the name of the joint venture clients and then when the company is incorporated, open a new client record for the company as a client in the normal way with the normal onboarding process and transfer the matter to the new client (including time recording, etc.). This can be administratively heavy and so an alternative is that when the company is incorporated, the matter description for the matter is changed to include the company name (e.g. purchase of 101 Commercial Road on behalf of Commercial Joint Venture Partners). This way a future conflict check should be picked up. Separately from this, the firm must ensure that the normal onboarding checks are completed. Whoever onboards clients in the firm will need to ensure that CDD is obtained and the normal checks conducted. Depending on how your firm operates, this second method may not work for you.

4. **Address changes:** Clients change address and so the firm's records should be amended. However, where an address changes, proof of address should be obtained.

Consider having a records policy that handles the above issues that the fee earners and support staff can refer to but also that the records team can use to guide them on what changes they can and cannot make without further input from the fee earner or risk and compliance.

7.8 Guidance and analysis

7.8.1 Guidance notes/articles and updates on risk news including Solicitors Disciplinary Tribunal cases

One of the benefits of a having a risk team is their ability to provide guidance notes/articles and updates on risk news including disciplinary cases.

There are of course many Law Society practice notes and SRA guidance pieces and warning notices and they should be utilised in the giving of guidance in the firm. However, there should be plenty of opportunity to provide short pieces of guidance to all those in the firm. The areas for guidance are too numerous to list here, but below are some ideas on how you might tackle getting these pieces of guidance out there:

1. Consider a newsletter or bulletin once a month or quarterly. This could come from the risk team or the COLP (maybe 'risk round up' or 'COLP corner' could be a title).
2. Keep pieces short (no more than one A4 page) and to the point – lawyers don't have time to read long pieces and therefore in my experience won't even try.
3. Rather than reporting on Solicitors Disciplinary Tribunal (SDT) cases one by one, do a roundup of cases once a quarter or by theme, e.g. misconduct of a harassment nature or conflicts or dishonesty.
4. Attend team meetings wherever possible and spread the message contained in the guidance note.
5. Try to bag a prominent place on the intranet for new guidance or news pieces and store previous guidance/news items on the intranet for future retrieval.
6. Aim for the amount of guidance or news that most suits your firm. Perhaps two pieces a month will be enough with one being guidance and the other news. The news item could be simply a short three-line report on a case and then a link to a fuller report in the *Law Society Gazette*, for example.

The trick is not to saturate your people so that they feel bombarded and switch off. Remember, though, that such guidance pieces can form part of the firm's defence when faced with disciplinary action and insurers are always keen to see you take risk seriously and communicate about it on a frequent basis.

7.8.2 Supporting the COLP and COFA in their decision-making

If you are fortunate enough to have risk and compliance people employed in your firm, then one of their main roles is to support the COLP and compliance officer for finance and administration (COFA) in all that they do.

The reporting obligations of the COLP and COFA have changed from reporting material breaches (for which there were a set of factors to take into account) to reporting facts or matters which the COLP or COFA reasonably believe could amount to a serious breach of the regulatory arrangements. Further, the 2019 SRA Code of Conduct for Solicitors, RELs and RFLs (paragraph 7.12) goes on to set out that solicitors will have discharged their reporting obligations if they have informed the COLP or COFA of their concerns on the understanding that the COLP or COFA will make that report. This could therefore lead to some debate between solicitors and the COLP or COFA about whether a report should be made.

The SRA Codes of Conduct go further (paragraph 7.8 of the Code of Conduct for Solicitors, RELs and RFLs; and paragraph 3.10 in the Code of Conduct for Firms) and state that notwithstanding the analysis that the COLP or COFA (or firm or solicitors) have made, if the reporter is of the view that the conduct is something that ought to be brought to the SRA's attention then the report should be made.

The reporting obligations on the COLP and COFA (and solicitors for that matter) are widely drawn and require careful consideration which must always be documented.

Often in firms the COFA is a person in finance and the COLP a busy full-time fee earner. Any help they can get to analyse the situation and document it must be welcomed. Ultimately the call whether to report something is down to those who have that obligation (it is not entirely clear where business services fit into this obligation and one must assume the SRA deliberately did not factor business services in its thinking or the obligation falls under the Code of Conduct for Firms) but any assistance in that decision-making process from the risk and compliance team should be given.

7.8.3 Trend analysis and forward risk planning

An important aspect of any risk management strategy is to look at trends and risks and plan how to mitigate those for the future. Not only is this just very good risk management, it also has the effect of impressing your insurers by showing them that you take risk management seriously.

I recommend that a yearly report is written which analyses trends and what is happening in the firm from a risk and compliance perspective and from this a forward-looking plan should be written with this analysis in mind.

As the data required to enable such a reflective report to be written is held by the risk and compliance team, my recommendation is that this report is written by those who handle such matters.

Below are some ideas of what you might like to include in any such analysis and forward-looking risk plans. Make sure you write the plan in a way which you would be happy to share with your insurers (but don't hold back, insurers like firms who recognise they have a problem and address it rather than dress the problem up so as to play it down).

1. **Complaints:** How many complaints has the firm received in the past year, how does this compare to the prior year, what reasons are given for complaints, are complaints being upheld, are they being referred to the Legal Ombudsman and what is the outcome. From this analysis, are there any lessons that can be learned, for example are there training needs about costs information being given to clients, are there any personnel issues around service.
2. **Claims:** How many notifications were made to insurers over the past year, how does that compare to the prior year, what are the reasons for the notifications, what proportion are purely precautionary notifications and what proportion are rectifications and claims. Also consider what the cost of these notifications has been to the firm. From this analysis, see whether you can spot any issues that are cropping up repeatedly and consider how they can be addressed. Insurers will want to know how you are going to ensure such claims do not arise again.
3. **Queries and guidance pieces given:** If possible, analyse the types of queries that have been raised by the firm with risk personnel. Also, document guidance pieces that have been written and shared and outline what guidance pieces you have planned.
4. **Training:** Outline the training that has taken place during the year and what

training you plan on rolling out over the following year. Make sure to include not only regulatory training but also training on claims avoidance.
5. **Regulatory changes:** Outline here the regulatory changes that have taken place during the past year and what effect this has had on the firm, i.e. what processes or policies have changed or whether the changes necessitated employing more people, etc. Outline here what regulatory changes are coming up, how you plan to tackle them and when.

My recommendation is to have a plan of action each year with areas of risk and compliance that you want to tackle. Don't bite off more than you can chew and make it realistic for you and your firm. If you are the only risk person in your firm then pick five aspects of risk and compliance to sort each year. It is far better to tackle five and feel good having achieved them than to push yourself to tackle 10 and be upset you only did five. Rome wasn't built in a day and neither were all risk problems solved in a day. Tackle them slowly and consistently and over time you will be surprised at the amount you have achieved.

Keep a record of those items that you have completed. You will see at **Appendix 35** a template risk and compliance action plan which you may wish to utilise. When items have been completed, do not delete them but instead move them to a completed space (maybe another tab in a spreadsheet, for example).

7.9 Inductions

The induction of new staff is a great way to get your risk and compliance messages in there early. Also, it is a great opportunity to speak to your newbie about how the firm they have come from handles various aspects of risk and compliance so you can get some new ideas.

What induction looks like is totally down to you and you may want to adopt a one size fits all approach or tailor your induction to suit the new starter's role. If you are a larger firm, then perhaps a one size fits all approach and a monthly slot that your new people are invited to is best. If you are a smaller firm, then a bespoke small group or one-to-one session may be possible. Below are some areas you may want to cover in your induction:

1. Who are the members of the team and who is the COLP, COFA, MLRO, DPO and whistleblowing officer (WBO).
2. What those people do and what you can go to them for.
3. Where the firm's risk management manual can be found and what policies it contains.
4. How files are opened (if this is part of a centralised function).
5. What is expected in terms of CDD – opportunity here to provide a short AML training session.
6. Conflicts and how they are run.
7. What to do if a client complains.
8. What to do if a fee earner thinks they may have made a mistake.
9. The firm's high-risk register and the checks that the firm does on clients or, if

this is not centralised, what the firm expects the fee earner to be checking – there is an opportunity here to run a training session on PEPs, sanctions and adverse media.
10. The firm's client and matter risk assessment, what it says, where it is and when it needs to be completed alongside ongoing monitoring requirements.
11. What the firm expects in terms of source of funds queries and where they should be recorded.
12. The firm's stance on how undertakings and key tasks are recorded.
13. Client care letters, where the templates are and the firm's stance on when they must be sent.
14. Any messages about the SRA Accounts Rules and perhaps rule 3.3 of the SRA Accounts Rules in particular – the non-banking rule.
15. Any other firmwide policy that may be relevant such as data protection, gifts or acting for family members and so on.

Do not see induction as just something risk and compliance impose on the fee earning population. Induction is an opportunity for everyone in the firm to understand what the risk and compliance team does in the firm and to do it effectively the risk function needs to be imbedded in every aspect of the firm, so take the opportunity when someone joins and sing about the risk function in the firm.

Finally, don't forget too about those who have been away and come back, for example after maternity leave. Re-induct them back in. A lot changes in risk and compliance in a few months and in my experience returners appreciate the refresher.

7.10 Engagement letter and terms of business ownership

7.10.1 Engagement letters

Sometimes hated, sometimes overlooked and sometimes under-baked, the engagement letter (or client care letter) is a vital aspect of all client work. Templates in firms can be long and unwieldy so that fee earners hate tackling them and may on occasion not bother.

Your firm's engagement letter evidences the contract between the firm and the client and when things go wrong it is the engagement letter which is first looked at whether that be by the firm's complaints handler to see what estimate was given, or a negligence lawyer advising the firm to see what the scope of the retainer was.

Why does such an important document get overlooked or fail to be sent? Length. I am not saying your engagement letters should therefore be one or two pages but what I am saying is that they should not have superfluous information in them. The letter needs to be to the point and unapologetic (so many times have I seen template engagement letters start by apologising for the length – just don't make it so long and stop apologising).

The content of your engagement letter will of course depend on the retainer but there are some aspects which need to be fed into by the risk and compliance function in the firm and my recommendation is that those aspects need to be owned by risk and compliance and any changes approved by them.

There is no Code requirement for an engagement letter to be sent. Nor are there many requirements now for certain information to be set out at the beginning of the retainer. However, it is good practice to share information at the outset and below you will find a list of items that I would recommend your engagement letter has (in no particular order):

- Introduction – thanking the client for instructions and stating who the fee earners are, supervisors, client relationship partner, etc.
- AML – what CDD is required to include source of funds where appropriate.
- Limitation of liability – if you are limiting your liability on the retainer then you must set this out in your engagement letter if you want to stand a chance of it applying in the event of a negligence claim.
- What is in scope.
- What is out of scope.
- Estimate of cost – remember that if an estimate is not possible, then this must be set out and details of hourly rates and any agreement on costs updates set out.
- Complaints internal process and Legal Ombudsman – you do not have to put these in your letter but some do. Personally I would put these in your terms and not the engagement letter.

Save for what is in scope, out of scope and the cost, the rest should remain pretty static, and amendments only made with the approval of risk and compliance.

Consider obtaining the client's signature at the bottom of the engagement letter to confirm understanding and acceptance. This is not mandatory, but is useful if a dispute arises.

Some firms have a view that the fewer the number of templates the better. However, it is far better to have a template for each type of work if this will make it easier for the fee earner to draft and send than insisting on, say, one template for the whole of your real estate department if this will discourage completion. In my experience, whether you want it or not, fee earners will find the easiest path they can and will quickly create their own templates. This is ok, and in fact I encourage it as long as they do not change the core risk and compliance aspects of the letter such as AML and limitation of liability. In my experience, fee earners are not interested in changing these parts anyway and are simply wanting a template that works for their practice area.

Consider creating a short engagement letter for those clients who provide you repeat work such as plots sales or lease renewals. This letter could contain just the risk and compliance aspects and be sent once a year with your terms and explain that for each specific piece of work a separate letter or email will be sent to set out the work and cost. It is far better to send a yearly engagement letter in this way than not at all for fear of bombarding your client with engagement letters.

7.10.2 Terms of business

Whereas I would encourage a short engagement letter, your terms of business are acceptable if long. Your terms of business are a vital aspect of your contract with your client and become relevant if a complaint or claim arises.

If you want to review your terms, I have set out a list of items for you to consider below. However, you can of course go to many other firms' websites and locate their terms there to compare yours to. The terms of business for a firm is a large document generally, and so if you feel you need a wholesale review, give yourself time to do it. Also, try not to push out changes frequently. Save up any non-urgent changes until you have four or five, and then update the terms and message to the firm that they have been updated and what has changed and why. Try to also keep a log of the changes. This becomes important if a complaint or claim turns on an aspect of the terms that have changed and so you will need to know when that change was made.

Some aspects of your terms for you to consider:

- Fees and how they are determined; what an estimate means; how frequently you will bill; how time is recorded; what disbursements are and how they will be billed; offset of monies held against bills and disbursements; how bills are delivered and when payment is expected; money on account expectations.
- Interest payable to the client and the firm's *de minimis* policy.
- Service commitments and complaints procedure as well as the right to complain to the Legal Ombudsman and the time limits for doing so plus the ability challenge a bill under the Solicitors Act 1974.
- Regulatory information, i.e. who you are regulated by and your authorisation number.
- Outsourcing of services and what that means.
- Audit enquiries from your client's auditors and that you may respond to those without recourse to the client.
- The client's responsibilities, i.e. to give clear instructions in a timely manner, tell the firm if the client's objectives change, inform the firm of any relevant information and provide accurate information and so on.
- Termination and suspension of services and when/why this may occur. Termination when it is clear that there has been a breakdown in the relationship between client and solicitor and suspension when for example outstanding fees have not been paid.
- Limitation of liability and the amount plus an explanation that the client accepts this limitation if they continue to instruct you (you may also wish to set out that you do not agree to third parties relying on your advice).
- Storage of files and for how long.
- Responsibility for acts or omissions of third parties such as counsel.
- Confidentiality and what that means. Here the terms should set out when client confidentiality does not apply, for example when information is required by regulators or law enforcement agencies, insurers, when instructing a third party on behalf of the client and so on.
- Limitations in the retainer. This could be that you only can advise on English law or that you do not provide tax advice.

- Successor practice – you need to set out what happens if the firm merges and whether the retainer terminates or transfers.
- Copyright clause which sets out who owns the copyright of any work that is drafted for the client.
- Data protection and in particular whether the firm is registered with the Information Commissioner's Office, why data is processed, the right to make a data subject access request and the right to erasure.
- AML and the firm's obligation to comply with the regulations and what is required from clients in terms of CDD to include source of funds information. Here you should also set out your obligations to inform the NCA of suspicious activities and further that any non-compliance by the client with the firm's requests for information required by the AML regulations can result in the termination of the retainer. You must also state here when CDD material will be destroyed (five years after the end of your relationship with the client).
- Status of the terms and that they replace the previous terms.
- Invalidity clause which sets out that if certain clauses are invalid then the remainder of the terms will continue to be in force.
- Governing law and jurisdiction for settling disputes.
- Acceptance of the terms – I would set out here that continued instructions means acceptance of your terms regardless of whether the engagement letter has been signed.

As you can see, your terms will be quite long and ultimately that is quite right as there is a lot to say.

7.11 Email disclaimer

Separate from the regulatory requirements as outlined in 6.9, there is an opportunity to expand your disclaimers at the bottom of your emails to include messages around fraud. Most firms do this and so if you are considering reviewing yours, look at the bottom of the emails you are sent by other firms to compare.

I would recommend that your disclaimer has the following in it:

1. A note saying that the content and attachments may contain confidential and privileged material and that if the email has been sent in error the recipient should not disclose the content to anyone, delete the email and let the sender know.
2. A message that email is not a secure medium and so while you have done your best to ensure cyber safety, emails can be intercepted and fraudsters can impersonate staff at the firm. You could say here that it is the duty of the recipient to check that the sender of the email is genuine.
3. A note setting out that the firm will never change bank account details during the matter and if the recipient receives an email purportedly from the firm changing bank account details it is likely to be a fraud and the recipient of the email should not send any funds and should call their contact at the firm immediately.

The disclaimer about bank account details not changing could also be replicated in your terms and also reconfirmed whenever bank details are sent to the client (consider creating a bank details one-page document with the disclaimer on a PDF protected document – not foolproof, but it helps). Tackling fraud is as much about educating clients about fraudsters as it is about educating your own staff. In my experience clients who understand how the firm operates, that the firm won't change bank account details and how fraudsters are trying to trick clients are more armed to spot a fraud when it is happening and stop it in its tracks.

7.12 How you send bank account details

How you send your bank account details to clients can assist in tackling fraud.

Fraudsters (currently) have a habit of emailing the client pretending to be the firm setting out that the firm's bank account details have changed and requesting that the client send the monies to this new account. Clients can fall for this because they do not spot that the impersonator is not the firm because they see nothing odd about the email. The task is therefore to educate your clients and to do that you need to tell clients that you never amend your bank account details and you never put bank account details in the body of an email. Further, you need to educate clients that if they receive an email which states that the firm has a new bank account and what that account details are, the email is likely to be a fraud and the client must call their contact at the firm. My experience (I am very happy to report) is that this works.

My recommendation for you therefore is that you create a letterhead document with the firm's bank details on with the disclaimer messaging set out at **3.2.4** and **7.11** and you make that document a PDF and you lock it down. You also then instruct everyone in the firm to not send bank account details in the body of the email and that they must use the PDF document instead.

This method is of course not foolproof and a fraudster may be able to hack the document, but it helps and it works to educate clients so that they can more readily spot a fraud occurring.

7.13 Business continuity

Vital to any legal practice is a well-documented and practised business continuity plan.

Well-looked-after business continuity plans are those that are owned by a specific business services area. That may be the risk team, but also consider it being owned by IT and/or facilities. Business continuity is a subject for a book all by itself and so I am just giving you some high-level ideas here.

If you do not have a business continuity plan, don't be daunted – start small and start somewhere. Some firms have all-singing, all-dancing documented business continuity plans but do not test them. My recommendation is to have a basic plan and regularly practise it and refine it each time. I discuss below some ways in which you may want to practise your plan.

Each area of the firm has a part to play and the size of your firm will dictate who does what. If you are a reasonably large firm then you will have business service teams who can undertake tasks. If you are a very small firm then just one or two people may be responsible for the lot. The first step is to think what kind of event could occur and then in each scenario what you would do to keep the firm running.

Events could be:

- unable to get into office for a short period, say two to three days;
- unable to get into office for a longer period, say two to three weeks or more;
- power outage for a short or long period of time;
- flooding or snow;
- loss of heating;
- transport issues which severely affect people's ability to get into work;
- terrorist attack;
- cybercrime attack, e.g. malware, ransomware.

Below are some ideas and issues for you to consider per business services area of your firm.

1. **IT:** In the event of a power outage, what happens? If you are unable to get into your office building, can people remotely access the firm's systems to carry on working? If you have a reciprocal arrangement with another firm for it to house you if a business continuity issue takes place will you be using its computers or will your people need to bring a laptop? How will the firm respond to a cyber-attack?
2. **Facilities:** If the office is not accessible, how will clients attend meetings with lawyers? How will the firm print, photocopy, scan and post? How will incoming post get to the firm and lawyers? How will the firm archive or retrieve archiving? Should an auto-message be placed on the firm's phoneline to say there has been an incident? What should reception be told to say? If you have an overflow reception service what should they be told to say?
3. **Accounts:** How will accounts process payments in the event of a business continuity situation? Will completions be able to happen?
4. **Business development/marketing/events:** What communications should be sent to clients, to your own people, put on the internet and intranet? What message should fee earners and support staff be told to give to clients?
5. **HR:** Are all your people safe? How will you check whether everyone is ok? Do you need calling trees where everyone is called by certain people to be communicated with? Do you need to designate floor walkers in your firm in the event of an office lockdown (perhaps due to a terrorist attack) to ensure everyone is ok? Do you need to offer counselling after an event?
6. **Risk:** Do regulators need to be told of the event? Do insurers need to be informed of the event? Consider whether client loss may occur.

Your business continuity plan should be tested in one shape or form two to three times a year. This doesn't have to be a full-blown evacuation of the office, and I have set out some ideas below.

- **Evacuation:** If you are a sizeable firm with multiple floors, you could test the evacuation of one floor to your off-site premises or by asking those on that floor to work from home. You could do this to the fee earner population or business services or a mixture of both (the latter is better in my view).
- **Round-table scenarios:** You may wish to get a core team of business services people or your board or management committee or fee earners or a combination of these people together and set out a scenario and discuss what the firm's steps should be. This is a useful way to run through some cybercrime scenarios also in the hope that when/if it does happen to your firm you are well practised in what you will do rather than in a state of shock. (See **3.2.9** for examples of cybercrime scenarios.)
- **Facilitated session:** There are companies that will facilitate a business continuity session with you to get you thinking.

If possible, ask a friendly firm that you know whether it would be prepared to share its business continuity plan with you to get you started on your own.

7.14 Technical training to ensure competence

The SRA Code of Conduct for Solicitors, RELs and RFLs provides that the solicitor is responsible for ensuring those that they supervise remain competent. Separate from this, with the eradication of the continuing professional development (CPD) hours requirement, there may be a relaxation in firms to ensure training is ongoing and kept up to date.

The COLP and risk and compliance team should take an interest in and feed into the firm's plans to ensure that solicitors remain up to date on their legal technical training. Often this is left to HR to administer or own, but technical training is required not only to comply with the Code but also to ensure as far as possible that mistakes are mitigated. Training does not have to be external and can be internally given by external or internal people, can be in the form of team talks or guidance notes. Whatever the method, the COLP should be aware of the technical training and the COLP and the risk team should feed into it especially if they have been able to spot a trend in errors that are being made which can be rectified with training.

7.15 Committees

You may decide that committees are a good idea for your firm. Committees are a good way of gathering the input from other areas of the firm, especially if the COLP is a lone COLP without a risk and compliance team for support. Each committee should have clear terms of reference.

Here are some ideas you may wish to consider:

- **Risk committee:** This committee could meet regularly to discuss complaints, claims, risk issues generally such as supervision, conflicts, ethics, Accounts Rules, training, regulatory issues and so on. The committee could represent a cross-section of the firm and provide feedback and input to the COLP.

- **Conflicts committee:** This committee could either meet regularly or when the need arises to determine whether the firm can act or continue to act in a given situation. Again, a cross-section of the firm could make up the committee. Time would be of the essence on this committee and it must be able to meet quickly.
- **Reputation committee:** There may be some clients for whom there is no regulatory reason why you cannot act but for which a question arises as to whether it would be right for the firm to act. These clients may be currently in the press for unsavoury reasons, accused of crimes or controversial figures. Alternatively, the client may be a competitor of a good client of yours and there is a dispute in the firm as to whether the firm should or should not take on the new client. These scenarios could be discussed through a committee comprising risk, business development, senior management and the fee earners concerned.

8 Additional areas to consider

8.1 Trainee secondment and work experience students

It is not the responsibility of the risk and compliance team to take on trainees or work experience students, but it is something that I think each risk and compliance team should consider.

8.1.1 Trainees

Trainees are future partners in the long term and in the short term will be fully qualified in a blink of an eye. Trainees will naturally form part of your induction and will receive training like all other fee earners. However, consider having trainees on a secondment for a short stint, even if it is just two weeks, so they can learn what the risk function does and can also lend a hand in complaints or claims handling, guidance writing, training delivery and so on. This secondment doesn't have to be limited to risk and compliance and could be shared with business development and finance, for example.

8.1.2 Work experience students

Pushing to the side whether you have to pay work experience students, if you are actually going to get them to work, consider taking a work experience student for just one day in their week-long stay with the firm. Those looking after the work experience person will appreciate this, and generally in my experience work experience students actually find the anti-money laundering (AML) aspects of risk and compliance fun. Subject to getting the right non-disclosure or confidentiality agreement in place (and consider what is appropriate for the work experience student to see if they happen to be the child of an important client – also consider whether they should be a work experience student in the firm at all), you could ask your student to undertake the following tasks:

1. **Reverse sanctions checking:** Ask your student to run recently released sanctions lists through your database to ensure that none of your clients have become sanctioned.
2. **Audits:** Ask your student to audit whether client and matter risk assessments have been completed by looking through a number of files, ideally electronically so as not to disturb fee earners.
3. **High-risk register:** Consider asking your student to run your high-risk register entrants through your checking platform for any updates – treat this with caution as you may not want the student who is the child of a client to know who you have on your high-risk register – otherwise it is really just akin to a new member of staff taking on such a task.
4. **Guidance or news pieces:** Students who are more advanced in their educational

stages are generally very happy to write a guidance piece or report on news. Cybercrime is a good topic and requires no prior knowledge of risk and compliance.
5. **Training modules:** If possible, make your online training modules or videos available to your student and ask that they undertake them.

8.2 Accreditation scheme maintenance – Lexcel and CQS

Depending on the type of firm you are, accreditation schemes can be an important aspect of your practice. If your firm practises residential conveyancing, for example, then membership of the Law Society's Conveyancing Quality Scheme (CQS) is a requirement for most banks for which the firm will also act. Some clients want to see membership of Lexcel (the Law Society's legal practice quality mark for practice management and client care) and/or ISO (quality management system accreditation).

There are excellent Law Society toolkits which help you obtain membership to Lexcel and CQS and so we will not go over that here.

The issue I want to address is who maintains membership, which can be incredibly time-consuming. As to lose such membership is a risk to revenue and fee earners are better spending their time fee earning, I would argue that such scheme memberships need to be looked after by the risk and compliance team (overseen in the case of CQS by the senior responsible officer for the scheme). Also, this makes sense when considering that a large portion of the information required to be accredited or reaccredited is held by risk and compliance, for example complaints and claims data or any regulatory issues.

If accreditation or reaccreditation is handled by the risk team, then so too should be the ongoing maintenance requirements. CQS, for example, requires an application to be made each time a new residential conveyancing person joins the firm and a Disclosure and Barring Service (DBS) check initiated. If the residential conveyancing team is of a reasonable size, then this can be a time-consuming task. CQS also requires training to be undertaken and this will require someone in the firm to arrange and nag (unfortunately).

8.3 Lender panel membership and maintenance

Just as the loss of membership of CQS can have an impact on revenue, so too can loss of membership of a lender's panel. Further, applying for membership of a lender's panel can be time-consuming and therefore a drain on fee earning time.

Again, as with accreditation schemes, the information that lenders want is often held by the risk and compliance team and so it makes sense for the application to be made from there. Further, most lenders now use a portal (sometimes shared with other lenders) to manage panel membership and like CQS expect to be updated when the workforce changes (some panels, for example, require partners' data to be provided when they join whether or not they practise residential conveyancing).

Lender panel membership and maintenance of that membership have become a time-consuming burden. As the loss of membership can affect revenue, I advocate if possible that maintaining such membership is undertaken by the risk and compliance team (if you are lucky enough to have one and if you are not then find a good safe pair of hands in the firm who can look after panel memberships such as a secretary/PA).

8.4 Responding to audit letters

Clients' auditors can write to firms and ask that information is provided for the purposes of the client's annual audit. The information they can ask for could be all outstanding fees; monies on account held; any outstanding litigation or pending claims; and any areas of non-compliance, for example.

There is very little guidance about how a firm should respond to such enquiries, but many moons ago on 16 March 2000 there was a short notice in the *Law Society Gazette* which provided guidance (and which in turn referred to guidance given in 1977 and 1970). On the basis of that guidance, the following should be considered when the firm receives an audit letter:

1. Ensure that you have client consent to respond – and also ensure that the client understands that privilege may be waived by responding and may alert auditors to report any issues to regulators.
2. Answer basic factual questions such as accountancy ones.
3. Decline to answer any far-reaching questions, such as those relating to any compliance breaches and any pending litigation, i.e. that there are no other material claims made or threatened against the company of which the solicitors are aware – this is for the client to answer and not the firm, as it may not be practicable for the firm to set out a list of all possible matters and the potential for success or failure and to do so may cause considerable time to be spent. Also note that if you do choose to answer but omit something, the firm may be held accountable later and so it is better to decline this line of questioning.
4. Consider declining to answer questions about any ongoing litigation the firm is handling. I say 'consider' because of course you want to help your client. However, you need to consider how accurately you are able to describe the litigation in a non-time zapping way and also whether you want to be held accountable for your summary or request for prospects of success analysis. You may therefore wish politely to decline this information request and suggest the auditors ask the client for detail.

To assist you when you receive any such letter, you will find a template response at **Appendix 36**.

8.5 KPIs, objectives and feedback on colleagues

To really imbed risk and compliance in a firm, you need to include the concepts in the language and vocabulary of all aspects of the firm. There is an opportunity to do this with key performance indicators (KPIs) in an individual's objectives or in firmwide career frameworks. They should be achievable and not drafted in such a way that openness is discouraged. So, for example, an objective could be to complete all risk training on time or to report when things have gone wrong in a timely way to the right people and to assist as much as possible in the rectification of the issue. An objective should *not* be to receive no complaints or to not make mistakes. We all make mistakes and if people are going to be measured on not making mistakes, then they may be inclined to bury their slipups, making the issue far, far worse. Objectives should be set to encourage the right behaviour.

There is an opportunity here for the compliance officer for legal practice (COLP) and/or risk and compliance to feed back to colleagues throughout the year and at appraisal time. Depending on the size of the firm, the feedback could be for those who need to improve and those who are commended for their behaviour and silence on everything in between. Of course, care needs to be taken with this feedback and it must be factually accurate and constructively given. It is an opportunity, however, for those in the firm to recognise that risk and compliance in the firm matters and it affects them.

PART 2
Addressing risk

9 Addressing risk in your firm

Now that you have considered some or all of the areas of risks outlined in **Part 1**, in this section we discuss how you might go about addressing the areas of risk and compliance in your firm.

9.1 Gap analysis

As outlined at the beginning of **Part 1**, the first step to ensuring compliance as far as possible is to conduct a gap analysis on your firm. There are many areas of risk and compliance as outlined in **Part 1**, and it is important to take heed of those areas but to prioritise areas to tackle as far as possible. If you are a small firm, then some of the areas outlined in parts of this book may not feel relevant to you or are above and beyond what you have resource for. That is ok. What is important is not to tick off as many areas as you can in tick-box exercise fashion, but rather pick your core and key areas to tackle and concentrate on them. I would recommend that you focus on areas of statutory and regulatory compliance to start with.

As outlined earlier in this book (see **Introduction**, 'Gap analysis of risks – why do it?'), don't underestimate the power of a good plan. It not only gets things done but it is a tangible document that insurers like to see and rather than it highlighting your issues to your detriment, it shows how serious you are about this subject.

So how do you go about conducting your gap analysis? Here are some ideas for you:

1. Review what you have by way of processes, policies and guidance. What is missing or lacking? You may want to focus on just three or four areas of compliance as this might be a large task.
2. Speak to colleagues and ask pertinent questions. If your policy says fee earners must do X, do they? Do they know they need to? Do they feel they understand the regulatory requirements of them?
3. How does your firm put policies and processes into practice? How are they communicated? How is compliance checked?
4. What is the firm's compliance training like? Is it up to date? Is it fit for purpose? Are staff members completing it or ignoring it?
5. Speak to brokers and insurers – what do they consider your firm's weaknesses are? Trust me, they will be pleased to be asked. Do they offer a gap analysis service? Do they offer risk management input? If so, take it up.
6. Has the firm had any regulatory feedback? What was that, and does anything need to change because of it?
7. Does the firm have any committees in the risk and compliance space? Are they working, are they made up of the right people, do they meet at appropriate times?
8. What do the complaints and claims against the firm tell you, if anything?

Ultimately what you are trying to do here is to assess what is missing against regulatory compliance and good risk management – hence why it is called a gap analysis.

9.2 Plan of action

Once you have conducted your gap analysis, it is time to put together your plan of action.

You will find a template action plan at **Appendix 35**.

Your action plan should set out:

1. what the compliance requirement or risk mitigation area is;
2. where the firm is currently at in terms of compliance or risk mitigation;
3. what needs to be done to bring the firm up to the level of compliance or to mitigate the risk;
4. who will undertake that work;
5. who needs to be liaised with in relation to the task, i.e. business service areas or partners and so on;
6. when the target date for completion is;
7. details of when completed.

You could also put in this plan your training schedule.

Your plan could cover tasks to be undertaken over the next year or years. However, I would recommend carving tasks up one year at a time and be realistic about what can be achieved in that time. For example, anti-money laundering (AML) compliance could be the main task for a whole year with a few ancillary tasks such as training through the year, some cyber awareness notices and articles and another couple of regulatory compliance areas such as anti-bribery and corruption or modern slavery. Some areas are naturally much larger than others and once you have brought the firm up to the right level of compliance or risk awareness you are then in a state of maintenance, auditing/checking/reviewing compliance, awareness and training.

By analogy, risk and compliance is like decorating a house in which every room needs decorating. When you have finished decorating the last room, the first room you decorated needs redecoration. Sometimes there are also leaks which need plugging, and extensions are put on the house on a regular basis for us to decorate. The work is never quite done. However, once you reach a state of compliance and risk awareness, the position is one of maintenance. If you are reading this and have become the compliance officer for legal practice (COLP) or a member of the risk team in a medium-sized firm that needs its compliance addressing, give yourself at least three years to do it. If you are in a smaller firm, then one to two years should be enough.

9.3 Risk registers

As outlined in 7.1.2, risk registers are a good way of analysing the risks faced at the firm and setting out the actions to be taken. The firm must have an AML firmwide risk assessment, but all other risk assessments are generally good practice rather than a legal requirement.

9.4 Risk roles – outline of COLP and COFA roles in the firm and other types of roles

To successfully address risk and compliance in your firm, you need to have the right people carrying out the right roles.

Each firm is required to have a COLP and a compliance officer for finance and administration (COFA). Depending on the size of your firm, you may need more people to support the efforts of the COLP and COFA.

The firm's COLP must take all reasonable steps to:

- ensure compliance with the terms and conditions of the firm's authorisation;
- ensure compliance by the firm and its managers, employees or interest holders with the regulatory arrangements which apply to them (except any obligations imposed under the Solicitors Regulation Authority (SRA) Accounts Rules) – these are:
    - authorisation;
    - practice;
    - conduct;
    - discipline;
    - qualification of persons carrying on legal activities;
    - accounts;
    - indemnification and compensation arrangements;
- ensure that the firm's managers and interest holders, and those they employ or contract with, do not cause or substantially contribute to a breach of the regulatory arrangements;
- ensure that a prompt report is made to the SRA of any facts or matters which may be a serious breach of the terms and conditions of your firm's authorisation, or the regulatory arrangements which apply to the firm, managers or employees.

The firm's COFA must take all reasonable steps to:

- ensure that your firm and its managers and employees comply with any obligations imposed upon them under the Accounts Rules;
- ensure that a prompt report is made to the SRA of any facts or matters which may be a serious breach of the Accounts Rules which apply to them.

Both the COLP and COFA fulfil their roles by analysing compliance and addressing any issues. The Law Society has toolkits for both COLPs and COFAs which will assist in your understanding of these roles. This book too will help significantly in fulfilling the roles of COLP and COFA.

There are other roles that firms do have and this depends on the size and need of the firm. I have outlined below the roles that firms may have:

1. **General counsel:** This person often will oversee the risk function as well as provide legal advice to the firm and contribute to the firm's strategy and vision. This person may be the COLP.
2. **Director of risk and compliance:** This person often sets the risk and compliance strategy for the firm and action plan and may be the COLP or support the COLP as well as oversee the risk function.
3. **Head of risk and compliance:** Often the same as the above but may not set the strategy or get involved with strategic decisions.
4. **Risk and compliance manager:** This is an operational role and this person often manages the risk team and will respond to all types of risk and compliance queries. They manage the risk function on behalf of the COLP and COFA.
5. **Risk and compliance solicitor:** This is a qualified person who will provide technical advice to the firm, the COLP, COFA and those in the firm. This person may respond to complaints and handle the firm's negligence claims.
6. **Risk and compliance analyst:** This is usually a non-legally qualified person who responds to queries and/or may look after certain areas of compliance such as data protection or AML.
7. **Risk and compliance officer:** Again usually a non-legally qualified person who will look after operational matters under the management of others in the team. They may deal with onboarding of clients or conflicts or administrative tasks.

This is a very high-level outline of what roles a firm may have, and there are of course many variations firm by firm. Please see below for details on how other firms tackle risk and compliance from a team perspective.

9.5 Convincing the firm to invest money in risk and compliance

If you are reading this as a risk and compliance team member, then your firm has already bought into the importance of risk and compliance. This is great. If you are reading this wondering whether you need to convince your firm to employ someone to assist you because you are the COLP or you are in the risk team and struggling with the workload, then you might feel you have some convincing to do. Compliance is expensive, and employing people in this area comes at a cost. Senior people in the firm may need some convincing to agree to expend revenue on this area of the business.

A law firm is a business, and one of the goals for partners or those at the top is to make money. Naturally a business should only spend what it needs to spend to secure as much profit as possible. If you are in a position where you need to convince the firm to spend money on risk and compliance, I have set out below some ideas as to what arguments you might wish to consider making. Ultimately where possible monetise your arguments so that people see the financial benefit.

1. **Complaints:** Complaints lead to time spent and money lost by fee earners handling complaints and/or writing off time and bills. How much has been lost from a financial perspective due to complaints? How much time has been spent over the last year or two years that could have been spent fee earning? How much in terms of fees has been written off or is unlikely to be paid because of complaints? Use these numbers to see whether your firm would benefit from employing a person who could handle complaints, train fee earners on how to avoid complaints (i.e. good costs information, good service, good communications) and advise fee earners how to handle correctly the situation where a client is looking like they might complain. Remember, that person is very likely to have lots of time to tackle other areas of compliance too.
2. **Claims:** The same analysis can be done here as above. If you were to employ a risk and compliance person, would they be able to assist in preventing claims from happening? Would they be able to handle the claim in-house, saving fee earning time or defence costs (this of course depends on your insurance arrangements)?
3. **Professional indemnity insurance (PII) premium:** As outlined earlier in this book, your premium is likely to go down if insurers can see good risk management in place. Is your premium currently high or too high? Would there be a benefit in employing a risk and compliance person to get your house in order? Speak to brokers here to gauge whether they think it will have an effect.
4. **Regulatory compliance:** Of course what should be done in terms of regulatory compliance should just be done and there should be no need for any convincing. However, if you feel that some convincing is needed, seek out some Solicitors Disciplinary Tribunal (SDT) cases with hefty fines for non-compliance and explain those to senior management.
5. **Risks:** Each risk to the firm will have a scary story that you can attach to it. Cyber and data protection, for example, are areas that need to be heavily invested in unless the firm wants to be a sitting duck to fraudsters. There are plenty of hacking stories to illustrate this. AML risk is prevalent in the legal market, and the firm would not want to be unwittingly involved or acting for unsavoury characters and not know it. It may be that the only way to undertake AML compliance properly is to employ risk and compliance people in the firm to undertake the day-to-day tasks (but remember: the fee earner acting is ultimately responsible). Again, there can be SDT cases found to illustrate what bad compliance can lead to.

There are plenty of good business and revenue generating or revenue protecting reasons for a firm to invest in risk and compliance, and in my experience if you can find a way to monetise your rationale, you will succeed in the firm agreeing to employ people in this space.

10 Risk management – how other firms do it

Now that you have considered how to tackle a gap analysis in your firm and the areas of risk and compliance that you may need to concentrate on, you might like to know how other firms are tackling risk and compliance in terms of whether they have a risk and compliance team and what they do.

Below you will see a snapshot of how some firms handle risk, categorised by the size of the firm. This detail was obtained by interviewing the risk and compliance team directly, and in the majority of cases there were plans for team expansion.

There are of course many ways to tackle risk and compliance and there is no right or wrong way.

10.1 Small to medium London firm

This small to medium-sized firm based in London, which has a practice consisting of corporate, dispute resolution, private wealth and real estate, has decided to put in place the following structure to handle all aspects of risk and compliance:

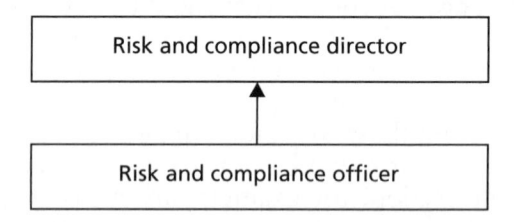

```
        Risk and compliance director
                    ▲
                    |
        Risk and compliance officer
```

Separate to this:

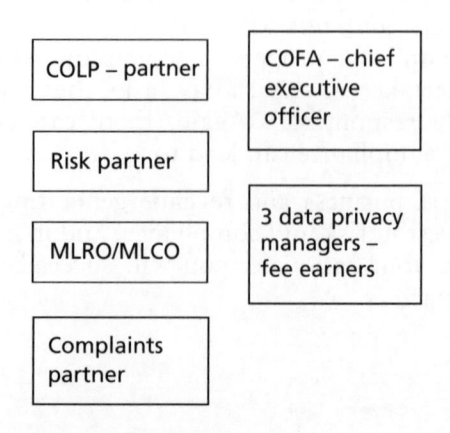

- COLP – partner
- COFA – chief executive officer
- Risk partner
- MLRO/MLCO
- 3 data privacy managers – fee earners
- Complaints partner

In this firm, the risk and compliance director oversees the entire function across the firm and deals with all aspects of risk that others do not. The risk and compliance director undertakes trend analysis to determine what improvements need to be made and then implements those changes. The director will also handle any queries on the Solicitors Regulation Authority (SRA) Codes of Conduct or ethics queries and undertakes training in the firm.

The risk and compliance officer handles the client onboarding, client due diligence (CDD) queries and checks the requisite forms that the firm requires to be completed. The officer also handles any ad hoc administration tasks and runs reports.

This firm has a separate complaints partner who handles all complaints that the fee earner is unable to resolve.

This firm also has a separate risk partner who handles the firm's professional indemnity insurance (PII) claims, notifications and renewal process and provides ad hoc support to the risk and compliance director.

This firm decided that it would not have a data protection officer (DPO) and instead has three data privacy managers recruited from within the firm, with one being a litigator who is able to assist with questions of privilege.

The money laundering reporting officer (MLRO)/money laundering compliance officer (MLCO) roles are handled by a separate partner in the firm with the risk and compliance director feeding in.

Practising certificate (PC) renewal and reauthorisation are handled by HR with the risk and compliance director feeding in.

This firm has Lexcel accreditation, and as such file reviews are done locally but overseen by the risk function.

Lender panel membership management is handled locally by the relevant lawyers, and risk and compliance assist where needed.

All SRA Accounts Rules queries are handled by the compliance officer for finance and administration (COFA) and the finance director.

The risk and compliance team use a product that continually monitors clients and flags any changes so that these can be actioned. The risk and compliance team also use an external product to check clients for politically exposed persons (PEPs), sanctions and adverse media.

The risk and compliance team undertake a roadshow each year to train the firm on matters of risk and compliance, preferring face-to-face training where possible.

The risk and compliance director will look at suppliers' contracts and review those.

10.2 Medium London firm

This firm, a medium-sized London law firm which practises in corporate, dispute resolution, private client and real estate, has decided to put in place the following structure to handle all aspects of risk and compliance:

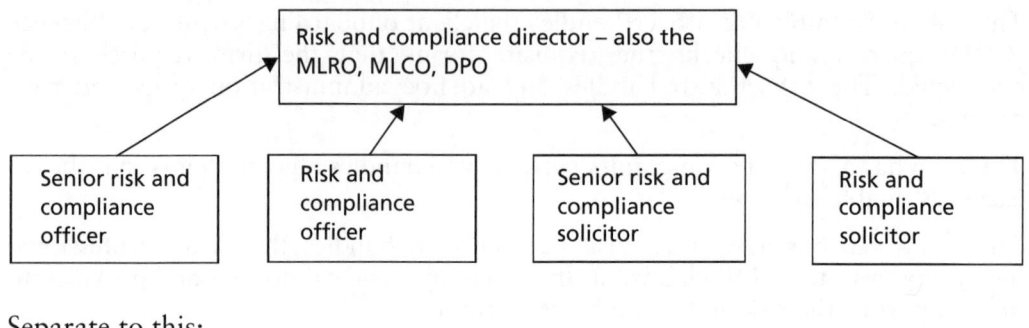

```
                    Risk and compliance director – also the
                    MLRO, MLCO, DPO
                    ▲         ▲         ▲         ▲
                    │         │         │         │
        ┌───────────┘         │         │         └───────────┐
   Senior risk and      Risk and         Senior risk and      Risk and
   compliance           compliance       compliance           compliance
   officer              officer          solicitor            solicitor
```

Separate to this:

```
   COLP –              COFA –
   partner             finance
                       director
```

In this firm, the risk and compliance director fulfils all regulatory roles save for the compliance officer for legal practice (COLP) and COFA roles.

The risk and compliance director sets the risk team's agenda each year in terms of what it is seeking to achieve. The risk and compliance director handles the firm's PII renewal with the assistance of the managing partner, advises the COLP and COFA on whether a regulatory breach has occurred and keeps them fully up to date with the team's activities.

The risk and compliance director also implements any policy changes and with the assistance of the entire team reports on trends and analysis.

The senior risk and compliance officer oversees the onboarding of all clients and together with the risk and compliance officer gathers CDD centrally; undertakes PEP, sanction and adverse media checks; risk assesses clients; and maintains the high-risk register. The senior risk and compliance officer also maintains the firm's membership of the Law Society's Conveyancing Quality Scheme (CQS); maintains all lender panels; runs the inductions for all staff; audits compliance with completion of client and matter risk assessments; and administers all online module training.

The senior risk and compliance solicitor and the risk and compliance solicitor (both of whom have been in private practice and one with the Law Society) handle all complaints, claims, notifications to insurers, queries on the SRA Codes, ethics and Accounts Rules; file audit; assist in regulatory investigations; and write guidance pieces.

This firm plans to expand its team's CDD/anti-money laundering (AML) compliance offering by recruiting another risk and compliance officer.

10.3 Large international firm

This is a large international firm for which the risk and compliance function is mainly based in the midlands with a limited number of people in its London office. The firm has decided to put in the following structure to handle risk and compliance:

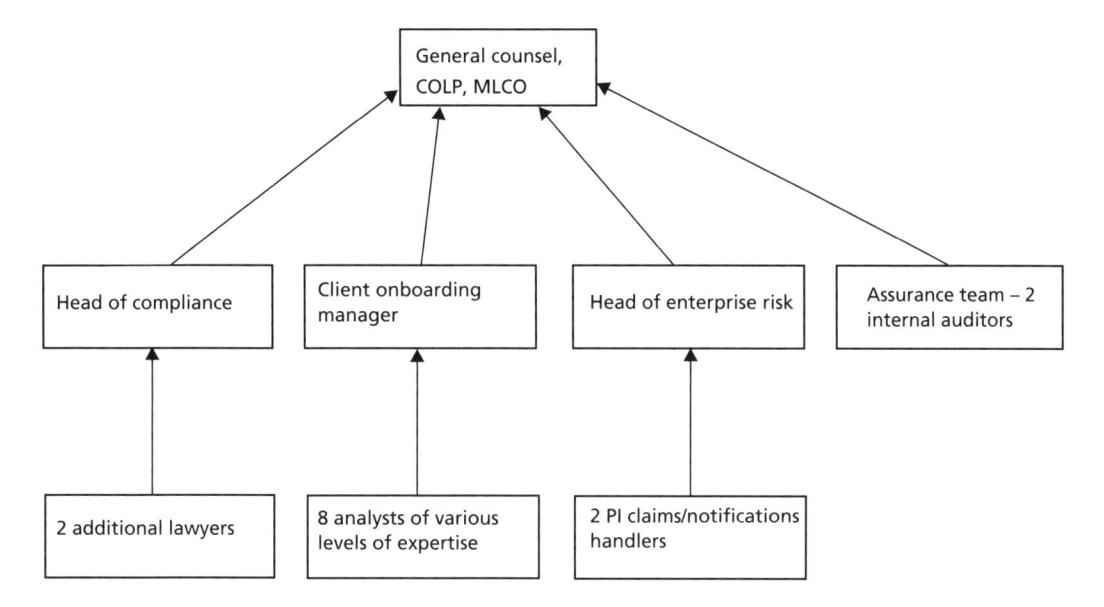

```
                    General counsel,
                    COLP, MLCO
           ┌───────────┼───────────┬──────────────┐
    Head of      Client onboarding   Head of          Assurance team – 2
    compliance   manager             enterprise risk  internal auditors
       ↑              ↑                   ↑
    2 additional  8 analysts of      2 PI claims/notifications
    lawyers       various levels     handlers
                  of expertise
```

The above is collectively called the general counsel team.

Separate to this team:

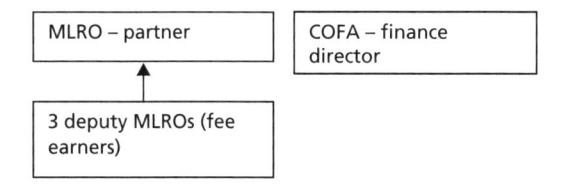

```
MLRO – partner          COFA – finance director
    ↑
3 deputy MLROs (fee
earners)
```

This firm has decided not to have a DPO. However, if there are any data queries or actions such as a data subject access request (DSAR) these go to the compliance team.

The firm's compliance team handle a large portion of the areas of risk and compliance outlined in this book. The firm's head of enterprise risk analyses risk across the firm and maintains the firm's risk registers. That person also assists with the firm's PI claims.

Interestingly, this firm has decided to implement an assurance team. This team consists of two non-lawyer auditors. These individuals will audit files on a random basis or conduct thematic reviews based on trends such as complaints or notifications. Where necessary, the general counsel team assist the assurance team to conduct these reviews.

The assurance team also look after the firm's accreditations where appropriate.

This firm also has a risk committee which is made up of some partners, the general counsel team and heads of business services. Trends analysis is reported to this committee.

This firm's onboarding personnel do not comprise qualified lawyers and any concerns are escalated to the head of compliance and the compliance team.

Cybercrime is looked after by the firm's information security officer and fed into by the general counsel team.

This firm has a procurement team that handles contracting with new suppliers and the firm's contracts manager reviews suppliers' terms. Any client's terms are reviewed by the general counsel team.

Training is done via online module and supplemented by targeted face-to-face sessions where possible.

10.4 Medium regional firm

This medium-sized regional firm with practice areas such as wills, trusts, probate, litigation, commercial property and residential property has put in place the following risk and compliance structure:

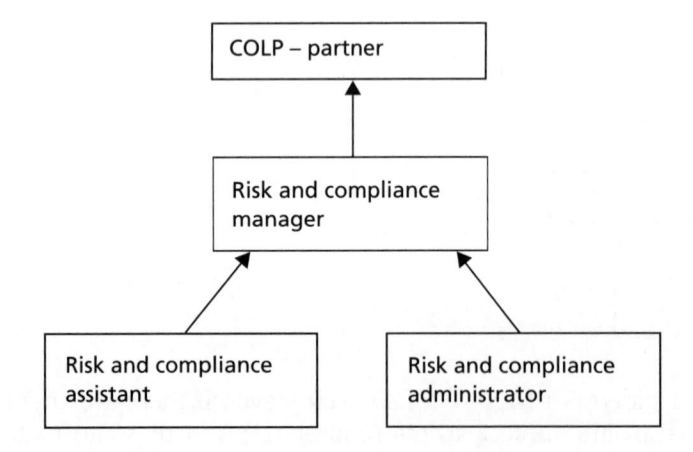

RISK MANAGEMENT – HOW OTHER FIRMS DO IT

Separate to this:

> MLRO, MLCO, COFA – head of client finance

This firm decided not to have a DPO, but any queries about data are handled by the risk and compliance manager.

The risk and compliance manager handles all complaints, notifications/claims, general risk and compliance advice, trend analysis; looks after the risk register for the firm; oversees Lexcel accreditation and maintenance; provides guidance, logs breaches; and so on.

The risk and compliance assistant has law firm paralegal experience and implemented the firm's EU General Data Protection Regulation (GDPR) compliance, handles policy updates and any other projects that are ongoing.

The risk and compliance administrator handles all administration tasks to include CQS maintenance.

The firm's MLRO handles all day-to-day AML queries to include CDD queries from fee earners. The MLRO also monitors the onboarding of PEPs.

The risk team does not undertake compliance file reviews and the firm has in place peer-to-peer file reviews where one fee earner per fee earning team has the job of undertaking the reviews and in return they receive a 50-hour target reduction.

Insurance renewal is led by the COLP with the risk and compliance manager completing the paper submission. Increases of limitation of liability are signed off by the COLP.

This firm has not adopted a centralised CDD gathering process but keeps this under review.

Cybercrime is jointly owned by IT, the MLRO, the COLP and the risk and compliance manager, and the firm has focused on its cyber security through some of the methods outlined in this book.

The MLRO also handled compliance with regulation that has a criminal flavour to it, for example anti-bribery and corruption and also Criminal Finances Act 2017 compliance.

Training is completed using online training resources and some training is conducted face-to-face where needed.

Business continuity in this firm is owned by the facilities and operations manager and fed into by other business services areas.

Finally, the risk and compliance manager feeds into all fee earner appraisals and risk and compliance key performance indicators (KPIs) are found in the firm's career frameworks.

10.5 Small regional firm

This small practice which provides a cross-spectrum range of services such as probate, litigation, employment and family has adopted the following structure (please note it has two managing partners):

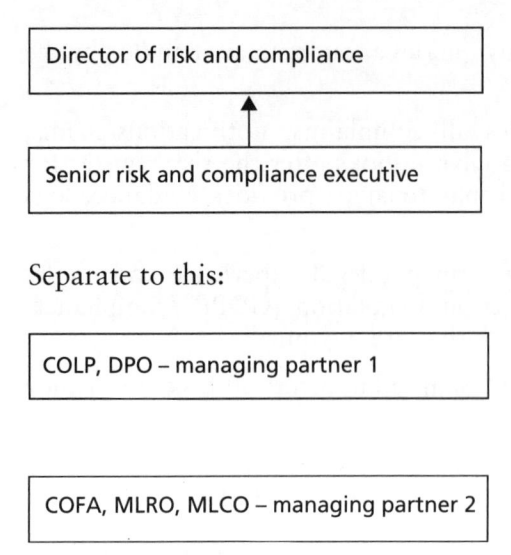

```
Director of risk and compliance
            ↑
Senior risk and compliance executive
```

Separate to this:

```
COLP, DPO – managing partner 1
```

```
COFA, MLRO, MLCO – managing partner 2
```

This firm has decided that it should have a DPO and interestingly has opted to take out cybercrime insurance which some might say demonstrates progressive risk management.

At this firm the senior risk and compliance executive undertakes most of the day-to-day operational activities which include a large portion of the areas of risk and compliance set out in this book.

This firm has not had to consider increasing its PI cover nor does it have many, if any, clients who seek an increase in the limit of the firm's liability. This is indicative of the value of the retainers/transactions it advises upon.

This firm's director of risk and compliance has historically undertaken the firm's SRA reauthorisation and PC renewal for the solicitors. The risk director and senior executive undertake file reviews.

The firm undertakes identification of clients electronically and supplements this with physical ID. Any queries as to this are sent to the senior executive, with all checks being done by fee earners in the first instance to include PEP, sanction and adverse media checks.

This firm recognises that it needs to conduct an independent AML audit but because of its size it will seek to do so internally and not pay for an external consultant to come in.

Supplier contract reviews and procurement generally are handled by the firm's operations manager and the risk team will feed in where needed. The firm's operations manager also looks after business continuity and again risk personnel feed into this.

The director and senior executive will provide guidance in the form of briefing notes and own all risk policies. The director and senior executive also run face-to-face training sessions on areas of compliance.

The firm plans on making it part of the trainee contract that trainees spend time in the risk and compliance team so that trainees can understand what the team do and also how to avoid complaints and how to handle things when matters go wrong.

10.6 Medium London firm

This medium-sized firm has approximately 120 fee earners and offers services in corporate, banking, charity, immigration and employment areas, to name a few. The firm has put in place the following structure when it comes to risk and compliance ('PSR' stands for professional standards and risk):

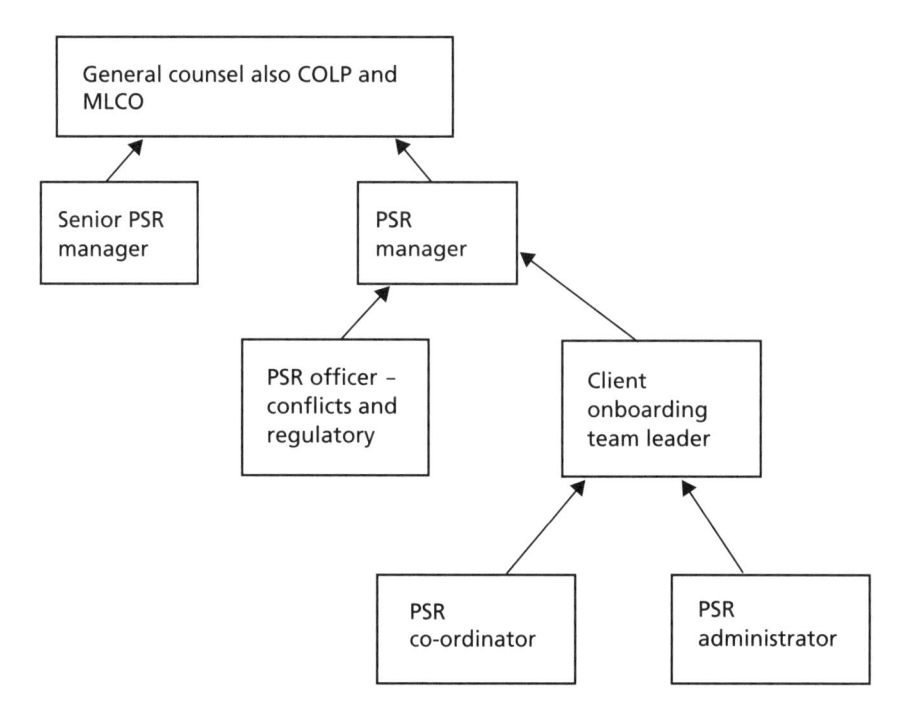

```
                General counsel also COLP and
                           MLCO
                   ↑                ↑
        Senior PSR              PSR
         manager             manager
                               ↑         ↑
                     PSR officer –    Client
                     conflicts and   onboarding
                     regulatory      team leader
                             ↑         ↑
                          PSR          PSR
                      co-ordinator  administrator
```

Separate to this:

| MLRO – partner | PII partner | COFA – finance director |

This firm decided not to have a DPO. The general counsel is responsible for data protection compliance and handles any data subject access requests that come in.

The general counsel describes their role as 50 per cent compliance, 30 per cent governance and contracts and 20 per cent risk. The general counsel gets involved with employee regulatory issues and arranges a quarterly HR and risk team meeting to understand any issues that come up.

This risk team handles Financial Conduct Authority (FCA) regulatory returns and training and maintains insider list management (as per insider trading rules) and maintains information barriers where they are appropriate.

The team also maintains an undertakings register.

Where appropriate, the general counsel will undertake process reviews for teams that are struggling to maintain profitability.

The PSR manager is responsible for handling complaints supervised by the general counsel.

This firm has a PII partner who handles PI notifications and claims. The general counsel handles insurance renewal.

This team handle PC renewal and reauthorisation without input from HR.

Cybercrime is shared between the general counsel and the information security manager. Procurement is handled by operations and generally any compliance that has a criminal aspect such as Criminal Finances Act and anti-bribery and corruption is 'owned' by the finance team with the risk team feeding in.

Training is done by way of online module and face-to-face where possible. The risk team conduct inductions for new staff.

Business continuity is handled by the firm's business innovation director with other business services areas feeding in to include the risk team.

This firm is in the process of centralising the undertaking of CDD and has already centralised conflict checking.

Interestingly, the general counsel feeds into partner appointments.

10.7 Large international firm

This large international firm with a plethora of practice areas has adopted the following structure for its risk team:

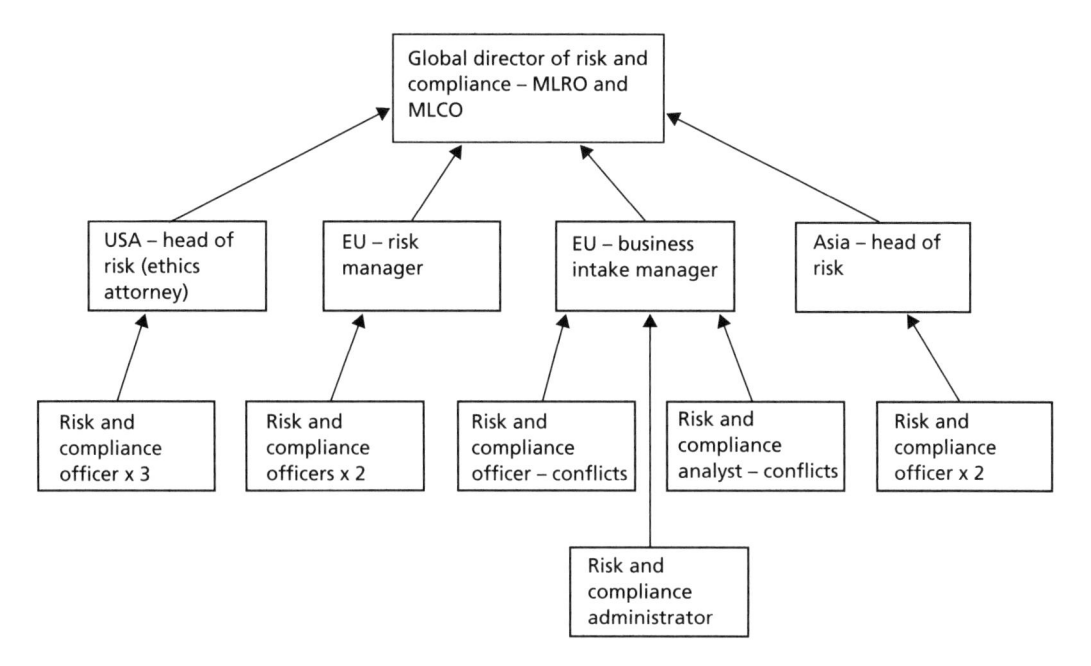

Organizational Chart

```
                    Global director of risk and
                    compliance – MLRO and
                    MLCO
                    ▲        ▲        ▲        ▲
        ┌───────────┘        │        │        └───────────┐
USA – head of        EU – risk        EU – business        Asia – head of
risk (ethics         manager          intake manager       risk
attorney)
    ▲                   ▲                ▲      ▲               ▲
    │                   │                │      │               │
Risk and          Risk and          Risk and   Risk and      Risk and
compliance        compliance        compliance compliance    compliance
officer x 3       officers x 2      officer –  analyst –     officer x 2
                                    conflicts  conflicts

                                    Risk and
                                    compliance
                                    administrator
```

Separate to this:

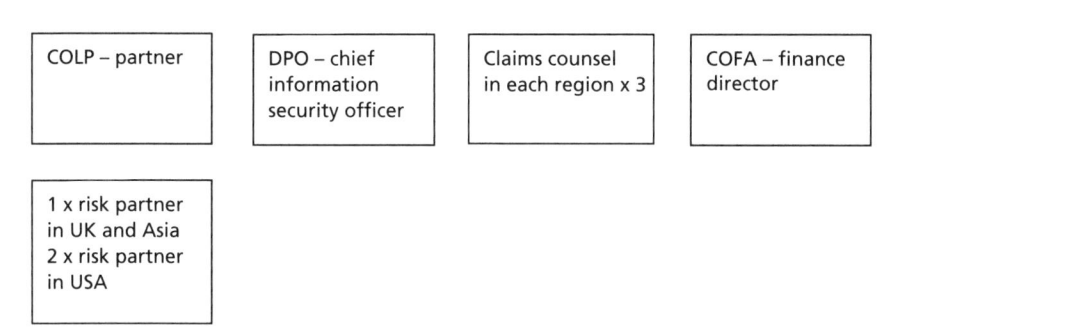

| COLP – partner | DPO – chief information security officer | Claims counsel in each region x 3 | COFA – finance director |

1 x risk partner in UK and Asia
2 x risk partner in USA

This is a very large international firm with offices in the UK/EU, USA and Asia. Each region has its own screening, onboarding and conflicts team. The US offices, for example, have a head of risk which oversees three officers who conduct screening and conflicts checks on new and existing clients. In the UK/EU, the risk manager has two reports, being one risk and compliance officer handling AML/financial crime, and the other any other non-new business intake areas. The business intake manager has an officer, analyst and administrator reporting to them and they handle all aspects of onboarding such as CDD gathering and checking and conflict checking. Likewise, the head of risk in Asia has two reports that handle AML compliance and conflicts.

This firm also has partners on hand to handle any reputation concerns with taking on clients and types of work.

This firm does not have membership of accreditation schemes that are maintained by the risk teams.

This firm did decide to have a DPO and aspects of compliance are handled by the DPO while being fully supported by the UK/EU risk team.

Cybercrime risk is handled by the global director of risk and compliance together with the firm's chief information security officer.

Training is done by way of online module and face-to-face where possible.

Business continuity is co-owned with other business service areas.

The team also handle any other reporting obligations such as to HM Revenue and Customs (HMRC) and the Information Commissioner's Office (ICO).

All aspects of risk and compliance as outlined in this book are covered by the teams as outlined above.

PART 3
Conclusion

I hope that you have found the contents of this book useful for your risk and compliance journey. Remember to undertake a gap analysis, draw up a plan and start somewhere – but most definitely do not bite off more than you can possibly chew. Start small and take areas that need to be tackled one at a time. Where possible, utilise the policies, plans, registers and guidance pieces annexed to this book and adapt them to suit your firm.

Above all else, try and make risk and compliance enjoyable by making it bite-sized, informative and where possible pepper your guidance with real-life examples provided in a non-lecturing way.

Good luck.

PART 3

Conclusion

Appendices

APPENDIX 1

Template client-facing complaints procedure

> See especially **1.1.2**.

Our complaints policy

We are committed to providing a high-quality service to our clients and we pride ourselves on our thorough and professional approach to our work.

While we rarely receive complaints, we believe that it is important to have procedures in place to help you in the unlikely event of your wishing to make a complaint.

The following procedure is intended to inform you of the way in which we handle complaints, and help you to decide the best approach to take. When something goes wrong we need you to tell us about it.

Our complaints procedure

The person with overall responsibility for managing complaints is [*name and any details of supervision or who assists this person*].

We ask that you communicate your complaint to us in writing setting out your particular concerns. This helps us to understand your complaint and respond to it.

If you want to raise a complaint under this procedure please email [*name and email address*]. Alternatively you can write to the lawyer with conduct of your matter or the supervising partner and request your complaint be forwarded to [*name*].

What will happen next?

1. We will send to you an acknowledgement of your complaint within three working days of receipt and enclose a copy of this procedure. We will at that stage decide who is best placed to respond to your complaint. This may be the head of department. We will also record your complaint in our central register. [*N.B. This section needs to describe what your firm has decided to do.*]
2. We will then investigate your complaint. This may involve inviting you to a meeting to discuss your concerns.
3. We will send you a reply to your complaint within 15 working days of receipt. If we are unable to respond to you within that time, we will inform you. The majority of matters are resolved at this stage. However, if you remain unhappy you are free to write to us again to set out your concerns.

If your complaint is not resolved to your satisfaction within eight weeks of it having been made to us, you have the right to complain to the Legal Ombudsman (LeO). Any complaint to LeO must usually be made within six years from the act or omission complained of or within three years from when you should have reasonably known of the cause for complaint. Further, you must raise your complaint with LeO within six months of our written response to your complaint. We hope that this will not be necessary but LeO can be contacted by telephone on 0300 555 0333, by email at: **enquiries@legalombudsman.org.uk** or by post at Legal Ombudsman, PO Box 6806, Wolverhampton WV1 9WJ. We will remind you of this right to complain to LeO at the conclusion of our complaints process.

Where we are unable to resolve your complaint you also have the option of contacting an alternative complaints body competent to deal with complaints about legal services should both you and our firm wish to use such a scheme.

We will inform you at the end of the complaints procedure whether we agree to the use of an alternative complaints body.

We are of course always glad to receive your comments on our service and to hear how we can help to improve it. Any complaint is always taken very seriously and if you do find cause for complaint you can be assured that it will be investigated thoroughly.

APPENDIX 2
Template internal complaints procedure

> See especially **1.1.3**.

Our complaints policy

We are committed to providing a high-quality service to all our clients and if something goes wrong, we will endeavour to rectify the situation as quickly as possible.

Our complaints handling process is intended to resolve clients' concerns wherever possible and to preserve their goodwill, even if things have gone wrong. It is also intended to minimise professional negligence claims.

The person with overall responsibility for managing complaints is [*name and any details of supervision or who assists this person*].

Some complaints may be well founded. We all make mistakes and we will expect honesty and realism from you if something has gone wrong. Equally, you will receive support from us. Complaints must be dealt with sympathetically and quickly. Our reputation depends on this as part of our commitment to treat clients fairly and to provide an excellent service.

Please note that this policy is an internal policy only and not to be disclosed to clients.

What is a complaint?

It is important to recognise what a complaint looks like.

A complaint is an oral or written expression of dissatisfaction which alleges that the complainant has suffered (or may suffer) financial loss, distress, inconvenience or other detriment.

You must bear in mind that complaints do not have to be formal and in writing but can equally be raised orally. In either case, they must be actioned in accordance with best practice and our complaints handling procedure and reported without delay. We recognise that a client may raise a concern which does not sound like a complaint but rather seems like a grumble. In this scenario it is more than likely appropriate that the conducting fee earner or supervisor handles this concern raised by the client outside this policy and procedure. This policy and procedure are intended for situations where it is appropriate for a complaint to be handled through a formal process such as this.

Common types of complaints include allegations of inadequate professional service, negligence and misconduct.

The Solicitors Regulation Authority (SRA) categorises complaints into the following areas:
- conduct;
- costs excessive;

- costs information deficient;
- criminal activity;
- data protection;
- delay;
- discrimination;
- failure to advise;
- failure to comply with agreed remedy;
- failure to follow instructions;
- failure to investigate complaint internally;
- failure to keep informed;
- failure to keep papers safe;
- failure to progress.

Information about complaints handling

Clients are notified in our terms of business of their right to complain including the right to complain about a bill and to refer the matter to the Legal Ombudsman (LeO) if they are not satisfied with the outcome of our internal complaints handling process.

We do not charge for handling complaints and they will always be dealt with in accordance with our complaints handling procedure.

As soon as you become aware of any complaint, you must consider what action to take. It is tempting to focus on formal complaints: letters or emails that clearly state that they are a complaint. However, many complaints are initially made informally, for example, a client telephoning to say that there is a drafting error in a document. While this person might not be making a formal complaint, they are expressing dissatisfaction.

Accordingly, you should explain how the problem might be resolved informally as well as highlighting details of our formal procedure. In this type of situation the best approach is to try to resolve the issue both informally and promptly to avoid escalation. For example, if there is a drafting error take immediate steps to acknowledge the error, apologise and correct it. Nobody's perfect and there will be times when clients are dissatisfied. If you pick up on this dissatisfaction and resolve issues as they arise, then clients are more likely to continue to instruct us and recommend us to others.

It is possible that a client may complain direct to LeO without first following our procedure. LeO will generally only consider a complaint after our internal complaints handling process has been exhausted and the matter will therefore usually be referred back to us. The normal complaints handling procedures will then be followed. Our complaints procedure can be accessed [*insert place*].

How we handle complaints

Once a complaint has been received, the matter should be referred to [*insert name*] in the first instance. If appropriate, the complaints procedure will be sent to the client and the complaint acknowledged within three working days. We will at that stage decide who is best placed to respond to the complaint. This might be the Head of Department, another partner or [*insert here who may handle the complaint*]. [*Name*] will record the complaint in our central register.

The complaint will then be investigated, which might involve inviting the client to a meeting to discuss their concerns.

Once the investigations are concluded the investigator [*consider putting the name of the person or person's role and amending this section accordingly*] will send a detailed reply to the complaint within 15 working days of receipt. If, however, the investigator is unable to comply with this time limit they will explain this to the client and confirm when a response will be prepared. We aim to resolve most complaints at this stage; however, if we are unable to do so then the client will be informed that we will be happy to consider any further concerns that they might have in order for us to try to reach a satisfactory conclusion.

If the complaint is not resolved to the client's satisfaction within eight weeks of it having been made to us, then they have the right to refer the matter to LeO whose contact details are: PO Box 6806 Wolverhampton WV1 9WJ or telephone 0300 555 0333 or via enquiries@legalombudsman.org.uk. Further guidance on the service can be found at www.legalombudsman.org.uk. Any referral to LeO must usually be made within six months of our final written response to the complaint.

The role of the Legal Ombudsman

After a complaint has been dealt with in accordance with our internal complaints handling procedure, the client is entitled to refer the matter to LeO if they are dissatisfied with the outcome. Accordingly, we aim to deal with complaints as quickly, objectively and sympathetically as possible so as to minimise the risk of a referral to LeO.

LeO accepts complaints from individuals and small businesses, charities, clubs, societies, associations and trusts. It can also consider complaints from other individuals and bodies not officially a client of the firm such as a beneficiary of an estate. It does not however accept complaints from larger corporate clients.

You should be aware that when investigating a complaint, LeO may contact you direct and without reference to [*name or position*]. If this happens you should notify [*name*] immediately.

Recording complaints

Complaints are recorded [*insert place*] which provides us with useful data allowing us to assess the effectiveness of our complaints handling process, identify trends and improve our service delivery. [*Optional but recommended:* This central record of complaints is analysed and reviewed annually.]

Complaints about others

If you believe you have grounds for raising a complaint to LeO, the SRA or any other regulatory body about another firm, lawyer or third party you should discuss your concerns with [*name*].

APPENDIX 3

Template professional indemnity insurance notification form

> See especially **1.2.2**.

Claimant name	
Claimant address	
Internal client reference	
Matter description	
Fee earner name and position, i.e. partner, associate, assistant	
Supervisor	
Department, team and practice area	
Purpose of retainer (what were we instructed to do)	
Date issue identified	
Date of alleged act	
Why has this date been selected for alleged act?	
Has a letter of claim been sent? Please confirm date	
Has a claim been issued? Please confirm date	
Is the file in the firm's possession? If not, where is it?	
If the file has been sent somewhere else does the firm have a copy?	
Circumstances that gave rise to notification. Please provide a full explanation and attach documents deemed necessary	
Views on liability and reasons why	
Rectification/mitigation steps to include where appropriate analysis of own interest conflict	
Proposed strategy/next steps	

Quantum and reasons	
What risk management strategies are being put in place to prevent reoccurrence?	
List of documents attached	

Name: ....
Position: ....
Date: ....

APPENDIX 4

Template attendance note – own interest conflict and professional indemnity notification and rectification

> See especially **1.2.3**.

Name: ....
Date: ....
Client: ....
Matter: ....
File no.: ....

Consideration of own interest conflict

We have carefully considered whether the firm has an own interest conflict pursuant to the Solicitors Regulation Authority (SRA) Code of Conduct for Firms paragraph 6.1, the SRA Code of Conduct for Solicitors, RELs and RFLs paragraph 6.1 and *SRA v. Howell Jones*.

In this matter the firm erred by [*insert facts of matter*].

It is proposed that the firm [*insert what action is to be taken, e.g. rectification*].

We do not consider our proposed actions to create an own interest conflict because [*insert reason*].

We will continue to keep under review whether we have an own interest conflict during the course of the matter.

APPENDIX 5

Template professional indemnity insurance declaration

> See especially **1.2.4**.

Please complete the attached form by [*date*] and return it to [*name*].

[*Optional:* N.B. You do not need to disclose matters which have already been reported to [*name*].]

1. Please confirm that you have reviewed carefully your current matters and that you are not aware of anything which should be reported to insurers, or if appropriate, give details.
2. Please give a detailed summary of any current or completed matter where the client has indicated any unhappiness or misgivings which might give scope for an allegation of negligence. Please note that something which may be seen as a client complaint may still have a negligence allegation lying behind it.
3. Please consider carefully whether you can recollect any act or omission of which the client may be wholly unaware, but which you acknowledge would be likely to be viewed as negligent if it emerges at some time in the future and confirm that you are not aware of any such matters or give details as appropriate.

Name: ……………………………………………

Signature: ……………………………………………

Position: ……………………………………………

Department: ……………………………………………

Date: ……………………………………………

[*Optional additional box*]

4. Please confirm that you have reviewed your matters and you are not providing any client or third party with a banking facility in breach of rule 3.3 of the Solicitors Regulation Authority (SRA) Accounts Rules.

APPENDIX 6

Template guidance to the professional indemnity insurance declaration form

> See especially **1.2.4**.

Dear fee earners

It is that time of the year when our brokers are starting discussions with insurers in the run up to the renewal of the firm's professional indemnity insurance (PII) at [*date*].

As part of the process each year, all fee earners are asked to identify all matters which might possibly result in a claim against the firm. As usual, we must be able to demonstrate to our insurers that we have carried out these enquiries diligently and to the best of our ability.

If we fail to notify our insurers of something which should be reported before the end of the current indemnity year, they may or may not accept it but even if they do, they could exercise a right of reimbursement against the firm.

Therefore, please reply to the questions found in the accompanying form. Please type your replies if more than single word answers.

[*Optional:* Please do not include those matters you have already notified to the risk team.]

As a reminder, our insurers require us to notify not only actual claims but also **circumstances which may give rise to a claim**. The definition of 'circumstances' includes an incident, occurrence, fact, matter, act or omission which may give rise to a claim in respect of civil liability. 'Circumstances' include not only an intimation of an intention to claim but also an awareness you may have of a failing or doubt as to the effectiveness of your work where such failing might give rise to a claim.

In other words, we must always notify circumstances where you are aware of a negligent act even if the client may be oblivious to the problem.

The following are examples of situations which would be likely to qualify as 'circumstances':

- A client complains or indicates unhappiness with our service. Even if you consider that the issue raised is no more than a complaint with or without substance, please tell [*name*] of this in any event so we can consider whether we need to notify it to our insurers.
- You realise that you have given negligent advice or in some other way breached the terms of your contract with the client even if the client is not yet aware of the error.
- The client has not complained and you do not consider you have done anything wrong, but nonetheless there is a possibility that a claim will arise.

If you are unsure whether a matter qualifies as a circumstance or not, please put it down in the accompanying form anyway and we can decide whether to inform our insurers or not. The number of notifications we make to our insurers does not increase the premium we pay and gives our insurers confidence that we are applying our minds to risk and take such matters seriously.

The requirement to disclose all claims and circumstances relates to all fee earners (including consultants, paralegals and trainees) at the firm. It is therefore most important that no one should fear holding up their hand when they have made a mistake. The consequences of not so doing could be severe and result in significant financial loss to the firm.

Please can you therefore send your named, signed and dated form, no later than [*date*], to [*name*] in the internal post or by email. If you do not have any circumstances to declare, you still need to complete the form.

Please do not inform your client if you have informed us of a circumstance involving their matter or reported the same to our insurers unless otherwise instructed.

[*Optional:* Finally, as part of our continuing compliance with the Solicitors Regulation Authority (SRA) Accounts Rules and rule 3.3 in particular, we have included a declaration for you to complete to confirm that having reviewed your matters you are not providing a banking facility to any client or third party.]

If you have any queries about the form or this guidance, please contact [*name*].

APPENDIX 7

Template client and matter risk assessment

> See especially **1.4.3** and **4.5.1**.
>
> N.B. There are many ways in which to conduct a client and matter risk assessment and this is just one way. The questions below have been designed based on the regulations and Solicitors Regulation Authority (SRA) guidance. The client and matter risk assessment below is based on your firm having a centralised onboarding process by a risk and compliance team. If this is not the case, you will need to amend the client assessment parts 1 and 2 to make it clear that the fee earner completes all client risk assessment questions.

Client and matter number: ....

Client name and matter description: ....

Solicitors are required to identify and assess risk on each and every client and matter as soon as possible and on an ongoing basis. This is not only to ensure compliance with the money laundering legislation but also part of firmwide good practice. The risk assessment is split into two parts: client and matter.

The risk and compliance team will complete the first client assessment section of this form as soon as possible after a new client is accepted. Fee earners should complete their sections as soon as possible and keep them under review and amend as necessary as the matter progresses.

The risk and compliance team will place this risk assessment in [*insert location*].

Client assessment for new clients or clients we have not acted for in past three years [*amend to suit your firm policy*].

Part 1 – initial assessment by risk and compliance

		Y/N/NA
1.	Is the client a regulated person or entity or is the client listed on a regulated market?	
2.	Is the client resident in, operating from or controlled from a high-risk jurisdiction set out in Schedule 2 below?	

		Y/N/NA
3.	Does the client operate in any of the following sectors which are regarded as potentially high risk? (a) high-end art/goods; (b) cultural artefacts; (c) public works contracts and construction; (d) real estate and property development; (e) oil and gas; (f) nuclear industry; (g) mining (of any sort); (h) tobacco products; (i) arms manufacturing/supply and the defence industry.	
4.	Is simplified due diligence satisfactory for this client?	
5.	Is the client, director or beneficial owner a politically exposed person (PEP)? This Includes UK and foreign PEPs, their family members and known close associates.	
6.	Is the client, director or beneficial owner sanctioned?	
7.	Is the client, director or beneficial owner resident in or a national of a country which is the subject of UK financial sanctions (refer to Schedule 1 below)?	
8.	Are we aware of any adverse media about the client, a director or beneficial owner?	
9.	Have any of the client's shares been issued in the form of bearer shares (corporates only)?	
10.	Has the client been evasive or obstructive in relation to our anti-money laundering (AML) checks (especially regarding beneficial ownership or source of funds or wealth)?	
11.	As far as you are aware, has the firm previously had to file a suspicious activity report (SAR) about this client?	
12.	If the client is unregulated, does the client's ownership structure seem unusual or unnecessarily complex/opaque?	
13.	Do we have satisfactory client due diligence (CDD) documentation?	
14.	Does the information provided by the client match the people with significant control (PSC) register? If not, consider obligation to report.	

RISK RATING given by risk and compliance

If any of the factors for questions 1–14 apply, the client may be assessed as being high risk.

Client risk rating by risk and compliance (high/med/low) – if all answers are of a favourable nature, then the risk is likely to be low. However, answers of an unfavourable nature may indicate a medium- or high-risk rating: [*insert rating*].

Reasons if necessary: [*insert reasons*].

Has this client been selected for ongoing monitoring? Y/N

Client assessment for new clients part 2 – to be completed by the conducting fee earner

		Y/N/NA
1.	Have we met the client (for companies this could be a director, beneficial owner or person with authority such as a general counsel)?	

		Y/N/NA
2.	Does the client's business involve dealing with large amounts of cash?	
3.	As far as you are aware, has another law firm refused to accept the client or terminated their retainer?	
4.	If the client is unregulated does the client's ownership structure seem unusual or unnecessarily complex/opaque?	

Matter assessment for all matters – to be completed by the conducting fee earner

When answering Yes to any question, enhanced due diligence should be considered. When answering Yes to a question denoted with a * enhanced due diligence must be applied as the regulations require this. Please see separate guidance.

		Y/N/NA
1.	Are instructions for this matter being given by a third party? If so, ensure you have identified and verified that third party as appropriate.	
2.	Does it make sense for us to be instructed? Is there an underlying legal transaction?	
3.	Is the client asking us to create a corporate structure or trust structure that is unnecessarily complex and/or could lead to tax evasion?*	
4.	Is the transaction unusually large or is there an unusual pattern of transactions?*	
5.	Does the transaction carry with it additional risk (e.g. it is handling high-value items such as art for which ownership is not clear) or does it create or facilitate anonymity of ownership or is the transaction unnecessarily complex?	
6.	Does the value of the transaction exceed our professional indemnity cover of £[amount]? Please ensure that liability is capped.	
7.	Is the transaction consistent with what you know about the client's business or level of wealth generally?	
8.	What is the source of funds for this transaction? Please document below. Do you understand the client's source of wealth? Does the information you are being given tally with what you know? **Please insert detail here.**	
9.	Will funds for the transaction be sent from a sanctioned jurisdiction OR high-risk country listed in Schedules 1 and 2 below? If yes, please inform [role or name].	
10.	If funds are coming from a third party, are you satisfied that you know who the third party is and why they are funding? Consider whether you need to undertake CDD.	
11.	Is the client insisting that you proceed on an urgent basis without a reasonable explanation and is this unusual for this client?	
12.	Is there anything else of concern to you? (Remember if you suspect money laundering please speak to the MLRO straight away.)	

RISK RATING given by conducting fee earner

Client and matter risk rating (high/med/low) – if all answers are of a favourable nature, then the risk is likely to be low. However, answers of an unfavourable nature may indicate a medium- or high-risk rating. If the latter, please inform [role or name]. Please see accompanying guidance to assist your rating: [insert guidance].

Reasons if necessary: [*insert reason*].

Remember you must tell [*role or name*] if your client changes address, ownership, directorship or corporate structure so that we can consider refreshing the CDD that the firm holds.

SCHEDULE 1

UK and UN financial sanctions regimes

Afghanistan (UK)	Mali (UN)	South Sudan (UK & UN)
Belarus (UK)	Republic of Guinea (UK)	Sudan (UK & UN)
Burundi (UK)	Republic of Guinea-Bissau (UK & UN)	Syria (UK)
Burma (UK)	Iran	Tunisia (UK)
Central African Republic (UK & UN)	Iraq (UK & UN)	Ukraine
Democratic Republic of the Congo (UK & UN)	Lebanon and Syria (UK)	Venezuela (UK)
Egypt (UK)	Libya (UK & UN)	Yemen (UK & UN)
Eritrea (UK & UN)	North Korea (Democratic People's Republic of Korea DPRK) (UK & UN)	Zimbabwe (UK)
ISIL (Da'esh) and Al-Qaida organisations (UK & UN)	Somalia (UK & UN)	

SCHEDULE 2

Other high-risk jurisdictions

Clients based in high-risk jurisdictions (individuals and corporates)

Transparency International publishes a list every year which ranks countries in order of their perceived levels of corruption (the Corruption Perceptions Index). The list of countries in the table below takes this into account together with the guidance on high-risk and non-co-operative jurisdictions published by the Financial Action Task Force (FATF).

The following list includes countries you are most likely to encounter. It is not intended to be exhaustive. To view the list visit: **https://www.transparency.org/en/news/corruption-perceptions-index-2017**.

Afghanistan	Kenya	Russia
Bahrain	Kuwait	Saudi Arabia
Bosnia and Herzegovina	Lao PDR	South Africa
Brazil	Lebanon	South Sudan
China	Liberia	Sri Lanka
Cyprus	Libya	Sudan
Democratic People's Republic of Korea	Kazakhstan	Syria
Egypt	Malaysia	Thailand
Ethiopia	Malta	Trinidad and Tobago
Ghana	Mauritius	Tunisia
Greece	Mexico	Turkey
Grenada	Morocco	Uganda
India	Nigeria	Ukraine
Iran	North Korea (DPRK)	Vanuatu
Iraq	Oman	Venezuela
Italy	Pakistan	Yemen
Jamaica	Panama	Zimbabwe

APPENDIX 8

Guidance to the client and matter risk assessment

> See especially **1.4.3** and **4.5.1**.
>
> This is a guidance note to the firm's client and matter risk assessment. Below is a summary of the purpose of the assessment, why it is in place together with guidance on each question contained within the assessment.

What is the assessment and why does it need to be completed?

It is a legal requirement under the Money Laundering, Terrorist Financing and Transfer of Funds (Information on the Payer) Regulations 2017 to undertake a documented risk assessment to understand and assess the level of risk arising from acting for the client.

To undertake this assessment we must take into account aspects such as whether our client is high risk (because they are politically exposed, sanctioned, reside or operate in a high-risk jurisdiction and so on) and we must also assess the level of risk contained in the work we are doing (for example, by asking ourselves whether it makes sense for us to be instructed, whether the work is consistent with what we know about the client and so on).

From this analysis we can assess the risk as being low, medium or high.

Please note this is not an exact science and each client and retainer must be reviewed on its own facts (so because we consider one type of client or work as low risk does not mean that all the same types of clients and work will be considered low risk).

Who needs to complete the assessment?

[*Amend as necessary to suit your firm.*]

The assessment is split into two parts: client and matter.

The risk and compliance team will complete the first part of the client assessment as indicated on the form. The conducting fee earner needs to complete the second part of the risk assessment and the matter assessment. Fee earners are asked not to change the assessment made by risk and compliance.

All new clients should have an assessment undertaken. For any new matter for an existing client, the matter assessment needs to be undertaken.

The assessment should take place as soon as possible and be amended on an ongoing basis where necessary.

You will find a copy of the assessment in [*insert location*]. When files are reviewed by [*role or name*] they will be checking to see whether the assessment has been completed.

GUIDANCE TO THE CLIENT AND MATTER RISK ASSESSMENT

Please remember, this is a legal requirement. This is not something which is a 'nice to have'. Systematic failure to complete the risk assessment puts the fee earner and the firm in breach of the law. That is so serious that it may warrant a self-report to the Solicitors Regulation Authority (SRA).

What do the questions on the assessment mean?

Below is guidance on each of the questions set out in the assessment.

Client assessment for new clients part 1 – initial assessment by risk and compliance

1. **Is the client a regulated person or entity or is the client listed on a regulated market?**

   Those who are regulated are considered to be lower risk. Those on the regulated market are also considered to be lower risk.

2. **Is the client resident in, operating from or controlled from a high-risk jurisdiction set out in Schedule 2?**

   Schedule 2 is found at the end of the risk assessment.

   Those who reside in or are operating from a high-risk jurisdiction are considered to be higher risk.

3. **Does the client operate in any of the following sectors which are regarded as potentially high risk?**

   (a) high-end art/goods;
   (b) cultural artefacts;
   (c) public works contracts and construction;
   (d) real estate and property development;
   (e) oil and gas;
   (f) nuclear industry;
   (g) mining (of any sort);
   (h) tobacco products;
   (i) arms manufacturing/supply and the defence industry.

   Those who operate in these sectors are considered to be higher risk.

4. **Is simplified due diligence satisfactory for this client?**

   To be able to apply simplified due diligence (this is where we are able to point to the regulated status or the entity's listing on a regulated stock market to identify the client) we have to assess the jurisdiction the client resides or operates in and the sector they operate in. We cannot automatically apply simplified due diligence any longer. To be able to apply simplified due diligence therefore we need to undertake this risk assessment.

5. **Is the client, director or beneficial owner a politically exposed person (PEP)? This includes UK and foreign PEPs, their family members and known close associates.**

   Those who are PEPs are considered to be higher risk as they may be susceptible to bribery and corruption. This includes UK PEPs as well as international PEPs. Where a PEP is present, this increases the risk and further information from the client should be sought about their source of funds for the transaction. Please note that money laundering reporting officer (MLRO) approval for the firm to act for a PEP is required by law.

6. **Is the client, director or beneficial owner sanctioned?**

    Sanctions are very serious. If a client is sanctioned then depending on the type of sanction we may not be able to act without an appropriate licence from HM Treasury. To act without a licence is a criminal offence.

7. **Is the client, director or beneficial owner resident in or a national of a country which is the subject of UK financial sanctions (refer to Schedule 1)?**

    Sanctions are imposed on countries as well as individuals and entities. If we are to act for those who reside in a country which is sanctioned by the UK, we need to consider what steps need to be taken, if any.

8. **Are we aware of any adverse media about the client, a director or beneficial owner?**

    Those who have allegations against them for criminal conduct may be higher risk to act for. Sometimes we may be fully aware of the media report and this is why we are engaged (business crime or defamation advice, for example). Each case is reviewed on its own facts.

9. **Have any of the client's shares been issued in the form of bearer shares (corporates only)?**

    Bearer shares pose a higher risk of money laundering as it is often difficult to identify beneficial owners and such companies are often incorporated in jurisdictions with lower anti-money laundering (AML) requirements. If our client is owned in the form of bearer shares, we will need to identify the holder of the shares. Please note bearer shares are banned in the UK.

10. **Has the client been evasive or obstructive in relation to our AML checks (especially regarding beneficial ownership or source of funds or wealth)?**

    This is considered to be a money laundering warning sign.

11. **As far as you are aware, has the firm previously had to file a suspicious activity report (SAR) about this client?**

    This means that we have had suspicions in the past. This doesn't mean we will not be able to act necessarily but we need to consider whether our suspicions are still prevalent.

12. **If the client is unregulated does the client's ownership structure seem unusual or unnecessarily complex/opaque?**

    Clients whose structure is not clear may be seeking to hide something. There may be a rational explanation for this complexity but we need to consider the position all the same.

13. **Do we have satisfactory client due diligence (CDD) documentation?**

    For each client, the risk and compliance team will assess whether the CDD is satisfactory.

14. **Does the information provided by the client match the people with significant control (PSC) register? If not, consider obligation to report.**

    Before establishing a business relationship with a:

- company (registered or unregistered as defined in the Unregistered Companies Regulations 2009);
- limited liability partnership (LLP); or
- Scottish partnership

we must collect proof of registration or an excerpt from the relevant register. Where there is a discrepancy between information collected from the PSC register and information collected from the client, the money laundering regulations require us to report it to Companies House. Where a discrepancy is found, we will endeavour to ask the client about it first and give them an opportunity to inform Companies House before we do.

Client assessment for new clients part 2 [to be completed by the conducting fee earner]

1. **Have we met the client (for companies this could be a director, beneficial owner or person with authority such as a general counsel)?**

    Not meeting the client increases the risk of identity fraud and may help facilitate anonymity. Therefore meeting a client lowers this risk. It may be perfectly normal not to meet the client on the particular transaction, but any evasive behaviour about meeting us might be a cause for concern.

2. **Does the client's business involve dealing with large amounts of cash?**

    The nature of the client's business might increase risk if it is cash-intensive and therefore presents a greater risk of disguising illegal funds within legitimate payments. The client's area of work may also pose a risk of money laundering, e.g. casinos. Please remember cash isn't 'bad', but it does increase risk.

3. **As far as you are aware, has another law firm refused to accept the client or terminated their retainer?**

    If another law firm has turned the client away or the client has 'fallen out' with their previous solicitor, this can be an indicator of a client that carries higher risk. Often clients who do not pay our bill and complain have done the same to previous solicitors. This should therefore be a warning sign to you.

4. **If the client is unregulated, does the client's ownership structure seem unusual or unnecessarily complex/opaque?**

    Clients whose structure is not clear may be seeking to hide something. There may be a rational explanation for this complexity but we need to consider the position all the same.

Matter assessment for all matters (new clients or repeat clients) [to be completed by the conducting fee earner]

When answering Yes to any question enhanced due diligence should be considered. When answering Yes to a question denoted with a * enhanced due diligence must be applied as the regulations require this.

1. **Are instructions for this matter being given by a third party? If so, ensure you have identified and verified that third party as appropriate.**

    It is a requirement of the law that we verify that the third party has the authority to give instructions on behalf of the client and that we also identify and verify the person giving those instructions (i.e. seek their certified copy photo ID and proof of address). This is to try to prevent fraud being committed on our client.

Our interpretation of this legal requirement is in line with that of other law firms in that this requirement is seeking to capture situations such as family members giving instructions on behalf of the client. It is not intended to capture, for example, a bank employee who clearly has the correct job role to provide us instructions on behalf of the bank.

2. **Does it make sense for us to be instructed? Is there an underlying legal transaction?**

    Asking the firm to act on matters it would not ordinarily undertake may indicate something untoward. Likewise, if there is no legal transaction at hand, instructing solicitors can give a criminal act an air of legality. We need to ask ourselves what we are doing, why and whether it makes sense.

3. **Is the client asking us to create a corporate structure or trust structure that is unnecessarily complex and/or could lead to tax evasion?***

    Clients that wish to structure a transaction in a complex way may be trying to hide something or avoid paying something (please note we are also subject to the Criminal Finances Act 2017 and you can find our relevant policy on the intranet).

4. **Is the transaction unusually large or is there an unusual pattern of transactions?***

    This is deemed to present a higher risk for which enhanced due diligence needs to be considered.

5. **Does the transaction carry with it additional risk (e.g. it is handling high-value items such as art for which ownership is not clear) or does it create or facilitate anonymity of ownership or is the transaction unnecessarily complex?**

    It is important that you consider whether there are any other additional risk factors associated with the transaction. There can be many aspects of the transaction and the question provides you with some examples but these are not exhaustive. What constitutes higher risk depends on the nature of the transaction itself and the client. There is no exact science.

6. **Does the value of the transaction exceed our professional indemnity cover of £[*amount*]? Please ensure that liability is capped.**

    This is self-explanatory.

7. **Is the transaction consistent with what you know about the client's business or level of wealth generally?**

    We need to consider whether the transaction fits with what we know about the client. If we understand the client to be of modest means and they are now buying a multi-million pound business, does this fit their profile? If you are unsure why, how or whether the client's position has changed then you need to ask the client about it. Clients with nothing to hide will not mind these questions.

8. **What is the source of funds for this transaction? Please document below. Do you understand the client's source of wealth? Does the information you are being given tally with what you know? Please insert detail here.**

    It is important to understand the client's source of funds for the transaction (where the money is from) and wealth (how the money came to be there) especially where the client is high risk. The question of evidencing source of wealth should be addressed on a risk sensitive basis. Please see the intranet for further guidance.

9. Will funds for the transaction be sent from a sanctioned jurisdiction OR high-risk country listed in Schedules 1 and 2? If yes, please inform [*role or name*].

    Schedules 1 and 2 are contained at the end of the client and matter risk assessment.

    Sending monies from these countries may be prohibited if they are sanctioned and so you need to consider this. Further, receiving monies from high-risk jurisdictions increases the risk of us receiving laundered monies.

10. If funds are coming from a third party, are you satisfied that you know who the third party is and why they are funding? Consider whether you need to undertake CDD.

    While we are obliged to undertake CDD on our own clients, where funds are being sent by a third party we should also undertake CDD on those third parties as well as understand why they are funding the client.

11. Is the client insisting that you proceed on an urgent basis without a reasonable explanation and is this unusual for this client?

    While it is normal for clients to want things done quickly, we need to consider whether that is reasonable in the circumstances. Is it normal for that client?

12. Is there anything else of concern to you? (Remember: if you suspect money laundering please speak to the MLRO straight away.)

    This is an opportunity to think about and put down any concerns that you may have.

Risk rating guidance

Whether a client and matter can be considered to be low, medium or high risk is a matter of judgment based on the information before you. There is no exact science to risk ratings but where the answers to the questions are unfavourable then the rating is likely to be medium or high. If on reflection it doesn't make sense for us to be instructed; the client is asking us to create an opaque structure; the transaction is dealing with assets that are considered to be higher risk such as mining, oil and gas; or an element of the transaction takes place in or emanates from a high-risk jurisdiction, the rating is likely to be high.

Remember, the law requires a risk assessment to be made and it is far better to give a rating even if someone else's judgment would be different from yours than to not give one at all. Please reach out to [*role or name*] if you wish to discuss a matter through. Please inform [*role or name*] if you rate a matter as high risk so they can consider ongoing monitoring. Please note, however, that [*role or name*] cannot provide the risk rating for you.

A note on enhanced due diligence

Enhanced due diligence may be required depending on your answers to the questions. Enhanced due diligence in its simplest terms means asking for more information and proof of what the client is telling you. What you ask for is based on the risk at hand.

APPENDIX 9

Template data protection policy

> See especially **2.1.1**.
>
> N.B. There are many different ways to write a data protection policy and this is just one. The main aim of the policy is to explain the firm's procedure for complying with the six principles under the EU General Data Protection Regulation (GDPR) and the firm's retention and erasure procedures. The Law Society produces a *Data Protection Toolkit* (2nd edition) which will be of use.

Introduction

We hold personal data about our people, clients, contacts and other individuals for a variety of business purposes.

This policy sets out how we seek to protect personal data and ensure that our people understand the rules governing the use of personal data to which they have access in the course of their work. In particular, this policy requires our people to ensure that the data protection officer (DPO) is consulted before any significant new data processing activity is initiated to ensure that the relevant compliance steps are addressed.

Scope of policy

This policy applies to all people. You must make yourself familiar with this policy and comply with its terms.

This policy supplements our other policies relating to [*insert name of other policies that you have*]. We may supplement or amend this policy from time to time. Any new or modified policy will be communicated before being adopted.

The law

Article 5 of the EU General Data Protection Regulation (GDPR) contains data protection principles which require that personal data shall be:

1. processed lawfully, fairly and in a transparent manner in relation to individuals;
2. collected for specified, explicit and legitimate purposes and not further processed in a manner that is incompatible with those purposes; further processing for archiving purposes in the public interest, scientific or historical research purposes or statistical purposes shall not be considered to be incompatible with the initial purposes;
3. adequate, relevant and limited to what is necessary in relation to the purposes for which it is processed;
4. accurate and, where necessary, kept up to date; every reasonable step must be taken to

ensure that personal data that is inaccurate, having regard to the purposes for which it is processed, is erased or rectified without delay;
5. kept in a form which permits identification of data subjects for no longer than is necessary for the purposes for which the personal data is processed; personal data may be stored for longer periods in so far as the personal data will be processed solely for archiving purposes in the public interest, scientific or historical research purposes or statistical purposes subject to implementation of the appropriate technical and organisational measures required by the GDPR in order to safeguard the rights and freedoms of individuals; and
6. processed in a manner that ensures appropriate security of the personal data, including protection against unauthorised or unlawful processing and against accidental loss, destruction or damage, using appropriate technical or organisational measures.

We need a lawful basis to process all data. Lawful bases are:

1. **Consent:** The individual has given clear consent for you to process their personal data for a specific purpose.
2. **Contract:** The processing is necessary for a contract you have with the individual, or because they have asked you to take specific steps before entering into a contract.
3. **Legal obligation:** The processing is necessary for you to comply with the law (not including contractual obligations).
4. **Vital interests:** The processing is necessary to protect someone's life.
5. **Public task:** The processing is necessary for you to perform a task in the public interest or for your official functions, and the task or function has a clear basis in law.
6. **Legitimate interests:** The processing is necessary for your legitimate interests or the legitimate interests of a third party, unless there is a good reason to protect the individual's personal data which overrides those legitimate interests. (This cannot apply if you are a public authority processing data to perform your official tasks.)

Responsibilities

[The DPO in the firm is [*name*]. / The person with overall responsibility for data is [*name*].] [N.B. *This policy proceeds on the basis that you have appointed a DPO.*]

The DPO has overall responsibility for the day-to-day implementation of this policy.

We must process personal data fairly and lawfully in accordance with individual rights. This generally means that we should not process personal data unless the individual whose details we are processing has given consent or we have other legitimate grounds for processing.

The DPO is responsible for:

- keeping the management committee/board/CEO [*amend as appropriate*] updated about data protection responsibilities, risks and issues;
- reviewing all data protection procedures and policies on a regular basis;
- arranging data protection training and advice for all people, board members and those included in this policy;
- answering questions on data protection from our people, board members and other stakeholders;
- responding to people and clients who wish to know which data is being held on them by the firm;
- checking and approving with third parties that handle the firm's data any contracts or agreement regarding data processing.

The IT director [*amend as necessary to fit your firm*] is responsible for:
- ensuring that all systems, services, software and equipment meet acceptable security standards;
- checking and scanning security hardware and software regularly to ensure that it is functioning properly;
- researching third-party services, such as cloud services the firm is considering using to store or process data.

The business development director [*amend as necessary to fit your firm*] is responsible for:
- approving data protection statements attached to emails and other marketing material;
- addressing data protection queries from clients, target audiences or media outlets;
- co-ordinating with the DPO to ensure all marketing initiatives adhere to data protection laws and the firm's data protection policy.

The processing of all data must be:
- necessary to deliver our services;
- in our legitimate interests and not unduly prejudice an individual's privacy.

In most cases this provision will apply to routine business data processing activities.

Our terms of business contain a privacy notice to clients on data protection. The notice:
- sets out the purposes for which we hold personal data on clients;
- highlights that our work may require us to give information to third parties such as expert witnesses and other professional advisers;
- provides that clients have a right of access to the personal data that we hold about them.

Sensitive personal data

In most cases where we process sensitive personal data, we will require the data subject's explicit consent to do this unless exceptional circumstances apply or we are required to do this by law (e.g. to comply with legal obligations to ensure health and safety at work). Any such consent will need to clearly identify what the relevant data is, why it is being processed and to whom it will be disclosed.

Accuracy and relevance

We will ensure that any personal data we process is accurate, relevant and not excessive, given the purpose for which it was obtained. We will not process personal data obtained for one purpose for any unconnected purpose unless the individual concerned has agreed to this or would otherwise reasonably expect this or we are able to rely on our legitimate interests in the use of the data.

Individuals may ask that we correct inaccurate personal data relating to them. If you believe that information is inaccurate, you should report this to [*role or name*].

Your personal data

You must take reasonable steps to ensure that personal data we hold about you is accurate and updated as required. For example, if your personal circumstances change, please inform the HR team so that they can update your personal records.

Data security

You must keep personal data secure against loss or misuse. Where other organisations process personal data as a service on our behalf, the DPO will establish what, if any, additional specific data security arrangements need to be implemented in contracts with those third-party organisations.

Storing data securely

In cases when data is stored on printed paper, it should be kept in a secure place where unauthorised personnel cannot access it.

Printed data shall be shredded when it is no longer needed.

Data stored on a computer shall be protected by strong passwords that are changed regularly.

Data stored on CDs or memory sticks must be locked away securely when they are not being used.

The DPO must approve any cloud used to store data.

Servers containing personal data must be kept in a secure location, away from general office space.

Data should be regularly backed up in line with the firm's backup procedures.

Data must never be saved directly to non-firm owned mobile devices such as laptops, tablets or smartphones.

All servers containing sensitive data must be approved and protected by security software and a strong firewall.

Data retention

We must retain personal data for no longer than is necessary. What is necessary will depend on the circumstances of each case, taking into account the reasons that the personal data was obtained, but should be determined in a manner consistent with our data retention guidelines. [*Cross-refer here to a policy or your terms of business which sets out the retention times for client data.*]

Transferring data internationally

There are restrictions on international transfers of personal data. You must not transfer personal data anywhere outside the UK without first consulting the DPO.

Data subject access requests

Individuals are entitled, subject to certain exceptions, to request access to information held about them.

If you receive a data subject access request (DSAR), you should refer that request immediately to the DPO. Where appropriate, we may ask you to help us comply with those requests.

Please contact the DPO if you would like to correct or request information that we hold about you. There are also restrictions on the information to which you are entitled under applicable law.

Processing data in accordance with the individual's rights

You should abide by any request from an individual not to use their personal data for direct marketing purposes and notify the DPO about any such request.

Do not send direct marketing material to someone electronically (e.g. via email) unless you have an existing business relationship with them in relation to the services being marketed.

Please contact the DPO for advice on direct marketing before starting any new direct marketing activity.

Training

Our people will receive training on this policy. New joiners will receive training as part of the induction process. Further training will be provided at least every two years or whenever there is a substantial change in the law or our policy and procedure.

Training will be provided through in-house seminars and via online learning on a regular basis.

It will cover:
- the law relating to data protection;
- our data protection and related policies and procedures.

Completion of training is compulsory.

Conditions for processing

We will ensure any use of personal data is justified in accordance with at least one of the conditions for processing and this will be specifically documented. All people who are responsible for processing personal data will be aware of the conditions for processing. The conditions for processing will be available to data subjects in the form of a privacy notice.

Justification for personal data

We will process personal data in compliance with all six data protection principles in the GDPR.

We will document the additional justification for the processing of sensitive data, and will ensure any biometric and genetic data is considered sensitive.

Consent

The data that we collect may be subject to active consent by the individual. If so, this consent can be revoked at any time.

Data portability

Upon request, an individual should have the right to receive a copy of their data in a structured format. These requests should be processed within one month, provided there is no undue burden and it does not compromise the privacy of others. An individual may also request that their data is transferred directly to another system. This must be done for free.

Right to be forgotten

An individual may request that any information held on them is deleted or removed, and any third parties who process or use that data must also comply with the request. An erasure request can only be refused if an exemption applies.

Privacy by design and default

Privacy by design is an approach to projects that promote privacy and data protection compliance from the start. The DPO will be responsible for conducting privacy impact assessments and ensuring that all IT projects commence with a privacy plan.

When relevant, and when it does not have a negative impact on the individual, privacy settings will be set to the most private by default.

Reporting breaches

All people have an obligation to report actual or potential data protection compliance failures. This allows us to:
- investigate the breach and take remedial steps if necessary;
- maintain a register of compliance breaches;
- notify the relevant regulatory authority of any compliance failures that are material either in their own right or as part of a pattern of failures.

Consequences of failing to comply

Failure to comply with this policy may lead to disciplinary action under our procedures which could result in dismissal.

If you have any questions or concerns about anything in this policy, do not hesitate to contact the DPO.

APPENDIX 10

Template password policy

> See especially **2.1.1**.

Introduction

The purpose of this policy is to define the firm's requirements regarding the setting of passwords for firm owned devices.

This policy applies to all people with a login account on the [*firm*] network.

Firmwide password requirements

All passwords must be complex. Using simple words, with or without numbers, such as 'Rebecca0', 'Monday19', or 'Password1', is prohibited.

Passwords must be at least 10 characters long and contain a combination of uppercase letters, lowercase letters, numbers and punctuation marks. These requirements will be enforced with software when possible.

If the security of a password is in doubt – for example, if there is any reason to believe that a password is known by an unauthorised person – then the password must be changed immediately.

Default passwords, such as those created for new people when they start employment at the firm, must be changed as quickly as possible.

You must never share your passwords with anyone else, including co-workers, line managers, IT service desk, etc. Any person who requires access to a specific system will be provided with their own unique password.

You must not write passwords down or keep them near your workstations.

Your network login password must be changed every 90 days [*amend to mirror the firm's process*].

IT service desk

Those who work on the firm's IT service desk must not ask a person for their password either verbally or in writing. If a member of the service desk team does need to login as another person for support purposes, then this must be agreed in advance and the person's password changed.

APPENDIX 11
Template email policy

> See especially **2.1.1**.

Introduction

The purpose of this email policy is to ensure the proper use of the [*firm name*] email system and make people aware of the difference between acceptable and unacceptable use.

This policy covers any email sent from a [*firm name*] email address and applies to all people.

Our policy

All business-related email must be sent to/from a [*firm name*] email account. The use of personal or third party email accounts for conducting any [*firm name*] business is strictly prohibited.

For the avoidance of doubt, you must never forward business-related emails to your personal email address for any reason, including remote working. If you are experiencing issues with remote working, please contact the IT service desk who will be able to assist you.

All use of email must be consistent with [*firm name*] policies and procedures, applicable laws and proper business practices.

[*Firm name*] email accounts should be used primarily for [*firm name*] business-related purposes; personal communication using a firm's email account is permitted as long as it does not interfere with business duties.

Using a [*firm name*] email address for non-[*firm name*] related commercial uses is strictly prohibited.

Email must be properly filed in the appropriate location if it is a [*firm name*] business record.

You must not use the [*firm name*] email system for the creation or distribution of any disruptive or offensive messages, comments concerning or images including pornography, race, sex, disability, age, sexual orientation, religion or religious belief and practice, political beliefs, national origin and other protected characteristics under the Equality Act 2010. People who receive any emails containing offensive content of this nature from any [*firm name*] people should report the matter to their supervisor or manager immediately.

You are strictly prohibited from automatically forwarding your [*firm name*] email to a third-party email system.

You are prohibited from using third-party email systems and storage servers such as Gmail, Hotmail, Yahoo, Dropbox, OneDrive, Google Drive, etc. to conduct [*firm name*] business to include any client work.

Personal email sent to your [*firm name*] email address that is in no way related to [*firm name*], its business operations or clients may be forwarded to a personal email address.

Any email sent to or stored on the firm's email system may be accessed by authorised personnel in line with the firm's published privacy notice and disciplinary policies as well as compliance with data subject access requests. [*Amend here as necessary.*]

All people must be aware of phishing emails and social engineering, and in the event of receiving a message that raises any suspicions, immediately [*set out steps that person should take*].

APPENDIX 12

Template privacy notice for employees and workers

> See especially **2.1.1**.
>
> N.B. There are many different versions of a privacy notice and this is just one. The purpose of the document is to describe how you collect and use data from employees and workers (such as partners and consultants). This template can be adapted to be client-facing. If you are adapting it to be client-facing, you will need to set out the circumstances in which you will collect client data and how you will use that data. The Law Society's *Data Protection Toolkit* (2nd edition) has a very good client-facing privacy notice.

Introduction

[*Name of firm*] is committed to protecting the privacy and security of your personal information.

This privacy notice describes how we collect and use personal information about you during and after your working relationship with us, in accordance with the EU General Data Protection Regulation (GDPR).

It applies to all employees and workers (including partners and contractors).

We are a 'data controller'. This means that we are responsible for deciding how we hold and use personal information about you.

This notice applies to current and former employees and workers. This notice does not form part of any contract of employment or other contract to provide services. We may update this notice at any time but if we do so, we will provide you with an updated copy of this notice as soon as reasonably practical.

Our data protection officer

[*If you have decided not to appoint a data protection officer, set out who is the person responsible for data protection compliance instead.*]

We have appointed a data protection officer (DPO) to oversee compliance with the data protection legislation and this privacy notice. Our DPO is [*name*]. If you have any queries about this privacy notice please contact the DPO.

Data protection principles

We will comply with data protection law. This says that the personal information we hold about you must be:

1. used lawfully, fairly and in a transparent way;
2. collected only for valid purposes that we have clearly explained to you and not used in any way that is incompatible with those purposes;
3. relevant to the purposes we have told you about and limited only to those purposes;
4. accurate and kept up to date;
5. kept only as long as necessary for the purposes we have told you about;
6. kept securely.

Information we may hold about you

Depending on the nature of your relationship with us, we will collect various aspects of data about you.

There are certain types of more sensitive personal data which require a higher level of protection, such as information about a person's health or sexual orientation.

We will collect, store, and use the following categories of personal information about you:

[*Set out the types of data that you may collect – this could be name, title, addresses, telephone numbers, personal email addresses, DOB, gender, marital status, bank details, salary, start date, leave date, performance information, sickness records, photographs, access card information, login information, CCTV and so on.*]

We may also collect, store and use the following more sensitive types of personal information:

[*Set out the types of sensitive information you may collect, such as race or ethnicity, religious beliefs, sexual orientation, political opinions and so on.*]

How we collect your data

We collect personal information about you through the application and recruitment process, either directly from candidates or sometimes from an employment agency or background check provider. We may sometimes collect additional information from third parties including former employers, credit reference agencies or other background check agencies [*insert name of any others*].

We will collect additional personal information in the course of job-related activities throughout the period of you working for us.

How we use the information about you

We will only use your personal information when the law allows us to (i.e. we have a lawful basis).

Most commonly, we will use your personal information in the following circumstances:

1. where we need to perform the contract we have entered into with you, such as your contract of employment;
2. where we need to comply with a legal obligation;
3. where it is necessary for legitimate interests pursued by us or a third party and your interests and fundamental rights do not override those interests;
4. where we need to protect your interests (or someone else's interests);
5. where it is needed in the public interest [or for official purposes].

If you do not provide us with the information we require

If you fail to provide certain information when requested, we may not be able to perform the contract we have entered into with you (such as paying you or providing a benefit), or we may be prevented from complying with our legal obligations (such as to ensure the health and safety of our workers).

Change of purpose

We will only use your personal information for the purposes for which we collected it, unless we reasonably consider that we need to use it for another reason and that reason is compatible with the original purpose. If we need to use your personal information for an unrelated purpose, we will notify you and we will explain the legal basis which allows us to do so.

Special categories of data and their use by us

'Special categories' of data consist of particularly sensitive personal information, such as information about your health, racial or ethnic origin, sexual orientation or trade union membership and require higher levels of protection.

We need to have further justification for collecting, storing and using this type of personal information. We may process special categories of personal information in the following circumstances:

1. in limited circumstances, with your explicit written consent;
2. where we need to carry out our legal obligations or exercise rights in connection with employment;
3. where it is needed in the public interest, such as for equal opportunities monitoring.

In general, we will not process particularly sensitive personal information about you unless it is necessary for performing or exercising obligations or rights in connection with employment. On rare occasions, there may be other reasons for processing, such as where it is in the public interest to do so. The situations in which we will process your particularly sensitive personal information are listed below.

[Insert reasons why you would process sensitive personal data such as occupational health.]

Sharing your data

We may have to share your data with third parties, including third-party service providers where required by law, where it is necessary to administer the working relationship with you or where we have another legitimate interest in doing so.

All our third-party service providers and other entities in the group are required to take appropriate security measures to protect your personal information in line with our policies.

Third parties that may process your personal data

Third parties that may process your data are [*set out here the names of these parties, e.g. payroll companies, HM Revenue and Customs (HMRC), health insurance companies, pension providers and so on*].

Transferring information outside the EU

[*Set out here whether the firm will be transferring data outside the EU or not; and if the firm will be, what measures are put in place to ensure security of data.*]

Keeping your data secure

We have put in place measures to protect the security of your information. Details of these measures are [*insert details or set out who can be spoken to about those measures*].

How long we keep your data for

We will only retain your personal information for as long as necessary to fulfil the purposes we collected it for, including for the purposes of satisfying any legal, accounting, or reporting requirements. We retain your data for [*insert length of time*].

In some circumstances we may anonymise your personal information so that it can no longer be associated with you, in which case we may use such information without further notice to you.

Your duty to inform us of changes

It is important that the personal information we hold about you is accurate and current. Please keep us informed if your personal information changes during your working relationship with us.

Your rights in connection with personal information

Under certain circumstances, by law you have the right to:
- request access to your personal information (commonly known as a 'data subject access request' (DSAR)). We have one calendar month to provide the data to you;

- request correction of the personal information that we hold about you;
- request erasure of your personal information. Please note there may be reasons why we are unable to fulfil your request;
- object to processing of your personal information where we are relying on a legitimate interest;
- request the restriction of processing of your personal information;
- request the transfer of your personal information to another party.

If you want to discuss any of the above rights, please contact [*name of DPO or appropriate person*].

Your right to withdraw consent for processing

In the limited circumstances where you may have provided your consent to the collection, processing and transfer of your personal information for a specific purpose, you have the right to withdraw your consent for that specific processing at any time. To withdraw your consent, please contact [*name*].

Future amendments

We reserve the right to update this privacy notice at any time, and we will provide you with a new privacy notice when we make any substantial updates. We may also notify you in other ways from time to time about the processing of your personal information.

APPENDIX 13
Template acceptable use policy

> See especially **2.1.1**.

Introduction

The purpose of this policy is to outline the rules and procedures of acceptable use of computer equipment at [*firm name*].

Inappropriate use of IT systems exposes the firm to risks including malware attacks, compromise of network systems and services, and may result legal claims against the firm.

This policy applies to the use of all electronic devices and network resources used to conduct [*firm name*] business, or interact with [*firm name*] systems or data.

General use

The firm's data stored in any format including both physical and electronic, and on any device, whether owned/leased by the firm, the person or a third party, remains the sole property of [*firm name*]. You must not bypass, or attempt to bypass or disable any security system, or use unauthorised software (e.g. mobile apps) to process data.

[*Firm name*] data may not be stored directly on any personal device unless within a designated secure container.

You must promptly report the theft, loss or unauthorised disclosure of [*firm name*] data [*insert reporting method*].

You may access, use or share [*firm name*] data only to the extent it is authorised and necessary to fulfil your assigned job duties.

We expect you to exercise good judgment regarding the reasonableness of personal use of IT systems. If there is any uncertainty on the personal use of IT systems, you should consult your supervisor or manager.

Security

If you have been issued with a firm's mobile phone, this must be used in accordance with the requirements of the [*insert any relevant policies*].

If you are using your personal mobile phone to receive firm email or store any [*firm name*], this must be used in accordance with the requirements of the [*insert any relevant policies*].

All passwords must comply with the firm's password policy.

Allowing unauthorised access to data to another individual, either deliberately or through failure to secure a device, is prohibited.

You must lock the screen of your device, or log off, whenever your device is left unattended.

You must use caution when opening email attachments, especially those received from unknown senders or those which contain external links. If you are concerned about the safety of any email or attachment, do not open it and [*insert process here*].

Unacceptable use

The activities contained in this section are, in general, prohibited. People may be exempted from these restrictions during the course of their legitimate job responsibilities (e.g. people responsible for network administration may need to disable the network access of a device, if it is disrupting business operations).

Under no circumstances are [*firm name*] people authorised to engage in any activity that is illegal under national or international law.

The lists below are by no means exhaustive, but attempt to provide a framework for activities which fall into the category of unacceptable use.

System and network activities

The following activities are strictly prohibited with no exceptions.

- Violations of the rights of any person or company protected by copyright, trade secret, patent or other intellectual property, or similar laws or regulations, including, but not limited to, the installation or distribution of 'pirated' or other software that is not appropriately licensed for use by [*firm name*].
- Unauthorised copying of copyrighted material including, but not limited to, scanning and distribution of photographs from magazines, books or other copyrighted sources, copyrighted music, and the installation of any copyrighted software for which [*firm name*] or the end user does not have an active licence.
- Accessing any data or IT system for any purpose other than conducting [*firm name*] business, even if you have authorised access.
- Introduction of malicious programs into the network (e.g. viruses, worms, Trojan horses, email bombs, etc.).
- Revealing your password to others or allowing use of your account by others. This includes family and other household members when work is being done at home. The IT service desk will never ask you for your password.
- Using a [*firm name*] device for any activity which is in violation of the Equality Act 2010 and/or would be considered bullying or harassment.
- Making fraudulent offers of products, items, or services.
- Making statements about warranty, expressly or implied, unless it is a part of normal job duties.
- Effecting security breaches or disruptions of IT systems.
- Port scanning or security scanning is expressly prohibited unless prior notification is given and approval has been received in writing from [*name*].
- Executing any form of network monitoring which will intercept data not intended for your device, unless this activity is a part of your normal job/duty.
- Circumventing user authentication or security of any host, network or account.

- Providing information about, or lists of, [*firm name*] people, processes or devices to anyone outside [*firm name*] unless this activity is a part of the person's normal job/duty.

Email and communication activities

When using firm resources to access and use the internet, you must acknowledge that you represent [*firm name*]. Whenever you state an affiliation to the firm, you must also clearly indicate that 'the opinions expressed are my own and not necessarily those of my employer'.

Any questions should be addressed to [*name*].

Sending unsolicited email messages, including marketing material or event invitations to recipients' private (non-company) email addresses is prohibited, unless that recipient has explicitly consented to receive such material.

If you require marketing material or event invitations sent to one or more of your contacts, you should refer this to [*name*].

Blogging and social media

The firm has an active presence on social media platforms including Facebook, Twitter, LinkedIn, Instagram and Passle [*amend as necessary*]. Business-related use of blogs and social media is encouraged, subject to compliance with the [*set out relevant policies such as a social media policy*].

APPENDIX 14

Data subject access requests – a practical guide – internal only

> See especially **2.3**.

Introduction

All data subjects have the right to make a data subject access request (DSAR) under UK data protection legislation. This document is an internal only guide to assist in responding to a DSAR. Under the EU General Data Protection Regulation (GDPR), recipients of a DSAR have one calendar month to respond (unless the DSAR is extensive and complex, by which we can give ourselves a further two months – more on that below) and there is no fee unless the request is 'manifestly unfounded or excessive' (whereas once there was a £10 fee no matter what). Given the short timescale, it is very important to spot a DSAR quickly and act swiftly upon it.

Determining whether you have a valid data subject access request

First things first. If you think you have a DSAR on your hands, inform the data protection officer (DPO) immediately. The DPO for the firm is [*name*].

It is important to remember that a person is entitled to information about themselves only. So first consider whether what is being asked for relates to the individual making the request. It is possible for third parties such as solicitors to make requests on behalf of others, but the recipient of such a request must be satisfied that the request is ultimately coming from the individual and may wish to get this confirmed by the individual directly.

The request for data should be in writing, but need be in no particular format. The request itself does not have to say that it is a request under the legislation or that it is a subject access request. The request should be treated as such a request if it is clear to the reader that an individual is asking for sight of their personal data. This can on occasions be quite tricky, as a request to see personal data can be made in among dealing with other matters such as a complaint or a grievance from an employee.

The request is also valid even if it is not sent to a designated person in the firm. An individual employee may consider it perfectly reasonable to send such a request to their line manager or supervisor.

Every request made should be acknowledged. If the request was made electronically then we must respond electronically unless otherwise agreed with the requester. Security of data should be considered.

Time limits, extending them and negotiating a narrow request

As indicated above, the time limit for dealing with DSARs is within one calendar month of receiving the request, calculated from the day of receipt. When acknowledging the request, it is good practice to confirm when the organisation considers the deadline expires.

It is important to carefully consider the request and ask for more information if you need it.

You can ask for enough information to judge whether the person making the request is the individual to whom the request relates. This could be, for example, asking for a certified copy of the individual's passport or driving licence.

You can ask for information that you reasonably need in order to action the request. This could be, for example, clarity on the request itself or more information about it. Until such information is provided, the organisation is not required to respond to the request and the time limit does not begin to run. This point should be made clear to the requester in writing. However, asking for more information where this is not needed should never be used as a tactic to buy more time.

Given that the timescale for responding to DSARs can be very tight, it is wise to narrow the request if possible by writing to the requester within seven days of receipt and proposing a narrowing of the search criteria.

You must, however, be cautious doing this. The requester is not obliged to respond to any such request from the organisation nor is the requester obliged to agree. The request can be as narrow or as wide as the requester likes. Do not therefore wait for agreement for too long, but prepare the material or you will run out of time.

If, however, the request can be considered to be extensive or complex, time can be extended by two months so long as it is explained to the requester within the initial one-month period.

Unfounded and excessive requests

We can decide to charge a requester a reasonable fee for responding to their DSAR if the request is unfounded or excessive. In addition, we do have the right to refuse to reply. However, this should not be a decision taken lightly and legal advice and/or advice from the DPO should be sought.

How to search for and sift information

The nature of the request often dictates where and how one should look for the personal data being requested. Below are some examples:

- **Files:** If we hold data about the requester in paper form, then we will need to consider whether the information is covered by the subject access request. Whether or not the data is relevant depends on the relevant filing system and whether you have been provided enough information to locate it. A relevant filing system is where the filing has been undertaken with reference to the individual and is structured in such a way that information about the individual can be found. An example of this would be a personnel file of an employee.
- **Emails:** As most communication is undertaken by email, most searches will involve searching incoming and outgoing emails. Our IT department should be deployed to assist. Depending on the DSAR, search terms could include the requester's name. If

you have been able to narrow the request by reference to an act, then a date range could be inserted which would decrease the number of emails returned significantly.
- **Other electronic forms:** A document search should be made using the relevant search terms which could be the name of the requester. Thought should be given to any other electronic system where personal data is recorded about the individual such as a HR system.

When sifting the information that has been returned from a search, we should document the agreed process internally. This is just in case a complaint is made by the requester later with the Information Commissioner's Office (ICO).

It is important that those who are to undertake the sifting process understand what they are looking for and that is personal data. Personal data is the data relating to the individual who can be identified from the data or from the data together with other information which is in the possession or likely to come into the possession of the organisation. This definition is not always easily applied and if in doubt you should seek guidance from the firm's DPO.

Depending on the nature of the DSAR but where thousands of emails have been retrieved, the following process could be adopted:

1. The emails are split between the persons reviewing the data.
2. Each person siphons those emails into three separate sub-folders as follows:

    (a) 'disclose' because the email contains personal data about the requester;
    (b) 'redact' because the email contains data about someone else (please see below);
    (c) 'review' because the sifter is unsure;
    (d) 'do not disclose' because the email does not contain any personal data or is privileged (please see below).

3. A designated person or persons within the group of people undertaking the sifting then spot-checks the disclose, redact and do not disclose folders and corrects any errors.
4. A designated person or persons within the group of people undertaking the sifting then reviews the items in the review folder and moves each item into one of the other three.
5. The emails contained within the redact folder are then printed and the data of others is removed by way of redaction.

The same process could be repeated for documents.

If the personal data that is retrieved is coded by reference to language that is used by the organisation, then the requester must be supplied with the relevant information to be able to read the information.

What to do if the information contains third-party data

Very often, your search results will contain the data of others. For example, an email from HR to a line manager confirms the sickness absence of four employees including the employee who has made the DSAR. This email will contain personal data about three other employees. If this is the case then that personal data of those individuals should be redacted.

Where the request involves providing information that relates to the requester and another person, there is no obligation on the firm to respond to the request unless the other person gives consent or it is reasonable in the circumstances to comply with the request without that consent. In these situations, the firm will need to balance the rights of the requester to see their personal data and the rights of the other party in having their data disclosed.

If consent is required from a number of people, it is wise to start seeking consent as soon as possible so as to meet the deadline.

If the third-party information is already known to the requester, say because the requester was the recipient of such information, then it can be disclosed.

Exemptions to providing the data

There are a number of exemptions to providing data. Some of these are:

- privilege – where either litigation or legal privilege applies, the data does not need to be disclosed;
- confidential references – this is information given in confidence. However, if we are in receipt of a confidential reference then it may be caught under the request;
- information publicly available;
- personal data processed for the purposes of crime and taxation, for example the prevention of crime or the prosecution of offenders;
- personal data that is processed for management purposes such as forecasting and planning in so far as to disclose such information would prejudice the organisation;
- negotiations with the requester – if negotiations are ongoing the firm does not have to comply with the subject access request if to do so would prejudice the negotiations.

We must remember to write down our reasons for deciding whether data is captured by one of the exemptions. This will be useful if we are asked to defend our position with the ICO.

Where to go for help

Please contact the DPO as soon as a DSAR is received (even if you are unsure whether it is a DSAR) or if you want to discuss any aspect of this note or data protection.

APPENDIX 15

Table of cybercrime events and whether insurance would cover any losses

See especially **3.2.12**.

Type of cybercrime	Most common threat	Current mitigations	Potential mitigation	Insurance
Crypto ransomware The threat of crypto ransomware is related to loss of access to data. Once a workstation is infected with ransomware and the malware is activated, it begins encrypting (i.e. converting into code) all data it can access.	Infection of a workstation with ransomware could destroy data on that workstation along with data held on common file shares and individual user's home drive.			
Unencrypted data exfiltration/insider data theft This risk refers to the removal of data from our systems. This could consist of email, documents or financial information. There are multiple possible causes including social engineering, malicious insider or virus infection.	• Staff members copying/pasting confidential data into personal email accounts (Gmail/Hotmail/etc.). • Staff members forwarding company email to personal accounts. • Virus infection allowing hacker to access a workstation and remove network data. • Unauthorised device being connected to the corporate network, e.g. IOT device (piece of hardware with a sensor that transmits data from one place to another over the internet), leading to security breach.			

APPENDIX 15

Type of cybercrime	Most common threat	Current mitigations	Potential mitigation	Insurance
	• Unauthorised person accessing offices and using an unlocked computer. • Staff sharing passwords with other people (including each other and IT). • Loss of mobile phone containing data without reporting it. • Unauthorised use of cloud services to store firm's data • Unauthorised use of personal email for firm's business. • Staff leaving employment without IT being informed.			
Distributed denial of service (DDOS) attacks This type of attack is when a server or website is bombarded with high amounts of internet traffic until it is overwhelmed and fails.	• The main risk is the internet connection being targeted and overwhelmed. This could cause the failure of our internet connection. • A secondary risk is one of the major cloud vendors being targeted in such an attack, e.g. Mimecast or Barclays.			
Weak/shared passwords Passwords are the main security factor safeguarding the majority of IT systems.	• Weak/easy to guess staff passwords. • Sharing passwords. • Old passwords. • Reusing passwords on different systems.			

Type of cybercrime	Most common threat	Current mitigations	Potential mitigation	Insurance
Social engineering This type of attack is an attack against a person rather than technology. A social engineering attack is when an attacker will attempt to persuade or trick a member of staff into revealing privileged or confidential information – for example, facilitating remote access to their workstation; revealing their password; revealing a client name or information. The results of social engineering are often then used as part of a second attack, for example data theft using the stolen credentials, or direction of funds.	• Attempt to persuade staff to reveal privileged information by email (phishing), telephone (vishing) or SMS (smishing). • Fake service desk call to user to allow remote computer access. • Fake supplier change of bank details. • Fake client change of bank details.			
Financial theft This is a secondary attack which is most likely to occur as a result of a previous attack, for example following ransomware, or a social engineering attack. A successful attack will result in loss of funds.	• Extortion – demanding payment after ransomware attack, or demanding payment not to release stolen client data. • Invoice fraud – sending a fake invoice for payment. • Client account fraud – fraudulently notifying a change to client bank details in an attempt to reroute outbound funds from client account.			
Vulnerable/unauthorised software or cloud services This threat can refer either to outdated/unauthorised software installed on firm's computers; or the unauthorised use of cloud services to store client data (shadow IT).	• Vulnerable software application. • Unsupported software application. • Unauthorised software installed. • Storing of client data on public cloud service. • Forwarding client information to personal email. • Automatically forwarding firm email to personal account.			

Type of cybercrime	Most common threat	Current mitigations	Potential mitigation	Insurance
Mobile phone breach This could range from loss/theft of an unsecured mobile device, through to malicious apps or a software breach.	• Loss/theft of an unencrypted/unsecured mobile device. • Malicious app resulting in data loss. • Malicious app resulting in interception/redirection of traffic. • Malicious app resulting in interception of camera/microphone/GPS.			

APPENDIX 16

Template anti-money laundering policy

> See especially **4.1**.
>
> N.B. This is a template anti-money laundering (AML) policy for you to use and adapt to suit your firm. You may find that this policy is long. It has been written to capture as many aspects of AML as possible, but will likely need to be amended to suit your firm's risk profile. Remember to amend the policy to sit in line with your firmwide risk assessment and also the Legal Sector Affinity Group (LSAG) 'Anti-money laundering guidance for the legal sector' (**www.lawsociety.org.uk/ policy-campaigns/articles/anti-money-laundering-guidance/**).

Introduction

Law firms are key players in the financial and business world, facilitating transactions that underpin the UK economy. As such, we have an important role to play in ensuring that our services are not used to further a criminal purpose. The objective of this policy is to help us all comply with our obligations under the UK anti-money laundering (AML) and counter-terrorism financing regime. All those who have any questions regarding this policy should speak to the money laundering reporting officer (MLRO) and where appropriate are encouraged to read the Legal Sector Affinity Group (LSAG) guidance, 'Anti-money laundering guidance for the legal sector' found on the Law Society's website (formerly known as the AML practice note) (**www.lawsociety.org.uk/policy-campaigns/articles/anti-money-laundering-guidance/**). This policy has been written taking that guidance into account as well as the firm's AML risk assessment.

This policy has been approved by the firm's MLRO and money laundering compliance officer (MLCO) and was last reviewed [*date*].

What is money laundering?

'Money laundering' is generally defined as the process by which the proceeds of crime, and the true ownership of those proceeds, are changed so that they appear to come from a legitimate source.

How are lawyers and law firms at risk?

Law firms are at risk of being used by criminals to launder the proceeds of crime by channelling money through client accounts to make it look as if it came from a legitimate source. 'Proceeds of crime' is widely defined and as well as covering things such as proceeds from the illicit sale of drugs, it can include small profits and savings from lower impact crimes, such as tax evasion and benefit fraud.

UK legislation applies to all 'proceeds of crime', however minor the crime and regardless of when it was committed. It may also apply if the criminal activity concerned took place abroad.

Our policy is that we will take no avoidable risks and will co-operate fully with the authorities where necessary. No matter how much we want to help our clients, we must not be a party to any form of dishonesty. We must be alert to the possibility that transactions might involve money laundering and follow our policy to reduce the risk. Any failure to do so could result in disciplinary action and put you at personal risk of prosecution under the Proceeds of Crime Act 2002 (POCA).

Appointment of money laundering reporting officer and money laundering compliance officer

Under the AML regulations (Money Laundering, Terrorist Financing and Transfer of Funds (Information on the Payer) Regulations 2017), we are required to appoint an MLRO to deal with the reporting/disclosure requirements and an MLCO to be responsible for compliance with the Regulations. We are also required to establish and maintain risk-sensitive policies and procedures in order to prevent activities related to money laundering and terrorist financing.

[*Name*] is our MLRO and [*name*] is our deputy MLRO. [*Name*] is the MLCO with overall responsibility for compliance with the AML regulations. Any questions about these guidelines or money laundering issues generally (including any queries from law enforcement agencies) should be addressed to [*name*] or in his/her absence [*name*] and in his/her absence [*name*] who will escalate it to [*name*] if necessary. [*Amend to suit your firm.*]

The Money Laundering, Terrorist Financing and Transfer of Funds (Information on the Payer) Regulations 2017

In accordance with the requirements of the AML regulations, we will carry out the following steps (this is not an exhaustive list):

- conduct an annual risk assessment which will assess the risk level particular to our firm and ensure we implement reasonable and considered controls to minimise those risks;
- review our policies, procedures and controls annually to ensure we fulfil our regulatory obligations. A review may also occur if a change in legislation occurs that requires a change to our approach;
- when a new client is onboarded all due diligence carried out on a client is checked and any concerns or issues reported to the MLRO;
- conduct risk assessments on our clients and their matters at the outset of the matter or as soon as practicable and where necessary conduct ongoing monitoring;
- screen all new relevant members of staff prior to them joining the firm; [*note you may wish to document this here or in a separate document*]
- undertake appropriate screening on existing staff; [*note you may wish to document this here or in a separate document*]
- regularly train staff about the law and our procedures regarding money laundering taking into account changes in legislation or practice. AML training is included as part of staff induction and must be completed within three months of starting [*amend to suit your practice*]. Refresher training will take place every two years and where

necessary (i.e. for high-risk practice areas) more frequently. Records of staff training are kept to ensure that no one is overlooked; and
- maintain records of evidence of identity for at least five years from the end of the client relationship.

Beware of potential risks

The money laundering process has traditionally been described as being divided into three stages:

1. **Placement:** Cash generated from crime is placed into the financial system.
2. **Layering:** Once the proceeds of crime are in the financial system, layering obscures their origins by passing the money through complex transactions. These often involve different entities, such as companies and trusts, and can take place in multiple jurisdictions.
3. **Integration:** Involves the translation of the laundered funds into a legitimate asset, such as the purchase of property through a conveyancing solicitor.

We can be targeted by criminals at any of these stages. We must therefore be vigilant to minimise the risks of:

- exposure to potential civil or criminal liability because of fraud, money laundering or the financing of terrorism, even where that exposure is as a result of innocent involvement in fraudulent transactions;
- reputational damage;
- claims from the true owner of property that we may have been involved in unlawful dealings;
- claims from the UK or other authorities; and
- disciplinary action from our professional regulator, the Solicitors Regulation Authority (SRA).

Your role

To protect yourself and us from potential prosecution for being involved in money laundering you should act as follows:

- During the course of any transaction you should be alert to the possibility of money laundering activity and satisfy yourself that the transaction in question is legitimate and does not involve criminal property.
- If, during the course of any transaction, you become aware or suspect that criminal property is involved, you should immediately discuss the circumstances with the MLRO. He/she will then advise you on the next steps after considering the circumstances. In particular, he/she will advise whether it is necessary to submit a suspicious activity report (SAR).
- Once you have referred your knowledge or suspicion to the MLRO, you must not take any further steps in the transaction unless authorised in writing by the MLRO.
- Having reported the circumstances, unless authorised by the MLRO, you must not discuss your concerns with the client or anyone else.

Confidentiality and privilege

Clients who instruct us are entitled to expect that their affairs are kept confidential. We have a duty, under the SRA Standards and Regulations, to keep clients' affairs confidential. However, this duty can be overridden in very limited circumstances and these include situations where we have a statutory obligation to report known or suspicious money laundering activity.

If anyone acquires knowledge or becomes suspicious about any form of activity which involves criminal property, they will have a statutory duty to report the circumstances to the MLRO. However, in certain circumstances, where the knowledge or suspicion is acquired in privileged circumstances, there will be no requirement to report.

The law relating to legal privilege is very complicated. You will not be breaching any privilege by discussing the circumstances of a case with the MLRO with a view to seeking his/her advice as to your disclosure obligations under POCA. The MLRO will be solely responsible for determining issues relating to privilege and external reporting obligations to the National Crime Agency (NCA).

Privilege and litigation work

In 2005 the Court of Appeal in the case of *Bowman* v. *Fels* effectively ruled that in general the money laundering offences do not apply to most forms of litigation including family work and mediation. While therefore (in litigation work) there will be no requirement formally to report knowledge or suspicions of activity involving criminal property, it will still be necessary to provide the MLRO with all the relevant details so that the information can be recorded against the particular client or the property in question. This will enable us to 'flag up' the relevant client and property in the event that we are ever instructed in the future outside the litigation context in relation to the property in question.

Detecting money laundering – general grounds for suspicion of money laundering

It is not possible to provide an exhaustive list of circumstances or situations that might give rise to a suspicion. However, please consider the following (this is not an exhaustive list and please also see the firm's client and matter risk assessment which sets out the risk factors you need to consider):

- Be vigilant at all times and be alert to the possibility of money laundering by clients or third parties. In most situations it should be obvious that the transaction in question is legitimate.
- Where a third party (such as the other person in a transaction) or a client we have not yet fully onboarded sends us monies, *never* send those monies back or use those monies for the transaction until we are satisfied as to the sender's identity and where appropriate source of funds and wealth. Sending the monies back can in effect clean them and you should be suspicious of any third party sending monies to us uninvited.
- Always take care when dealing with a client who has no obvious reasons for using our services, e.g. clients with distant addresses who could find the same service nearer to home; or clients whose requirements do not fit into the normal pattern of our business and could be more easily serviced elsewhere.
- If you are in any way suspicious about the circumstances of a particular transaction, discuss it with the MLRO before getting involved.

- Be aware of higher risk factors such as handling high-value items such as art for which ownership is not clear, or dealing with a transaction that is creating or facilitating anonymity of ownership; or a transaction which is unnecessarily complex, unusually large or has an unusual pattern of transactions within it. What is considered to be complex or unusually large should be judged in relation to the normal activities of the firm and client and there is no exact science to this assessment.
- The view of the SRA is that we should also be aware of clients who combine services. These can be services that may not be inherently risky but when combined with other services may become so. For example, setting up a company to purchase a property and disguise beneficial ownership. Combining services may also be where the client is using our firm for one aspect of a transaction and another firm for a different aspect of the transaction. This may obscure what would otherwise cause suspicion.
- The SRA also sets out that we should be cautious of transactions or products that facilitate anonymity or that do not fit in with our profile as a firm or the client's normal type of transaction.
- There may be good reasons why a client wishes to pay money to us in cash. However, it should be a warning signal to you if this happens. You must satisfy yourself that there is a good and legitimate reason for this method of payment. Do not be afraid of asking the client for a full explanation. Always make a note on the file of the explanation and if in any doubt seek guidance from the MLRO.
- Cash payments from clients will only be accepted for sums up to £*[amount – suggest £500]* but even then, enquiries will be made as to why the payment has to be made in cash. Where any larger cash payments are offered the matter will be referred to the MLRO and only accepted with his/her authorisation.
- Under no circumstances must our client account be used except in cases where there is a genuine underlying legal transaction or some other valid reason for client's money to be held. This is a fundamental requirement and must be observed at all times.
- Where possible, meet new clients in person. Be very cautious about third parties introducing clients whom you do not meet.
- If anything about the circumstances of a transaction gives cause for concern, then ask more questions. The answers may deal with your initial cause for concern. If they do not, then the answers may give foundation to a suspicion and you may have to consider whether or not the circumstances need to be reported.
- Sometimes it is the details of 'the deal' itself that just do not make sense. Try to get full details of the transaction, its structure and its funding source before you become involved. If your instructions change dramatically or they change at the last minute, be very wary. Watch out if it appears on the face of it that the client is overpaying for something or selling something at a significant loss.
- Another area which should raise warning signals is where the transaction involves the client insisting on paying monies direct to the other party as opposed to through solicitors.
- People may wish to avoid paying tax. Sometimes they attempt to achieve this by laundering money through a solicitors' firm. You must be careful not to become unwittingly involved in such activity.
- A client who refuses to co-operate with you about identification and other 'client due diligence' (CDD) procedures should not remain a client and their reluctance should be considered suspicious.
- A client who gives confusing and/or misleading identification and other required information about the source and flow of funds should be questioned.
- Be vigilant if a client wishes to use offshore funds for a particular transaction. There may be a very good and legitimate reason why offshore funds are being used. If in doubt, please refer to the MLRO.

- Be wary if the client tells you that they have just 'won the lottery' or inherited a large sum of money. It may be true, but you should seek information to satisfy yourself that it is.
- A flow of funds through our client account that is out of character with your actual knowledge of the financial standing of the client or with the circumstances of the transaction may give rise to suspicion and should be reported to the MLRO.
- There may be cases where the client provides instructions and transfers funds to us and suddenly, for no obvious reason, the matter becomes abortive and the funds are returned to the client. We are not suggesting that all abortive work should be regarded as suspicious, we are simply saying that you should be careful. It is well known that money launderers often use solicitors in this way.
- Be on your guard if a client asks you simply to prepare paperwork to reflect the transfer of an asset in circumstances where the client has already paid the full consideration to the other party.
- If you know that your client is bankrupt or you have suspicions about the client's financial position, be wary if they wish to deal in cash.
- Money launderers do go to the extremes of inventing legal disputes. This type of money laundering is often difficult to detect, but if a case suddenly takes an unexpected turn and settles quickly without any apparent reason, your suspicions may be raised.

The due diligence information that you have obtained should ensure that you know enough about your client and your client's normal expected activities to recognise unusual or suspicious instructions or matters. A suspicious instruction or matter should give rise to further enquiry.

Reporting a suspicious activity

If you do have any concerns of whatever nature, that either your client or any third party is engaged in money laundering, then you should immediately discuss the matter with the MLRO. Under no circumstances should you discuss your suspicion with your client or any third party or generally in the office. To do so could amount to the criminal offence of 'tipping off'.

If you have concerns about the client, any other party to the transaction or any aspect of any matter you *must*:

- Review and immediately follow our procedures, which requires you to discuss the matter with the MLRO. Your suspicion or concern can relate to a major or minor crime and it matters not where or when it was committed, so long as it would have been a criminal offence if it had happened in the UK.
- Do not fail to report your suspicion or concern because you believe the matter may be privileged. This is a matter for the MLRO to determine.
- If you continue to have concerns, you *must* report your concerns to the MLRO as a suspicion following our firm's procedures.
- If you have reported to the MLRO and he/she considers the report to be justified, he/she will report to the NCA and if appropriate, obtain a defence to a money laundering offence that may be committed. In the meantime, you should take no steps to progress the transaction without the MLRO's consent.
- Any enquiries from the SRA, NCA or the police must be referred to the MLRO immediately to allow him/her to deal with the enquiries.
- Keep the fact that a report has been made confidential, even within the office.
- Take care as to what is recorded on the client file.

- You *must not* do anything to indicate to the client, or anyone else, that a report has been made to the MLRO or to the NCA.
- You *must* strictly and fully observe our firm's reporting procedures in order to gain the protection afforded to you personally by the legislation.
- In particular, you *must not* report directly to the NCA.

Client due diligence

The AML regulations require us to carry out CDD and 'ongoing monitoring' on clients who retain our services. Clients we can identify are less likely to be conducting money laundering.

The importance of thorough CDD

Our reputation is our greatest asset. Thorough CDD will not only ensure compliance with the law, but will tend to deter undesirable clients from instructing us.

When taking instructions from new clients you must explain your obligation to carry out due diligence and the reason why this must be done. Where appropriate, ask questions about the source of the client's wealth and how any transaction is to be financed. Few honest clients will resent such questions. Our client care letter explains our CDD obligations, and you may wish to draw that explanation to your clients' attention when you speak or meet with them.

Elements of CDD

CDD involves a number of elements. These are:

1. identifying the client and verifying their identity on the basis of documents, data or information obtained from a reliable and independent source (this can be on a simplified, standard or enhanced due diligence (EDD) basis);
2. identifying the beneficial owner of a client and taking adequate measures, on a risk sensitive basis, to verify their identity so that you are satisfied that you know who the beneficial owner is. This includes understanding the ownership and control of a legal person, trust or similar arrangement;
3. identifying where clients operate in a high-risk jurisdiction and taking appropriate ongoing monitoring measures;
4. verifying the identity of those who purport to act on behalf of the client;
5. undertaking sanctions, politically exposed persons (PEPs) and adverse media checks;
6. understanding the source of funds and wealth (for example, when dealing with the purchase of assets and also handling assets which were made/created/bought in a high-risk jurisdiction);
7. obtaining information on the purpose and intended nature of the business relationship; and
8. where appropriate, implementing ongoing monitoring of the CDD outlined above.

In relation to point 4 above, our interpretation of this legal requirement is in line with that of other law firms in that this requirement is seeking to capture situations such as family members giving instructions on behalf of the client. It is not intended to capture, for example, a bank employee who clearly has the correct job role to provide us instructions on behalf of the bank. [N.B. *You may not agree with this interpretation of the regulations and so amend as necessary.*]

Our procedure

[N.B. Below are processes that will need to be amended to suit your firm. The processes below are just a suggestion.]

It is our policy to verify the identity of all new clients and all existing clients that we have not acted for within the last three years at the start of a new matter.

For all matters, the client's full name, address and telephone number should be obtained and recorded correctly on our database. For companies, we also require the full names of those who sit on the board; the senior people responsible for the operations of the body; and the usual entity information such as registered address, company number and the laws to which it is subject.

Particular care must be taken when acting on the instructions of someone on behalf of the true client or where our client is clearly an agent for a third party. In those circumstances you must ensure that steps are taken to establish and verify the identity of both parties.

A client's identity must be verified within [*number*] working days of a file opening (when work begins) or files will be locked with no ability to time record or bill. [*Amend to suit your firm.*]

No client money should be accepted from the client for payment into client account until the verification process has been satisfactorily completed.

You should be satisfied that any documents offered to verify identity are originals so as to guard against forgery. Ensure that any photographs provide an actual likeness of the client. Take copies of the relevant evidence and sign and date the copies to certify that they have been compared with the originals. If you do not see the originals, you can accept copies provided they have been certified by a regulated professional.

We categorise our clients into three risk levels: low; medium; high. Low-risk clients might include financial institutions, listed companies and public authorities where the work that is being conducted can also be considered to be low risk and the client operates in a low-risk jurisdiction. High-risk clients can include those where there is no face-to-face meeting or where the client is a PEP.

If a client is a PEP, then their details must be passed to the MLRO so he/she can approve the firm acting for the PEP and so that the PEP may be to be added to our high-risk register. At the outset of a matter, [*person or role*] will conduct a PEP check using an online database. However, if you are aware early on in your interaction with a potential client that they are or may be a PEP, you must contact [*person or role*] as soon as possible so that they may conduct checks at an early stage. This will help prevent any delays in onboarding a client later on.

When acting for a PEP, you must also consider whether it is appropriate to:

- seek further verification of the client or beneficial owner's identity;
- obtain more detail on the ownership and control of the client;
- request further information on the purposes of the retainer or the source of the funds; and
- conduct enhanced ongoing monitoring.

Please note you can only act for a PEP with the approval of the MLRO as required by the AML regulations.

Our CDD checks include identifying whether clients are subject to sanctions. This is done by [*insert process*].

Financial sanctions aim to safeguard international security and prevent terrorism. **It can be an offence to do business with someone who is subject to sanctions.** We conduct a sanction check on all clients at matter inception and any adverse results are reported back to the fee earner with conduct of the case. Identifying whether a client is subject to counter-measures by the Financial Action Taskforce (FATF) or the UK Treasury, where the Treasury has imposed financial restrictions, can be checked by accessing the 'Financial sanctions targets: list of all asset freeze targets' at: **www.gov.uk/government/publications/financial-sanctions-consolidated-list-of-targets/consolidated-list-of-targets**. Identifying whether clients are subject to financial sanctions following designation by the United Nations or the European Commission can be checked by accessing the full list at: **www.gov.uk/government/publications/financial-sanctions-consolidated-list-of-targets**. If you have any concerns relating to sanctions you should speak to [*person or role*].

Enhanced due diligence

EDD is required to be undertaken under the following non-exhaustive circumstances:

- the client is a PEP and we are undertaking a transaction for them;
- the transaction is complex;
- the transaction is unusually large;
- there is an unusual pattern of transactions, or the transaction or transactions have no apparent economic or legal purpose;
- there are unfavourable answers to the client and matter risk assessment meaning the client and matter are not deemed low or medium risk.

Whether a transaction is 'complex' or 'unusually large' should be judged in relation to the normal activity of the firm and the normal activity of the client.

The Fifth EU Money Laundering Directive (which was implemented on 10 January 2020) sets out additional factors to take account of in deciding whether EDD should be applied:

- whether the person is a beneficiary of a life insurance policy (whether the person is a beneficiary of a life insurance policy is only likely to be indicative of higher AML risk where the retainer bears direct relevance to the policy);
- whether the person is seeking residence/citizen rights in exchange for investments in that EEA state;
- whether you act without face-to-face meeting and without electronic identity systems to mitigate this;
- whether the person is involved in the trade of oil, arms, precious metals, tobacco products, cultural artefacts, ivory and other items related to protected species, and other items of archaeological, historical, cultural and religious significance, or of rare scientific value.

Client has changed

Where the client has changed (for example, the underlying client has altered which purchase vehicle will be used or formed a new purchase vehicle), the CDD process must be repeated for that new client and the new client set up in the appropriate way.

Beneficiaries of trusts

There are additional requirements in relation to the identification of beneficiaries. Before we are able to make any distribution or the beneficiary is able to exercise their rights in the trust, we must ensure that we have established and verified the identity of that beneficiary.

There are also additional obligations for reporting the details of trusts and beneficial owners to HM Revenue and Customs (HMRC) as set out in the AML regulations and our private client team are aware of these obligations.

Third party reliance

As a firm, our starting point is that we do not rely on a third party's analysis of a client's due diligence documentation. The reason for this is that we will be liable for any failure by the third party to carry out the identity checks properly. If a third party – such as another solicitor, financial institution or accountant – has obtained CDD, you may ask that the CDD is sent to you for you to analyse to see whether it is satisfactory according to the firm's standards.

A third party may request to rely on [firm name] due diligence documents for the purpose of satisfying their money laundering requirements. These third parties can be other solicitors or estate agents, for example.

While we consider that we satisfy our due diligence requirements accurately, there is always the chance that we could get it wrong. By allowing a third party to place reliance on our due diligence, we may become liable to them if the documents we hold are not accurate. **We do not therefore allow others to rely on our assessment of the CDD.**

Subject to the client's consent, we would be willing to provide the third party with the CDD documents. However, it is for the third party to decide whether or not to rely on the documents for satisfying their money laundering requirements.

If you receive such a request, you are asked to adopt the following wording in your response:

> 'Subject to obtaining our client's consent, we will provide you with a copy of the due diligence we hold on our file to assist your due diligence requirements under the money laundering regulations. However, it is for you to form your own opinion of these documents.
>
> For the avoidance of doubt, [firm name] does not consent to the application of regulation 39 of the Money Laundering, Terrorist Financing and Transfer of Funds (Information on the Payer) Regulations 2017 and you cannot place reliance on this firm's assessment.'

If you have any queries, please contact [person or role].

Identification requirements

Please note that the AML regulations do not allow the firm automatically to apply simplified due diligence where a client is regulated or listed (i.e. use their regulated or listed status as evidence of identity) without first assessing the risk (by analysing the type of operation the client undertakes and jurisdiction of the client and its operations). The firm's client and matter risk assessment therefore covers this requirement when completed.

We recognise that more and more clients do not have physical/original proof of address because it is held electronically only. We will accept an electronic proof of address but only where the client is unable to provide physical/original proof of address.

The importance of obtaining documentary evidence

Evidence of identity must be kept with the individual client file and uploaded [*insert place if this applies*]. This ensures that any other fee earner wanting to check the identity documents for a client will know where those documents are located.

It needs to be borne in mind at all times that the dual objectives of seeking CDD are to meet statutory requirements as well as to 'know your client' and understand its business.

A common-sense approach should be adopted. For example, you should check the client's correspondence address against the verification evidence and any discrepancy must be satisfactorily explained. It may not be possible to obtain all of the documents specified and there will be some circumstances in which judgment needs to be exercised. If you are in any doubt, [*person or role*] is on hand to help you make the correct judgment call.

Where you inspect an original document, a copy should be taken and the copy should be marked 'original seen' and signed by the relevant fee earner or the fee earner should apply the usual certification.

Documentary evidence from prospective and actual clients and information from other sources obtained when undertaking client due diligence form an essential record of the steps we have taken as a firm to comply with our money laundering obligations. Such records may be subject to inspection by the regulatory authorities.

Failure to comply with these regulatory requirements can amount to an offence, irrespective of whether any money laundering has taken place.

The requirements should be applied to all new clients but we are also under an obligation to monitor client relationships.

We are required to retain documentary evidence of ID for a minimum period of five years after the end of the client relationship.

Renewing ID evidence

Once we have evidence of identification on file for a particular client, there will be no need to obtain similar evidence if we are instructed by that client on a new matter unless we have not acted for them in the last three years, in which case fresh identification evidence should be obtained. [*N.B. You may decide to refresh CDD more frequently than this, and so amend as required.*] If we become aware during a matter or at the beginning of a new matter that the structure of the client has changed or the client's name or address has changed, then we must refresh our CDD regardless of the three-year rule. [*Amend as required.*]

If you are in any doubt about what evidence to obtain or whether the evidence that you have is adequate, you should inform [*person or role*].

Where joint instructions are received, identification procedures should be applied to each client. If joint clients have the same name and address (e.g. spouses) the verification of the address for one client only is sufficient.

Risk assessments

As part of our assessment of the client and the matter at hand, we conduct a risk assessment at the outset of a matter and where necessary select the client for ongoing monitoring.

The risk assessment is split into two parts – client and matter. The first part of the client risk assessment is conducted by [*person or role*] as soon as possible after file opening and includes the PEP, sanctions and adverse media check and a thorough review of the client identification documents. The conducting fee earner is tasked with completing the second part of the client assessment and matter risk assessment as soon as possible and within five working days of the file opening or work beginning whichever is the earliest.

Depending on the client and/or matter assessment, the client may be selected for ongoing monitoring by [*person or role*] or the conducting fee earner. If this is the case, that decision will be recorded and the method of ongoing monitoring selected and carried out. Please see the firmwide client and matter risk assessment and guidance for more information.

If you have any queries about this policy, please speak to the firm's MLRO or MLCO.

APPENDIX 17

Template anti-money laundering firmwide risk assessment

See especially 4.4.

Firmwide anti-money laundering risk assessment

Review notes by MLRO – enter these on this row or in a different tab								
Area of risk	Type of risk	Explanation of risk and likelihood of it occurring	Policies	Procedures	Controls	Next step	Completion notes	Completion date
Clients								
	High turnover of clients v. stable client base							
	Politically exposed persons (PEPs)							
	Sanctioned individuals							
	Adverse media							
	Large cash operators							
	Offshore companies							
	Complex corporate structures							
	Reside or operate in high-risk jurisdiction							

Operate in a high-risk sector	Require work done urgently unnecessarily – behavioural warning signs	Evasive when providing client due diligence (CDD)	Size and value of transaction (from Solicitors Regulation Authority's (SRA's) risk assessment)	Transactions that don't fit with the firm's or client's normal transaction type (from SRA's risk assessment)	Transactions or products that facilitate anonymity (from SRA's risk assessment)	New products, delivery mechanisms or technology (from SRA's risk assessment)	Complex transactions (from SRA's risk assessment)	Combining services (from SRA's risk assessment)

TEMPLATE ANTI-MONEY LAUNDERING FIRMWIDE RISK ASSESSMENT

Area of practice/type of transaction		
[Insert here your practice areas and associated risks]		
Geographical areas in which we operate		
[Insert here the geographical areas you operate in and assess the risk of each.]		
Delivery channels		
[Suggestions to the right.]	Non face-to-face	
	Face-to-face	
	Through intermediary	
Other aspects considered		
[Insert here other risks you considered. To the right are some suggestions.]	Suspicious activity reports (SARs)	
	High-risk register	
	Monies being received before full CDD being completed	
	Misuse of client account	

APPENDIX 18

Template ongoing anti-money laundering/risk monitoring form

> See especially **4.5.3**.

Name of reviewer	
Fee earner	
Date	
Client name	
Client number	

[*Name*] has carried out the following:

- Politically exposed persons (PEPs), sanction, adverse media check [*N.B. Via a third party provider if this is possible*] – results are: [*insert results*].
- Google search – results are: [*insert results*].

[*Option 1:* [*Insert name if not the fee earner completing this form*] has spoken to [*name of fee earner*] and asked the following questions, responses underneath each point:]

[*Option 2:* I am the fee earner on this matter and I have considered the questions below and set out my answers:]

- Is the transaction consistent with knowledge of client/business and risk profile?
- Has the structure of the company changed? If so, obtain evidence.
- Has the nature of the work changed?
- Source of funds, if appropriate?
- Do you have any concerns?

Please save this form [*insert place*].

APPENDIX 19

Template money laundering compliance officer audit questions

See especially **4.7**.

Client name	
Matter description	
File number	
Fee earner	
Department/team	

Question	Answer	Action
Has the client and matter risk assessment been completed in full with rating given?		
Does the risk assessment look accurate?		
Do we hold the correct client due diligence (CDD) for the client?		
If we made any CDD concessions or deviated from the norm is it documented?		
Did we conduct politically exposed person (PEP), sanction and adverse media checks?		
Were any PEP, sanction, adverse media results flagged with the fee earner and money laundering compliance officer (MLRO)?		
If the client was considered to be high risk were they entered on to the high-risk register?		
If client was selected for ongoing monitoring, is there evidence of this on the file?		

Audit completed by: [*name*] ....
Date: [*date*] ....

APPENDIX 20

Flowchart from Legal Sector Affinity Group anti-money laundering guidance

See especially **4.8**.

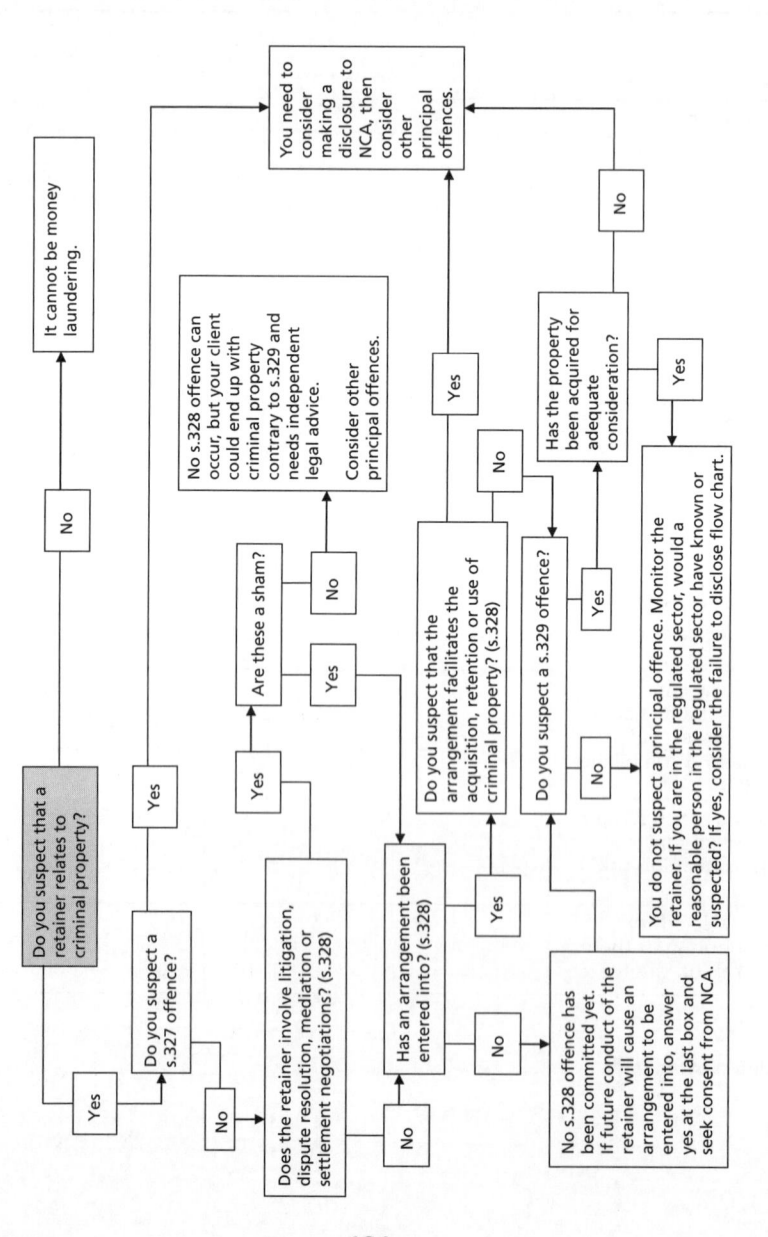

Flowchart A. Legal Sector Affinity Group, 'Anti-money laundering guidance for the legal sector', March 2018

APPENDIX 21

Template suspicious activity report

> See especially **4.8**.

We, [*name of law firm*], are a law firm located in [*insert location*] and we provide a wide range of legal services for our clients [*amend as necessary*]. We make this disclosure under section 330 of the Proceeds of Crime Act 2002 (POCA).

The proposed activity to which we seek a defence is [*set out the actual act you are seeking a defence for as succinctly as possible*].

We suspect these monies may be proceeds of crime for the reasons outlined below and that offences under sections [*insert specific sections that apply – s.327 and/or s.328 and/or s.329*] of POCA may be committed.

In this matter [*outline the matter including: who the firm acts for; details of the retainer; monies in; monies out; proposed activity and when it will be taking place*].

For the avoidance of doubt, this suspicious activity report is being filed in discharge of our obligation to make disclosure of suspected money laundering pursuant to section 330 of POCA.

APPENDIX 22

Template modern slavery and human trafficking statement

> See especially **5.2.4**.
>
> N.B. There are many ways to write this statement and there is no set format. This is just one suggested way and is quite straightforward and basic. Have a look at other firms' statements and if the statement is especially important to your firm because of the nature of clients or work that you do, look at the statements of charities for inspiration.

This statement is made on behalf of [*firm name*] ('the firm') pursuant to section 54(1) of the Modern Slavery Act 2015 ('the Act').

It constitutes the firm's modern slavery and human trafficking statement for the financial year ending [*date*].

The firm is registered in [*country*] and has its office in [*location*]. The firm employs approximately [*number*] people and provides a wide range of legal services to its clients.

The firm is committed to the highest standards of ethical behaviour and complies with all laws, regulations and rules applicable to its business. Furthermore, it is committed to taking steps to ensure that modern slavery and human trafficking do not occur in any part of its business or in its supply chains.

The firm's approach

To ensure adherence to the Act and to ensure that no slavery or human trafficking exists in the firm's own business or, so as far as reasonably possible, in its supply chains, the firm has undertaken the following steps:

[*N.B. Here you need to outline the steps you have actually taken. This is unique to your firm and the items set out below are just a suggestion of the steps you may wish to take.*]

- a review of the firm's own recruitment policies and practices and its contracts of employment; and
- an analysis of the firm's suppliers and their business practices by requiring 20 of them to complete the firm's Modern Slavery Act questionnaire.

  Suppliers were selected to participate based upon the following criteria:

  (a) the value of supplies made to the firm;
  (b) the type of supply and whether goods provided are produced in jurisdictions that are high on the modern slavery index or services via personnel; and
  (c) physical location of the supplier, i.e. is it located in a jurisdiction that is high on the modern slavery index.

The responses to these questionnaires have been analysed by the firm and it is satisfied that as far as it is aware, no modern slavery or human trafficking can be detected in any of the firm's supply chains.

Supplier due diligence [N.B. Again this is just a suggestion and you need to amend this to explain the true position for your firm.]

New suppliers are reviewed to assess whether they comply with the Act and other legislation generally and to that end the firm has implemented a procurement process requiring the supplier to explain its own compliance with various laws and regulations not limited to modern slavery.

The firm does not knowingly engage with businesses involved in modern slavery or human trafficking and will report any organisations where there are reasonable grounds to suspect their involvement. All of the firm's suppliers are expected to adhere to all laws and regulations applicable to their business.

Staff awareness

The firm has implemented a slavery and human trafficking policy which sets out the firm's stance in relation to modern slavery and human trafficking and its processes and procedures for minimising the risk of slavery and human trafficking in its own workforce and supply chains. A reminder of the firm's policy is communicated each year when our statement is released.

The firm has also provided training to those in the business who deal with either suppliers or the recruitment of staff and also operates an effective whistleblowing policy.

Responsibility

It is the responsibility of [*title and/or name*] to ensure adherence to the slavery and human trafficking policy.

[*Space for signatures here.*]

APPENDIX 23

Template modern slavery and human trafficking policy

> See especially **5.2.6**.
>
> N.B. This template is for compliance with the Modern Slavery Act 2015.

This policy does not form part of any employee's contract of employment and we may amend it at any time.

1. Policy statement

1.1 Modern slavery is a crime and a violation of fundamental human rights. It takes various forms, such as slavery, servitude, forced and compulsory labour and human trafficking, all of which have in common the deprivation of a person's liberty by another in order to exploit them for personal or commercial gain. We have a zero-tolerance approach to modern slavery and we are committed to acting ethically and with integrity in all our business dealings and relationships and to implementing and enforcing effective systems and controls to ensure modern slavery is not taking place anywhere in our own business or in any of our supply chains.

1.2 We are also committed to ensuring that there is transparency in our own business and in our approach to tackling modern slavery throughout our supply chains, consistent with our disclosure obligations under the Modern Slavery Act 2015. We expect the same high standards from all of our contractors, suppliers and other business partners, and as part of our contracting processes, we include specific prohibitions against the use of forced, compulsory or trafficked labour, or anyone held in slavery or servitude, whether adults or children, and we expect that our suppliers will hold their own suppliers to the same high standards.

1.3 This policy applies to all persons working for us or on our behalf in any capacity, including but not limited to employees at all levels, directors, officers, agency workers, seconded workers, volunteers, interns, agents, contractors, external consultants, third-party representatives and business partners.

2. Responsibility for the policy

2.1 [*Role and/or name*] has overall responsibility for ensuring this policy complies with our legal and ethical obligations, and that all those who are required to comply with it do.

2.2 [*Role and/or name*] has primary and day-to-day responsibility for implementing this policy, monitoring its use and effectiveness, dealing with any queries about it, and auditing internal control systems and procedures to ensure they are effective in countering modern slavery. [N.B. *This may be the same person as named in para.2.1 and so you may wish to combine these paragraphs.*]

2.3 Management at all levels are responsible for ensuring those reporting to them understand and comply with this policy and are given adequate and regular training on it and the issue of modern slavery in supply chains. [N.B. *This is optional and may not be how you decide to determine responsibility. Please amend these paragraphs as you see fit.*]

3. Compliance with the policy

3.1 You must ensure that you read, understand and comply with this policy.

3.2 The prevention, detection and reporting of modern slavery in any part of our business or supply chains is the responsibility of all those working for us or under our control. You are required to avoid any activity that might lead to, or suggest, a breach of this policy.

3.3 You must notify [*role and/or name*] as soon as possible if you believe or suspect that non-adherence with this policy has occurred, or may occur in the future.

3.4 You are encouraged to raise concerns about any issue or suspicion of modern slavery in any parts of our business or supply chains of any supplier at the earliest possible stage.

3.5 If you believe or suspect a breach of this policy has occurred or that it may occur you must speak to [*role and/or name*] or your manager as soon as possible.

3.6 If you are unsure about whether a particular act, the treatment of workers more generally, or their working conditions within any of our supply chains constitutes any of the various forms of modern slavery, raise it with your manager or [*role and/or name*] as soon as possible.

3.7 We aim to encourage openness and will support anyone who raises genuine concerns in good faith under this policy, even if they turn out to be mistaken. We are committed to ensuring no one suffers any detrimental treatment as a result of reporting in good faith their suspicion that modern slavery of whatever form is or may be taking place in any part of our own business or in any of our supply chains. Detrimental treatment includes dismissal, disciplinary action, threats or other unfavourable treatment connected with raising a concern. If you believe that you have suffered any such treatment, you should inform [*role and/or name*] immediately. If the matter is not remedied, and you are an employee, you may consider raising it formally using our grievance procedure which can be found [*insert location*].

4. Communication and awareness of this policy

4.1 Training on this policy, and on the risk our business faces from modern slavery in its supply chains, forms part of the induction process for all individuals who work in HR and areas of procurement, and regular training will be provided as necessary. [N.B. *These are suggestions and you will need to adapt these to suit your firm.*]

4.2 Our zero-tolerance approach to modern slavery must be communicated to all suppliers, contractors and business partners at the outset of our business relationship with them and reinforced as appropriate thereafter. [N.B. *Think about how you will do this. You may wish to provide an explanation when you send suppliers your procurement questionnaire which sets out your zero tolerance to such activities.*]

5. Breaches of this policy

5.1 Any employee who breaches this policy will face disciplinary action, which could result in dismissal for misconduct or gross misconduct.
5.2 We may terminate our relationship with other individuals and organisations working on our behalf if they breach this policy.

6. Review

This policy was reviewed [*date*] by [*role and/or name*].

APPENDIX 24

Template Modern Slavery Act 2015 guidance note

> See especially **5.2.6**.
>
> N.B. Consider providing this note as a method of training those in the firm who need to be aware of this piece of legislation such as HR, any employment fee earning team or those who handle procurement for the firm.

This guidance note is aimed to assist those who read it in understanding modern slavery and the firm's obligations. This note is to be read in conjunction with the firm's modern slavery statement found on the firm's website, the firm's slavery and human trafficking policy and procurement process.

What is modern slavery?

Modern slavery is defined by the UK government as the recruitment, movement, harbouring or receiving of children, women or men through the use of force, coercion, abuse of vulnerability, deception or other means for the purpose of exploitation.

What forms does modern slavery take?

You may think of slavery as something from the 19th century that ended a long time ago. Unfortunately, this is not the case and slavery exists around the world today, even in the UK.

Forms of modern slavery can be:

- being forced to work – through coercion, or mental or physical threat;
- being trapped and controlled by an 'employer', through mental or physical abuse or the threat of abuse – this may also be because of 'debt bondage' where the worker borrows money that they then have to work off for little or no pay to repay;
- being dehumanised, treated as a commodity or bought and sold as 'property';
- being physically constrained or having restrictions placed on their freedom of movement;
- being trafficked – involving transporting, recruiting or harbouring people for the purpose of exploitation, using violence, threats or coercion;
- child slavery – child trafficking, child soldiers, child marriage and child domestic slavery.

What does the Modern Slavery Act 2015 require us to do?

To tackle this worldwide problem, the UK enacted the Modern Slavery Act 2015.

The Act seeks to tackle modern slavery by creating criminal offences of:

- slavery, servitude and forced or compulsory labour;
- human trafficking: arranging or facilitating the travel of another person with a view to that person being exploited;
- exploitation: slavery, servitude and forced or compulsory labour; certain sexual offences; removal of organs or tissue; and obtaining services or benefits by threats, force or deception.

The provisions apply whether or not the offences take place in England and Wales.

The Act seeks to address the role of businesses in preventing modern slavery from occurring in their supply chains and organisations.

The Act requires businesses in the UK with a total annual turnover of £36 million or more to report annually (by way of statement – see our website) on steps taken by the business to ensure that slavery and human trafficking are not taking place in either its business or its supply chains.

Our process at [insert name of firm]

The firm has reviewed its employment practices and does not consider it has a modern slavery risk.

To ensure that as far as possible we are not engaging with a supplier who may be engaging themselves or have a supplier who supplies to them engage in modern slavery, the firm has devised a procurement process which requires suppliers to complete a questionnaire setting out their stance and policies on modern slavery and other aspects of compliance.

Further, the firm will not engage a supplier who is established and runs its operations in a country deemed to be high risk for modern slavery.

It is important therefore that all those who are engaging a supplier follow the procurement process set out by the firm.

If you have any queries about this guidance note please contact [name].

APPENDIX 25

Template Criminal Finances Act 2017 risk assessment

> See especially **5.3.3**.

The risk assessment below has been carried out by [*name*] and forms the firm's risk assessment further to the implementation of the Criminal Finances Act 2017. This risk assessment will be revisited and expanded upon, if appropriate, each year on the anniversary of the legislation coming into force or during the year if necessary. The last review of this risk assessment was [*date*]. [*N.B. The frequency of review is a matter entirely for you and this is just a suggestion.*]

[*Steps for use – complete the assessment below by ticking or marking with a cross where appropriate. Then decide whether your firm has a low, medium or high risk of being involved with tax evasion and write down the steps you will take to mitigate these risks. There are some suggested steps below.*]

Our clients	Never	Rarely	Sometimes	Often
Do we act for clients whom we have reason to suspect of past or present involvement in tax evasion?				
Do we otherwise act for clients who may pose particular tax evasion risks? For example: • cash-based businesses or their owners; • clients with assets in high-risk jurisdictions; • clients who hold assets through complex or obscure ownership structures.				
Do we have clients who for some other reason present a substantial tax-evasion risk?				
Our services				
Do we set up arrangements which have as a major objective the minimisation of tax?				
Do we assist in creating corporate or trust structures which may be sought by clients in order to facilitate tax evasion?				
Do we act in matters with connections to tax havens, or other jurisdictions which may provide facilities for tax evasion?				
Do we otherwise act in matters which may involve substantial tax liabilities? For example: • purchases of property subject to land tax; • sales of businesses or property subject to capital gains tax (CGT); • inheritance and estate matters involving inheritance tax (IHT) issues.				

Our people				
Does any member of staff or partner display ignorance of or indifference to their ethical and legal obligations?				
Do we lack appropriate oversight of anyone in the firm?				
Do we recruit people without suitable references or other checks upon their ethical record?				
Does our bonus and remuneration system encourage a win-at-all-costs approach to doing business?				
Do we use third parties to carry out work on our behalf, where that third party may be involved in facilitating tax evasion?				

Overall assessment

Overall, we regard the firm as being [*insert risk rating*].

Risk areas

The following types of client are considered to be higher risk:
[N.B. These are examples for you, but your firm may be exposed to different risks.]

Private clients who engage us to advise on mitigating their tax position.
Corporate clients who engage us to advise on mitigating their tax position.
Family clients who do not wish to disclose certain assets or income in order to avoid tax.

The following practice areas are considered to be higher risk:
[N.B. These are examples for you but your firm may be exposed to different risks.]

Private client and tax team – tax mitigation planning.
Corporate – corporate structuring so as to mitigate tax liability.
Family – clients who do not wish to disclose assets or income to their spouse so as to avoid tax.

We have the following other significant risks:
[N.B. These are examples for you, but your firm may be exposed to different risks.]

In respect of billing when clients ask us to change the name of the client/entity to be billed.

Mitigation

[*Set out here your mitigation for the risks you have identified. Below are some suggestions.*]

- Billing guide will be written and circulated by [*date*]. This provides guidance relating to billing third parties.
- Anti-tax evasion policy will be published to all staff by [*date*].
- A reminder to all staff as to that policy will be made [*date*].
- Training will be mandatory for all relevant personnel [*N.B. Consider here who should receive the training as it may not be necessary to train all*] and will take place by [*date*].

- The file review process will have a question added as to whether there are any tax evasion concerns on the file.
- A procedure will be put in place requiring third parties who provide services to high-risk clients through the firm to demonstrate their anti-tax evasion credentials and where necessary commit to improving them. [N.B. *This is a suggestion and you will need to consider how practically to implement this. You may decide where that third party is itself regulated that the risk is mitigated and no further steps are needed. However, if it is unregulated you need to consider what steps should be taken.*]

APPENDIX 26

Template anti-tax evasion policy

> See especially **5.3.3**.

This is the firm's anti-tax evasion policy and applies to all staff in the firm.

This document has been approved by the firm's money laundering reporting officer (MLRO) and compliance officer for legal practice (MLCO). They are collectively responsible for this policy. [*N.B. It is up to you who approves the policy but it needs to be someone in senior management in the firm.*]

If you have any concerns about this policy or are aware of any tax evasion, please contact either of these people or your supervisor (if appropriate) in the first instance.

Failure to adhere to this policy may be treated by the firm as gross misconduct and could result in formal disciplinary action, in addition to any other professional or criminal sanctions which may apply.

1. Criminal Finances Act 2017

The Criminal Finances Act 2017 came into force on 30 September 2017 and creates a criminal offence for any entity that fails to prevent the criminal facilitation of tax evasion by associated persons. The offence is not so much about tax law but about behaviours and indicators which are dishonest.

The offence of tax evasion will be committed where an associated person:

1. is knowingly concerned in, or takes steps with a view to, the fraudulent evasion of tax by another person; or
2. aids, abets, counsels or procures the commission of a UK tax evasion offence by another person; or
3. is involved in the commission of an offence consisting of being knowingly concerned in, or taking steps with a view to, the fraudulent evasion of tax.

There are three stages to the offence:

1. the criminal evasion of UK tax, i.e. the underlying tax evasion offence;
2. the criminal facilitation of this offence by an associated person to the firm;
3. the firm failing to prevent the associated person from committing that facilitation.

An associated person is defined as a person who is an employee of the firm who is acting in the capacity of an employee (this includes partners and consultants), an agent of the firm who is acting in their capacity as an agent or any other person who performs services for and on behalf of the firm who is acting in the capacity of a person performing such services.

Those who act as an agent may be experts that we instruct including counsel. These parties may therefore be construed as being associated persons. Most if not all such persons themselves will be regulated persons and so will be subject to their own regulators' requirements and the Criminal Finances Act 2017 and therefore we consider these associated persons as being low risk. [N.B. *You need to make this assessment for your firm, but this is my suggested stance.*]

However, if you are instructing a non-regulated person to provide a service which may cause them to be seen as associated persons and they are providing advice which may include tax advice, you need to consider whether we should ask questions concerning their own anti-tax evasion policy.

For further guidance please consult the Law Society's Criminal Finances Act 2017 practice note.

If in doubt, please speak to [*name*] in the first instance.

2. Our commitment

Our firm is committed to doing business ethically and in accordance with our professional and legal obligations.

Our commitment to avoiding facilitating tax evasion is one aspect of that.

Moreover, under Part 3 of the Criminal Finances Act 2017, the firm is expected to have reasonable procedures to prevent the criminal facilitation of tax evasion by staff or other associated persons. Without such procedures, the firm may be exposed to criminal sanctions.

This document explains those procedures.

3. What we expect of you, and why

Your work for the firm may present you with opportunities to facilitate tax evasion by clients or others.

We expect you to resist any temptation to engage in such behaviour and immediately to report any improper behaviour by others.

If you were to facilitate tax evasion you would commit a serious criminal offence.

You would also leave yourself open to professional sanctions and internal disciplinary action and you could expose the firm to liability.

4. What is 'facilitation of tax evasion'?

Tax evasion is fraudulent activity.

Tax evasion is quite different from tax avoidance or mitigation (the lawful minimisation of tax liability). It is also different from honest errors in tax affairs, even where such errors amount to an offence.

To be more specific, fraudulent activity intended to divert funds from the public revenue constitutes the common law offence of cheating the public revenue.

There are also statutory offences of 'fraudulently evading' various taxes.

It is not necessary that any tax actually be successfully evaded.

Facilitating tax evasion is a crime, if done deliberately and dishonestly.

That can apply even if you are outside the UK at the time. Facilitating the evasion of foreign tax may likewise be a crime. It is not necessary for your client to be convicted for you to face conviction.

5. Your duty to report

It is not enough merely to avoid personally facilitating tax evasion. As with all aspects of your professional work, you should be open, report any concerns about questionable behaviour, past or present and, if in doubt, seek guidance.

If someone within or outside the firm suggests anything which might be regarded as tax evasion, you must report it.

6. Whistleblower protection – our promise to you

As per our whistleblowing policy, you will not be subject to any retaliation or retribution for reporting your concerns about a suspected breach of this policy.

Anyone who retaliates against someone who has made such a report will be subject to disciplinary action.

While we would prefer you to report any concerns openly, you may do so anonymously.

Whistleblower protection applies even if your concerns turn out to be unjustified, so long as you made the report in good faith. It may not apply in other circumstances, for example if someone maliciously makes allegations which they know to be false.

If you do have such concerns, please report them to the firm's whistleblowing officer (WBO), [name].

7. Examples

The following are non-exhaustive examples where opportunities to facilitate tax evasion might arise within our practice areas and to which you should be alert.

If you are in any doubt, please contact [name] for guidance.

In any practice area:

1. Delivering a misleading or inaccurate bill which enables a client to evade tax. For example, billing a company for work actually done for its directors or shareholders in order to assist clients to claim a tax deduction to which they are not entitled. This is VAT fraud and if you engage in it you will face internal disciplinary action and possibly external disciplinary action.

Property:

2. Preparing documents which misstate the price of a property to enable a client to evade land tax or capital gains tax (CGT).
3. Assisting in a property being bought using nominees or other structures to enable a client illegally to avoid tax.

Corporate:

4. Assisting in creating corporate or trust structures designed to conceal a client's taxable income or assets.
5. Referring clients to third parties in tax havens to set up accounts or structures which you know are to facilitate tax evasion, rather than tax avoidance.
6. Using side letters so that aspects of a transaction with taxable effects are not apparent from reading the main agreement in order to enable a client, or anyone else, to evade tax.

Wills and probate:

7. Assisting in creating trust or other structures designed to conceal a client's taxable income or assets.
8. Giving clients advice on how to make lifetime transfers in ways which HM Revenue and Customs (HMRC) will find difficult to detect.
9. Preparing documents which misstate the value of an estate in order to avoid inheritance tax (IHT).

Family law:

10. Helping a client to put forward figures which you know to be false will involve a number of offences, possibly including conspiracy to pervert the course of justice and tax evasion offences.
11. Clients who have been ordered to disclose their earnings in connection with family proceedings may tell you that they have committed tax evasion in the past. That information will normally be privileged and is not normally reportable under money laundering law. However, in such cases discuss the matter with the MLRO or compliance officer for legal practice (COLP) to ensure that your involvement in the case will not create any liabilities or concerns.

APPENDIX 27
Template anti-bribery and corruption policy

> See especially **5.4.7**.

Introduction

We value our reputation and are committed to maintaining the highest ethical standards in the conduct of our business.

This policy applies to all employees, partners, agents, consultants, contractors and to any other people or bodies associated with the practice.

The legislation

The Bribery Act 2010 came into force on 1 July 2011. It creates three main offences:

1. bribing a person to induce or reward them to perform a relevant function;
2. improperly requesting, accepting or receiving a bribe as a reward for performing a relevant function; and
3. improperly using a bribe to influence a foreign official to gain a business advantage.

Bribery is not always a matter of handing over cash. Gifts, hospitality and entertainment can be bribes if they are intended to influence a decision.

Under the Act, bribery by individuals is punishable by up to 10 years' imprisonment and/or an unlimited fine. If the firm is found to have taken part in bribery or to lack adequate procedures to prevent bribery, it too could face an unlimited fine.

A conviction for a bribery or corruption related offence would have severe reputational and financial consequences for us.

Managerial responsibilities

The anti-bribery and corruption officer (ABCO) is [*insert name; and consider whether you would like to name a deputy*]. The ABCO is responsible for overseeing our policy on anti-bribery and corruption and ensuring it is upheld in both word and spirit.

This responsibility includes:

- an annual review of the policy;
- an annual risk assessment of issues relating to the policy;
- overseeing training and communications relating to the topic.

The ABCO has authority to make amendments to this policy but ultimately all partners of the practice remain accountable for its implementation.

Third party due diligence

The scope of the Bribery Act 2010 requires us to identify third-party business relationships which may give opportunities for that third party to use bribery while acting on our behalf. Appropriate due diligence should be undertaken before a third party is engaged. Third parties should only be engaged where there is a clear business rationale for doing so, with an appropriate contract. Any payments to third parties should be properly authorised and recorded. [N.B. *You may wish to cross-refer to your procurement process.*]

Gifts and hospitality

Gifts and hospitality are commonly used in business circles to build relationships and market services or products. Hospitality often takes the form of entertainment, meals or tickets to events. If the provider of the hospitality does not attend, then it should be regarded as a gift. Businesses often pay expenses for a potential client to attend business-related conferences or events.

While this is all normal practice, it is recognised that gifts and hospitality can be used to influence and corrupt third parties and on occasion to manoeuvre employees into a position of obligation. When considering whether to accept a gift, what matters is the intention behind it. If it is offered as a bribe it should be refused, but if it is offered as a genuine gift it may be accepted provided that all aspects of this policy are complied with.

We want to prevent the giving or receiving of gifts, hospitality or paying of expenses if it might influence or be perceived to influence a business decision. Accordingly, gifts, entertainment and hospitality over the value of £[*insert value which fits your firm – this might be say £100 or maybe £500*] either given or received must be reported to the ABCO and logged in the [*insert place of logging*] by either the ABCO or the business development team as appropriate. This allows us to monitor both the level and the number of instances to assess whether the nature of the relationship is appropriate.

Risk assessment

We will conduct a risk assessment to assess the extent and nature of the risk of bribery or corruption to which we might be liable in our activities. This assessment will record the type of risk and the means by which we can prevent or mitigate our exposure to such risk. [N.B. *You may wish to create a document setting out your risk assessment or combine it with your firmwide anti-money laundering (AML) risk assessment.*]

Communication and training

It is important that we are all aware of this policy and for this reason we will ensure that:
- it is available via our intranet;
- you are notified of any amendments via email and the intranet;
- new staff are made aware of the policy as part of their induction;
- training will be provided, as necessary.

Personal responsibilities

We must all take personal responsibility for upholding the principles of this policy. Aside from the risk of criminal liability, you should be aware that any breach of procedure in relation to its letter or spirit may be interpreted as a matter of misconduct and could result in disciplinary proceedings.

You should not hesitate to contact the ABCO if you have any questions about the anti-bribery and corruption policy, its implementation or implications.

You are all actively encouraged to contact the ABCO if you have any suspicions about another member of staff or any third party in relation to bribery and corruption. Such reports will be dealt with on a strictly confidential basis.

APPENDIX 28

Template whistleblowing policy

> See especially **5.5**.

This policy does not form part of any contract of employment and it may be amended at any time. This policy was last reviewed by the whistleblowing officer (WBO) on [*date*].

Introduction/background

At one time or another you may have a concern about what is happening at work.

Whistleblowing is the reporting of suspected malpractice, wrongdoing or dangers in relation to the firm's activities which have a public interest element.

This may include the following (this is not an exhaustive list):

- bribery of clients, staff or third parties; potential fraud or other criminal activity;
- any breach or potential breach of our legal, professional or regulatory obligations such as breaches of the Solicitors Regulation Authority (SRA) Codes of Conduct for firms and solicitors;
- potential health and safety risks, e.g. failure to maintain properly fire exit routes or train staff on health and safety procedures.

You can also use this policy if you believe that any of the above have been deliberately concealed.

[*Name of firm*] takes fraud and malpractice very seriously. Our partners are committed to conducting business with honesty and integrity, and expect all of our people to maintain high standards too. We encourage open communication from all those who work for us and want everyone to feel secure about raising concerns.

We have introduced this policy to reassure you that it is safe and acceptable to speak up and to enable you to raise any concern you may have at an early stage and in the right way.

Be assured that you do not have to prove the allegation you are making – but you must reasonably believe that raising the concern is in the public interest and that the information tends to show some malpractice.

This policy applies to all those who work for the firm – whether full-time or part-time, including employees, consultants, contractors, partners, interns, casual workers and agency workers.

There is a difference between whistleblowing and raising a personal grievance:

1. Whistleblowing concerns are when you have a concern that has a public interest aspect to it – for example, because it threatens clients, a large number of staff, third parties or the public generally.

2. A grievance is a complaint that generally relates to your own employment position or how you have been treated at work. In these cases, employees should use the firm's grievance procedure.

If you have a concern about bullying, please refer to [*name of appropriate policy*].

How to raise a concern internally

If you are concerned about any form of malpractice, we hope you would feel able to raise it with your manager or supervisor.

If you feel unable to speak with your manager or supervisor for whatever reason, you should raise the issue with your head of department.

If you feel the matter is so serious that you cannot discuss it with the persons named above, you should raise the matter with the WBO, [*name*].

You can raise a concern by telephone, in person or in writing. If possible, please put your concerns in writing. It would be useful to provide the following:

1. the nature of the concern and why you believe it to be true; and
2. the background and history of the concern (giving relevant dates where possible).

How we deal with your concern

We are committed to ensuring that all disclosures raised will be dealt with appropriately, fairly and professionally.

We will arrange a meeting as soon possible to discuss your concern. We may ask for further information about the concern, either at this meeting or at a later stage.

You may bring a colleague or trade union representative to any meeting that takes place. Please note that your companion must respect the confidentiality of the disclosure and any subsequent investigation.

After the meeting, we may need to make internal enquiries first or carry out an investigation. We will endeavour to complete investigations within a reasonable time. We will keep you informed of the progress of our investigation (where possible) and notify you when it is completed.

Please note that we will not be able to inform you of matters which would infringe any duty of confidentiality owed to others (for example, notifying you of disciplinary action taken against other members of staff).

Our assurances to you

We are committed to good practice and to being supportive to anyone who raises genuine concerns under this policy, even if they turn out to be mistaken.

If you suffer any detriment as a result of raising your concern please contact [*name*], the firm's WBO immediately. If the matter is not dealt with to your satisfaction, you can raise it formally using the grievance procedure.

Nobody must threaten or retaliate against you for raising a concern and the firm will not tolerate any such harassment or victimisation. Any person involved in such conduct may be subject to disciplinary action.

To ensure the protection of our people, those who raise a concern, maliciously or make an allegation they do not reasonably believe to be true may also be subject to facing disciplinary action.

We hope that you will feel able to voice your concerns openly under this policy. Although a concern may be made anonymously, we encourage individuals to put their name to their allegation whenever possible, as it will be much easier for us to protect the individual's position or to give feedback on the outcome of investigations.

All concerns raised will be treated in confidence and every effort will be made not to reveal your identity if that is your wish. However, there may also be circumstances where we are required to disclose your identity by law.

If disciplinary or other proceedings follow the investigation, it may not be possible to take action without your help. In these instances, we will discuss with you how best the matter can proceed.

Independent advice

If you are unsure about raising a concern, you can get independent advice from the whistleblowing charity Protect on 020 3117 2520 or by email at: **whistle@protect-advice.org.uk**. Protect's advisers can talk you through your options and help you raise a concern about malpractice at work.

External disclosures

We would hope that in most cases raising concerns internally would be the most appropriate course of action, for example by raising your concerns with the WBO or the firm's compliance officer for legal practice (COLP). However, we recognise that there may be circumstances where you can properly report a concern to an external body.

If you feel you cannot raise concerns internally and reasonably believe the information/allegations are substantially true, you may raise the matter with the appropriate regulator such as the SRA or a prescribed person (see **www.gov.uk/government/publications/blowing-the-whistle-list-of-prescribed-people-and-bodies–2**).

We encourage you to seek advice before reporting a concern to anyone external.

Further information and contacts

If you have any queries about the application of this policy, please contact [*name*], the firm's WBO.

APPENDIX 29

Template conflicts of interest policy

> See especially **6.2.2**.

Conflicts of interests

Conflicts of interests are dealt with in paragraphs 6.1 and 6.2 of both the Solicitors Regulation Authority (SRA) Codes of Conduct (SRA Code of Conduct for Solicitors, RELs and RFLs and SRA Code of Conduct for Firms).

All fee earners have a personal responsibility to be familiar with the Codes as they relate to conflicts of interests.

Own interest conflict

You cannot act if there is an 'own interest' conflict or a significant risk of such a conflict (paragraph 6.1. of both Codes). An own interest conflict is defined in the SRA Glossary as:

> ... any situation where your duty to act in the best interests of any client in relation to a matter conflicts, or there is a significant risk that it may conflict, with your own interests in relation to that or a related matter.

Circumstances that can give rise to an own interest conflict or a significant risk of one include:

- any financial interest;
- a personal relationship;
- the appointment of you, or a member of your firm or family, to public office;
- commercial relationships; or
- your employment.

Client conflict – where acting for two or more clients creates a conflict of interest or a significant risk of one

You should not act in a matter where you have a conflict of interest or there is a significant risk of one arising between two or more clients, subject to certain specified exceptions (paragraph 6.2 of both Codes).

A conflict of interest means a situation where your separate duties to act in the best interests of two or more clients in the same or a related matter conflict. The most obvious example of a conflict is where the matter itself concerns a dispute between two or more current or intended clients. For example, paragraph 6.2 of the Codes will prevent you from acting for both sides in litigation. Other less direct examples include:

- acting for two clients seeking separately to purchase a particular asset or to be awarded a particular contract;
- acting for an investor and the scheme in which they will be investing;
- acting for both clients where one is selling or leasing an asset to the other;
- agreeing a commercial contract between two clients.

Paragraph 6.2 of both Codes allows two exceptions to the prohibition on acting for more than one client where there is a conflict of interest or significant risk of one, where:

- the clients have a substantially common interest in relation to the matter or the aspect of it, as appropriate; or
- the clients are competing for the same objective.

A substantially common interest is defined as a situation where there is a clear common purpose between the clients and a strong consensus on how it is to be achieved.

Competing for the same objective would be where two clients are attempting to buy the same asset or win the same contract.

You can only rely on either exception if the following conditions are met:

1. all the clients have given informed consent, given or evidenced in writing to you acting;
2. where appropriate, you put in place effective safeguards to protect your clients' confidential information; and
3. you are satisfied it is reasonable for you to act for all the clients.

Evidence of confirmation of the relevant factors should be clearly documented on the file along with your assessment of the risks and benefits to the client. [Role or name] is on hand to assist in any conflict of interest consideration.

In deciding whether to act within the scope of the exceptions under paragraph 6.2, you should consider factors such as the respective knowledge and bargaining power of the clients; the extent to which there will need to be any negotiations between the parties; and any particular benefits to the clients such as speed, convenience and costs. One way to remove the risk of a conflict or potential conflict is to restrict your retainer so that you are only acting on those aspects where a conflict is unlikely to arise.

If you are ever in any doubt about a potential conflict situation, you should seek guidance from [role or name] before acting or continuing to act. Please also consider the SRA's guidance on conflicts of interest which was used to write this policy (**www.sra.org.uk/solicitors/guidance/ethics-guidance/conflicts-interest/**).

Our procedure relating to conflicts of interest

Conflicts of interests must be considered at the earliest opportunity before accepting instructions and must not be seen as an 'admin task' to be done before file opening as it is often too late by that time and we may have acted where there is a conflict.

Information should therefore be obtained from the client before any meeting takes place to check for conflicts with existing clients. You should take the client's name, address and telephone number; the field of law involved; and details of the opponent or others involved in the matter, if applicable. This information will enable you to conduct a conflict check in line with the procedure set out in the file opening process.

If you are unsure whether a conflict has arisen or is likely to arise, please speak to [role or name] in the first instance.

If, as a result of a conflict check, it is considered that instructions should be declined or we should cease to act, the client should be informed as soon as possible and in any event before any meeting takes place or instructions are taken.

APPENDIX 30

Template guidance: Am I providing a banking facility to the client?

> See especially **6.4**.

It is important that we do not allow the firm's client account to be used as a banking facility in contravention of the Solicitors Regulation Authority (SRA) Accounts Rules. This note sets out the rule itself and what this means in practice. For any queries about this note or if you have a non-banking rule query, please contact [*name*].

What does SRA Accounts Rules rule 3.3 say?

Rule 3.3 itself sets out the following:

> You must not use a client account to provide banking facilities to clients or third parties. Payments into, and transfers or withdrawals from a client account must be in respect of the delivery by you of regulated services.

'Regulated services' is defined as the legal and other professional services that you provide that are regulated by the SRA and includes, where appropriate, acting as a trustee or as the holder of a specified office or appointment.

What does it mean?

Effectively the rule means that we cannot make or receive payments on behalf of our clients or any other party that do not relate to our regulated services.

What does this mean in practice?

There are some clear and obvious examples.

If we are acting on the sale of a residential property, the following will generally be ok:

- payment to redeem the mortgage;
- payment to the estate agent;
- payment for the surveyor.

However, in that same transaction it would not be ok to make the following payments:

- for the client's children's school fees;
- payment to a garage for the purchase of a car;
- the client's gambling debt.

The reason why the above are not acceptable to make is because they are not linked to our regulated services, i.e. the residential property sale.

We may be asked by wealthy foreign individuals with a UK residence to pay their household bills for them, i.e. gas, electricity, water, council tax, cleaners. While we may have been instructed to purchase the property in question, payment of household bills does not form part of our regulated services. Making these payments therefore breaches the rule.

There are instances, however, where these types of payments are permissible because they relate to underlying work such as the administration of estates, trusts or where we are acting under a power of attorney. Often at first glance it may appear that the payment wouldn't be connected to work we would be undertaking. However, payment of a gas bill in relation to a property within the estate being administered is linked to the underlying work we are undertaking and so this payment is ok and does not breach the rule.

Further, when we are acting as an attorney, a trustee or acting on their instructions, any payments will generally not fall foul of the rules as long as it can be shown the payment relates to the underlying legal work or the payment forms part of our normal regulated activities.

Not all scenarios are clear and when in doubt please do seek guidance from [*name*].

APPENDIX 31

Guidance note: SRA reporting obligations – what are they and when do they kick in?

> See especially **6.7.4**.

On 25 November 2019 the new Solicitors Regulation Authority (SRA) Codes of Conduct came into force. This brought with it a change in the reporting obligations for both the firm and solicitors. You will find the new Codes on the SRA website (**www.sra.org.uk/solicitors/standards-regulations/**) and you are encouraged to read them.

The reporting obligations are as follows:

- You report promptly to the SRA, or another approved regulator, as appropriate, **any facts or matters that you reasonably believe are capable of amounting to a serious breach** of their regulatory arrangements by any person regulated by them (including you).
- Notwithstanding the paragraph above **you inform the SRA promptly of any facts or matters that you reasonably believe should be brought to its attention** in order that it may investigate whether a serious breach of its regulatory arrangements has occurred or otherwise exercise its regulatory powers.
- **You do not subject any person to detrimental treatment** for making or proposing to make a report or providing or proposing to provide information based on a reasonably held belief under the first paragraph above irrespective of whether the SRA or another approved regulator subsequently investigates or takes an action in relation to the facts or matters in question.

[Emphasis added.]

The Code of Conduct for Solicitors, RELs and RFLs further sets out that a solicitor's obligation to report will be fulfilled if they have informed the compliance officer for legal practice (COLP) or compliance officer for finance and administration (COFA) of the matter on the understanding that they will make a report.

When considering whether an obligation to report has occurred, you need to consider whether the facts or matters before you could amount to a **serious breach**. What therefore needs to occur is an assessment of what is serious.

The SRA will not define what serious means, but it does inform us via its enforcement strategy (this sets out the SRA's approach to regulation in order to meet the regulatory objectives: **www.sra.org.uk/sra/corporate-strategy/sub-strategies/sra-enforcement-strategy/**) what factors it takes into account when it decides whether something is serious. These factors include but are not limited to:

1. nature of the allegation – some types are inherently more serious than others, for example dishonesty, taking unfair advantage of clients, sexual misconduct;
2. intent and motivation – conduct may be more serious because of the intent behind it;
3. harm and impact – has there been significant impact on the victim or little/no impact at all;

4. vulnerability – was the victim vulnerable and did the solicitor take advantage of that;
5. role, experience and seniority – is the individual junior or well seasoned;
6. regulatory history and pattern of behaviour – has this happened before;
7. remediation – is there a risk of future harm or has any risk been mitigated.

What should you do if you are concerned you have a reporting obligation?

To begin with, consider whether you have facts or matters before you that could amount to a serious breach taking into account the above factors. If you are unsure or believe that you do have such facts or matters before you, please speak to [*insert name and role such as risk and compliance manager or COLP*].

Please do not make any reports to the SRA about any other person inside or outside the firm without speaking to [*name and role*] first.

APPENDIX 32
Firmwide risk register

See especially 7.1.2.

RISK DETERMINATION

Reference	Risk area	Risk identified	Impact	Risk owner	Likeli-hood	Impact	Risk rating
1. Operational risks	[N.B. These might be business continuity, personnel leaving, lack of supervision, negligence, complaints, succession panning issues and so on.]	Step 1 – Determine the risk and rate it using the chart below.			Put in rating as per chart below.	Put in rating as per chart below.	Put in rating as per chart below.

COUNTER MEASURES

Existing controls	Action to be taken	Owner	Due date	Review date	Likeli-hood	Impact	Risk rating
	Step 2 – Decide what actions to take in accordance with risk and its rating. If very low risk then minimal or no steps needed. If high risk then consider what steps need to be taken.			Step 3 – After implementation of the steps – review and re-rate the risk using the chart below. Has it changed or do further steps need to be taken?			

APPENDIX 32

RISK DETERMINATION							COUNTER MEASURES						
Reference	Risk area	Risk identified	Impact	Risk owner	Likeli-hood	Impact	Risk rating	Existing controls	Action to be taken	Owner	Due date	Review date	Likeli-hood	Impact	Risk rating
2. Regulatory risks	[N.B. These might be AML risk, sanctions, PEP exposure, data protection and breaches, code breaches, accounts rules breaches and so on.]														
3. Financial risks	[N.B. These might be client monies handling, overhead increases, loss of large client billing and collections and so on.]														

FIRMWIDE RISK REGISTER 215

RISK DETERMINATION									COUNTER MEASURES						
Reference	Risk area	Risk identi-fied	Impact	Risk owner	Likeli-hood	Impact	Risk rating	Existing controls	Action to be taken	Owner	Due date	Review date	Likeli-hood	Impact	Risk rating
4. Practice area risks	*[N.B. Here assess risks associated with your practice areas.]*			Impact											

			Negli-gible (1)	Minor (2)	Moder-ate (3)	Major (4)
Likeli-hood	Almost Certain (5)	5	10	15	20
	Likely (4)	4	8	12	16
	Possible (3)	3	6	9	12
	Unlikely (2)	2	4	6	8
	Rare (1)	1	2	3	4

APPENDIX 33

Annual declaration of business/organisation interests [*year*]

> See especially **7.3.3**.

Name ....
Job title ....
Department ....

Individuals should include interests of both themselves and any member of their immediate family (including partners). Please see guidance notes for more information.

If neither you nor your family (including partners) have any interests in any business or organisation, please tick here ☐ and then sign and date below.

If you or your family members have interests in any business or organisation, please complete the table below.

Name of person – and if not you, their relationship to you	Name of business/ organisation	Nature of business/ organisation	Nature of interest – both you and family member, i.e. director, board member, owner	Date interest started	Date interest ends or confirm ongoing

I confirm that I have declared all interests which I or my immediate family (including partner) have with businesses or organisations which may have dealings with [*firm name*]. I will also inform [*firm name*] of any change in these interests.

Signed: [*signature*] ....
Date: [*date*] ....

Guidance notes to declaration of business/organisation interests form

What is this form all about?

We are asking **all employees (including partners and consultants)** to complete the form to confirm whether or not they themselves have an interest in a business/organisation outside the workplace. The form also extends to immediate family members of the employee and the employee's partner, i.e. mother, father, grandparents, siblings and children.

What kind of information are we seeking?

We need to know about any interest that you or your immediate family (and partner) may have in relation to any business or organisation. For example, you or your immediate family may act as a governor of a school, sit on a board of some kind or be a director of a company or own shares in it. This interest does not have to be financial and we do not require information about your immediate family member's place of work. If in doubt, declare it to us and we can take a view as to whether it is relevant.

Why are we asking for this information?

When deciding whether to take on a piece of work we need to consider whether there is a conflict of interest. So for example, if an employee owns part of a business that a client has instructed us to issue proceedings against, it is likely that we will have a conflict and we cannot act. We therefore need the information we are asking for from you to be able to conflict check properly.

What do we propose to do with the information you give to us?

The information you give to us is strictly confidential and will be held by [*name*] only. So that we can easily ascertain whether there is a conflict we will [*insert process here – example process as follows – place the name of the business/organisation into our database [name] as a contact but not link it to you. In place of the address we will place the words 'Please refer to risk and compliance – employee interest'. The user will then need to contact [name] who will then check the data held and advise whether a conflict of interests exists. It is very likely that we will not be able to tell the person conducting the conflict search why we cannot act nor will the person who has the interest be consulted*].

More information

If you would like more information or if you have any concerns, please contact [*role or name of person*].

APPENDIX 34

Template procurement/supplier questionnaire

> See especially **7.4**.
>
> N.B. These are suggested questions and you may decide not to ask them all. Adapt this form to suit your firm and the likely supply.

At [*name of firm*] it is important to us that we work with suppliers who are compliant, responsible and hold the same values as we do. We have a zero-tolerance policy to breaches of any laws, regulations or rules.

To enable us to consider you/your company as a supplier to [*firm*], we ask that you please complete the form below within 14 days and return this to us with your contract/terms. It is possible that some sections of this form are not applicable. Where it is felt that this is the case we ask that you indicate this and set out the reasons why.

	Question/information required	Supplier response
1.	**SUPPLIER INFORMATION**	
	Supplier name	
	Company address	
	Contact details of individual responsible for this procurement exercise	
	Company registration number	
	VAT registration number	
	Please briefly outline: • the ownership structure of your company; • the names of persons of significant control.	
	Turnover of business	
	Number of people employed	
	Has the company been the subject of criminal proceedings or regulatory investigation in the past five years?	
	Please provide your bank details	
2.	**THIS SUPPLY**	
	Please outline the supply you are proposing to make to [*firm*]. Please attach the contract and terms of business.	
3.	**RISK, POLICIES AND PROCEDURES**	
	Business continuity and information security	
	Do you have a business continuity plan?	

Question/information required	Supplier response
Would you be prepared to send that business continuity plan to [firm] for viewing?	
Do you have a data protection policy?	
Please outline your data security measures – i.e. what software is used to protect data.	
Regulatory compliance	
Do you have an anti-money laundering policy?	
Who is your money laundering reporting officer (MLRO)?	
Do you have a modern slavery statement? Please provide a copy or direct us to its location on your website.	
Do you have an anti-modern slavery and human trafficking policy?	
How do you assess that those in your supply chain are not involved with modern slavery or human trafficking?	
Do you have an anti-bribery and corruption policy?	
Do you have an anti-bribery and corruption officer (ABCO)? Please provide their name.	
Do you have a whistleblowing policy?	
Do you have an equality and diversity policy?	
Do you have an anti-tax evasion policy?	
Health and safety and environment	
Do you have a signed health and safety policy for all locations? If yes, please provide a copy of statement or policy.	
What is the name and title of the person in your organisation with executive responsibility for health and safety?	
Are written risk assessments in place for areas of significant risk? If yes, please provide an example.	
Please provide your company's accident statistics (under Reporting of Injuries, Diseases and Dangerous Occurrences Regulations 2013 (RIDDOR)) over the last three years.	
Please give details of any prohibition, improvement notices or prosecutions that have been issued against your company in the last three years.	
Do you have a signed environmental policy? If yes, please provide a copy of your statement or policy.	
Do you hold an environmental management accreditation, e.g. ISO14001? If yes please attach a copy of the certificate.	

Question/information required	Supplier response
Are you energy savings opportunity scheme (ESOS) compliant? If yes, please attach a copy of your certificate.	

Declaration

I believe that the facts stated in this document are true and accurate.

Signed　　　　　　..
Position　　　　　　..
Company name　..
Date　　　　　　　..

APPENDIX 35

Template risk and compliance action plan

See especially 7.8.3 and 9.2.

Template risk and compliance action plan [*date*]

Area of risk or compliance	Current position	Desired position	How are we going to achieve the desired position?	When by?	Has this been actioned, what is the result and next steps	Allocated to?	Done or carry over?

APPENDIX 36

Template letter to auditors

> See especially **8.4**.

[*Insert your usual letterhead and address etc.*]

[N.B. *The firm may decide to provide all of the information that auditors are asking for. However, the firm is not obliged to and may be exposing itself by confirming detail which the client company itself should confirm. Below is some wording therefore which you may wish to adopt when responding to those aspects of the auditor's request that you do not consider you should respond to.*]

In relation to the points raised in the letter, our representative body, the Law Society of England and Wales, has advised that it is the responsibility of the company and not its solicitors to provide such information. Accordingly, I am afraid that we are unable to answer these questions and I would ask that you contact the entities directly in this regard.

Please accept our apologies that we are unable to provide all the information requested.